The
Favourites

The Favourites

Layne Fargo

Chatto & Windus

LONDON

1 3 5 7 9 10 8 6 4 2

Chatto & Windus, an imprint of Vintage, is part of the
Penguin Random House group of companies

Vintage, Penguin Random House UK, One Embassy Gardens,
8 Viaduct Gardens, London SW11 7BW

penguin.co.uk/vintage
global.penguinrandomhouse.com

First published in Great Britain by Chatto & Windus in 2025
First published in the United States of America by Random House in 2025

Printed and bound in Great Britain by Clays Ltd, Elcograf S.p.A.

The authorised representative in the EEA is Penguin Random House Ireland,
Morrison Chambers, 32 Nassau Street, Dublin D02 YH68

A CIP catalogue record for this book is available from the British Library

HB ISBN 9781784745486
TPB ISBN 9781784745493

Penguin Random House is committed to a sustainable
future for our business, our readers and our planet. This book
is made from Forest Stewardship Council® certified paper.

For Katarina, Tonya, Surya,
and all the other badass women who've shown me
what it means to win on your own terms.

Today is the tenth anniversary of the worst day of my life.

As if I could forget, when millions of strangers have been so eager to remind me. I'm sure you've seen the news stories, the magazine covers, the social media posts. Maybe you're planning to snuggle up on your sofa tonight with a bowl of popcorn and binge the documentary series released to commemorate the occasion. Schadenfreude and chill.

Go right ahead. Enjoy the show. But don't fool yourself into thinking you know me. By now, I've heard it all: Katarina Shaw is a bitch, a diva, a sore loser, a manipulative liar. Cold-blooded, a cheater, a criminal. An attention whore, an actual whore. Even a murderess.

Call me what you want. I don't give a damn anymore. My story is mine, and I'll tell it the same way I skated: in my own way, on my own terms.

We'll see who wins in the end.

NARRATOR: They were an obsession.

American ice dancers Katarina Shaw and Heath Rocha smile and take their bows in front of a crowd of screaming fans at the 2014 Winter Olympics in Sochi, Russia.

NARRATOR: Then a scandal.

Shaw and Rocha, surrounded by a crowd again—only this time, it's paparazzi shouting their names, a flurry of shutters and flashbulbs as they leave their Sochi hotel. The couple pushes through the throng with grim expressions, Heath's arm around Katarina's shoulders.

NARRATOR: And ultimately . . . a tragedy.

NBC Sports commentator Kirk Lockwood reports live from the Sochi Olympics. "In all my years covering skating," he says, shaking his head solemnly, "I've never seen anything like this."

NARRATOR: Now, for the first time, those closest to Katarina Shaw and Heath Rocha will share their stories, shedding new light on what led to the unprecedented events of that fateful Olympic final.

Former Olympic ice dancer Ellis Dean speaks to an interviewer in a West Hollywood bar.

ELLIS DEAN: We used to joke they were going to die in each other's arms or kill each other with their bare hands. Nothing in between.

Figure skating coach Nicole Bradford is interviewed in her suburban Illinois kitchen.

NICOLE BRADFORD: They were the most talented skaters I've ever worked with, no question. But looking back . . . yes, I could see the signs of trouble to come.

U.S. Figure Skating judge Jane Currer addresses the camera from an ice rink in Colorado.

JANE CURRER: How could we have known? How could anyone have known?

In quick flashes, a series of images: Katarina and Heath skating together as children. Then older, standing on top of a podium, smiling, gold medals around their necks. Finally, shouting at each other, Katarina's makeup ruined, her hand pulled back to strike.

ELLIS DEAN: I know one thing for sure. There'll never be another team like Kat and Heath.

Slow dissolve to a photo of the ice rink in Sochi. Bright red spatters stain the Olympic rings.

ELLIS DEAN: And you know what? Maybe that's a good thing.

NARRATOR: This is . . .

THE FAVOURITES:

The Shaw & Rocha Story

PART I

The Hopefuls

CHAPTER 1

Once I was satisfied, I handed him the knife.

Heath stood up on his knees, and I stretched out in the warm spot he'd left on the bed, watching him: the way his black hair shone in the moonlight, the press of his teeth on his lower lip as he concentrated, making his first mark with the tip of the blade. He was more precise than I had been, drawing curved, graceful lines underneath my savage slashes.

Shaw & Rocha, the carving read when he finished. It was the way our names would be written on the scoreboard at our first U.S. Figure Skating Championships in a few days' time. The way they'd be announced in medal ceremonies and reported in newspapers and entered in the record books. We'd cut the letters into the center of my antique rosewood headboard, deep enough that no amount of sanding could remove them.

We were sixteen, and so sure of everything.

Our bags were already packed for the National Championships, costumes and skates in a neat stack next to my bedroom door. As many years as we'd been waiting, working, preparing for this moment, those few final hours felt like torture. I wanted to leave right then.

I wished we never had to come back.

Heath left the knife on my bedside table and settled down beside me to admire our handiwork. "Are you nervous?" he whispered.

I looked past him, at the pictures collaged around the drafty leaded glass window—all images of my favorite figure skater, Sheila Lin. Two-time Olympic gold medalist in ice dance, living legend. Sheila never seemed nervous, no matter how much pressure she faced.

"No," I told him.

Heath smiled and slid his hand up the back of the stretched-out Stars on Ice 1996 sweatshirt I always wore to bed. "Liar."

Nosebleed seats to see that tour were the closest I'd ever come to Sheila Lin in real life. My father sprung for a signed commemorative photo of her too, which was tacked up on my wall with the rest of my shrine. She was the woman, and the athlete, I wanted to be—not when I grew up, but as soon as possible.

When Sheila and her partner, Kirk Lockwood, won their first U.S. title, she was still a teenager. Winning was a long shot for Heath and me, since we'd never been to Nationals before. We had qualified the previous season but didn't have the means to travel to the competition venue in Salt Lake City. Luckily, the championships were in Cleveland this time, a comparably short and affordable Greyhound bus ride away. I was certain the competition would change everything for us.

I was right. Just not in the way I imagined.

Heath kissed my shoulder. "Well, *I'm* not nervous. I'm skating with Katarina Shaw." He said my name slow, reverent, savoring the sound. "And there's nothing she can't do."

We stared at each other in the shadows, so close we were sharing breath. Later, we'd become world famous for that: stretching out the moment before a kiss until it was almost unbearable, until every member of the audience felt the quickening of our pulses, the pure want reflected in our eyes.

But that was choreography. This was real.

Heath's mouth finally met mine—soft, unhurried. We thought we had all night.

By the time we heard the footsteps, it was too late.

Nicole Bradford, a middle-aged blond woman wearing a sparkly cardigan and heavy makeup, sits at the center island in her white-on-white suburban dream kitchen.

NICOLE BRADFORD (Figure Skating Coach): There's always a surge after the Winter Olympics. All these girls who think they're destined to become stars. Though they usually aren't *quite* as intense about it as Katarina Shaw.

Family photos show Katarina as a little girl in various skating costumes. In one, she's in front of a wall covered in pictures of Sheila Lin, imitating Sheila's pose in the central image.

NICOLE BRADFORD: At her first lesson, Katarina said she was going to be a famous ice dancer like Sheila Lin. The other girls hated her instantly.

Four-year-old Katarina skates alone with a serious expression, her hair in two messy pigtails.

NARRATOR: Though her name eventually became synonymous with ice dance, Katarina Shaw spent her early career as a singles skater, since no boys were available to partner with her.

Ellis Dean perches on a stool at a chic cocktail bar, holding a martini glass. He's in his early forties, with an impish smile and carefully coiffed hair.

ELLIS DEAN (Former Ice Dancer): There are *vanishingly* few guys who want to do ice dance. At least pairs has jumps, plus hurling pretty girls into the air and catching them by the crotch. If you like that sort of thing.

NARRATOR: Ice dance is perhaps the least understood figure skating discipline.

Archival footage of skaters competing in the ice dance event at the 1976 Winter Games in Innsbruck, Austria—the first year ice dance was contested as an Olympic sport.

NARRATOR: Drawn from ballroom dancing, ice dance focuses on intricate footwork and close partnering between skaters, rather than the acrobatic lifts and athletic jumps seen in other events.

ELLIS DEAN: A lot of female ice dancers start out skating with their brothers, cause those are the only dudes they can manage to guilt into it. That was not an option for Kat Shaw.

CHAPTER 2

The door banged open, and my bedroom filled with the mingled stench of Marlboros, Jim Beam, and body odor.

My older brother, Lee.

Heath and I leapt up. My brother didn't want Heath in the house, let alone in my room. Which only inspired us to find more creative ways to sneak him inside. If Lee was sober—an increasingly rare occurrence—he limited his objections to snide remarks, maybe the occasional inanimate object hurled against the wall.

When he was drunk? He had no limits at all.

"What the hell's he doing here?" Lee staggered across the threshold. "I told you—"

"*I* told *you* to stay out of my room."

I used to lock the door and leave the tarnished brass key in place, so Lee couldn't spy on us through the keyhole either. Until he kicked the door in and busted the lock.

"It's *my* house." Lee jabbed a finger in Heath's direction. "And he's not welcome."

Heath moved in front of me, smooth as a dance step, and smiled in a way we both knew would only incense Lee further. "Katarina wants me here," he said. "And so did—"

Lee surged forward, seizing Heath by the arm and yanking him toward the hallway.

"Stop it!" I shouted.

Heath gripped the doorframe, fingernails sinking into the cracked trim. As a competitive athlete, he was in far better shape, but Lee had several inches of height and many pounds of bulk on him. One brutal wrench, and Heath was forced to let go.

"Lee! That's *enough*."

Not for the first time, I wished we had neighbors close enough to hear the commotion, to call the police. But our house was in the middle of nowhere, bordered only by old-growth forest and the cold expanse of Lake Michigan.

No one was coming to help us.

I chased after them, snatching at the collar of Lee's shirt, pulling his greasy hair, anything I could think of to slow him down. He jabbed an elbow into my rib cage, knocking me back.

Heath made a valiant effort to stomp on Lee's toes, and Lee slammed him into the banister. They were close—treacherously close—to the top of the staircase.

Gruesome images flashed through my mind: Heath, in a crumpled heap at the bottom of the steps, a pool of blood spreading. Bones protruding through skin, shattered so thoroughly he'd never be able to stand, let alone skate.

I scrambled back to my feet. I ran into the bedroom.

I didn't realize what I was doing until the knife was already aimed at my brother's face.

"Get your hands off him." I jabbed the blade toward Lee's stubbled chin. He regarded it with a lazy grin. He didn't believe I was capable of hurting him.

Heath knew better.

"Katarina." The lower Heath's voice, the raspier it sounded, rustling the edges of every word like a breeze through tree branches. "Please. Put the knife down."

It was only a little paring knife, taken from a dusty drawer in the kitchen. Sharp enough to carve wood, but not to seriously maim someone, let alone murder them. Still, I did want to hurt Lee, just a little. Just enough to make him afraid of me for once.

I looked at Heath, like we were standing at center ice, our music about to start. *Ready?*

He winced and shook his head. I held his gaze, tightening my grip on the knife. I could tell he thought this was a terrible idea—and also that he didn't have any better ones.

Heath's chin dipped, almost imperceptibly. *Ready.*

I lunged at Lee, swiping the knife across his bicep. He let out an enraged yelp—and let go of Heath so he could take a swing at me. I managed to duck the blow but dropped my weapon as I shoved past my brother, racing down the steps. Heath hauled open the front door, letting in a blast of cold wind, then stopped on the other side of the threshold to wait for me.

Lee spat out a flurry of curses as he tripped on the last step and stumbled into the foyer. I kept running, eyes locked on Heath. I was almost there.

But Lee got there first. With one hand, he slammed the door and threw the deadbolt.

With the other, he pressed the blade to my neck.

NICOLE BRADFORD: Katarina and Heath met at the rink, but he wasn't a skater.

NARRATOR: Heath Rocha grew up in foster care. By the time he was ten years old, he'd lived with six different families.

NICOLE BRADFORD: I don't know for sure what Heath's home life was like, so I don't want to cast aspersions. I'll just say his foster parents didn't seem very . . . involved. He first came to the rink through a charity organization that offered free sports programs for local kids.

Slow zoom in on a photograph of young boys in hockey gear, highlighting ten-year-old Heath. He's the only child in the photo who isn't white.

NICOLE BRADFORD: Heath signed up for hockey, and after his lesson, he'd hang around the rink, like he didn't want to go home. When he thought no one was looking, he sat in the stands and watched Kat skate. It was clear he had a crush on her. I thought it was cute.

A photograph of nine-year-old Katarina practicing at the North Shore Ice Rink in Lake Forest, Illinois. Zooming in reveals a blurry figure behind her in the bleachers: Heath.

NICOLE BRADFORD: Eventually they struck up a friendship, and he started going home with her for dinner. Even sleeping over at the Shaw house. She hadn't mentioned her ice dancing aspirations for a few months; I thought maybe she'd finally gotten over it and was ready to go all-in on singles. I should have known she wouldn't give up so easily.

Stock footage of Lake Michigan in the dead of winter, the waves frozen solid.

NARRATOR: Katarina taught Heath to figure skate in secret, on the lake near the Shaw home.

ELLIS DEAN: I took up skating at seven, and that was late. Heath Rocha was almost *eleven*.

Jane Currer, a severe-looking woman in her seventies with curly hair dyed bright red and a silk scarf in a clashing hue, sits rinkside at the Olympic Training Center in Colorado Springs.

JANE CURRER (U.S. Figure Skating Official): While ice dancers do tend to peak at an older age, skaters who start any discipline past the average age are at a disadvantage. Basic skating skills lay the foundation for future success.

NICOLE BRADFORD: I'll admit it, I was extremely skeptical. Until I saw them skate together.

CHAPTER 3

I didn't fight anymore, as Lee dragged me back upstairs and threw me into my bedroom. As soon as his shuffling steps faded down the hall, I ran to the window. Heath stood on the lawn below, bare feet in the frost-covered grass. His shoulders dropped with relief when he saw me.

For January, it was reasonably pleasant outside: no snow on the ground, the lake still unfrozen. Heath had been chased out in far worse weather. I used to toss things down to him—clothing, food, clean blankets—but Lee got wise to that and screwed the window casing shut.

Heath waved, then turned and walked toward the woods. Lee might not have been able to lock my door anymore, but I was still as good as trapped until he passed out, which could happen anytime between midnight and the break of dawn. I knew where Heath went to hide on nights like this, and I couldn't risk my brother ruining that too.

I pressed my hand against the pane, like I could touch Heath from a distance, and kept it there until he'd disappeared beyond the twisting branches of the locust trees. When I pulled away, my palm left a streak of red on the glass.

I hoped my brother was still bleeding.

Since our father's death, Lee was in charge—though he was only five years my senior, and barely capable of looking after himself—and he thought Heath was a bad influence. Bold of him to worry about Heath's "influence," when Lee brought a different girl home every week. I'd lost count of the nights I spent with a pillow over my ears, trying to drown out the sounds of those poor girls' obviously faked orgasms.

The media likes to make my younger years with Heath out to be some sordid *Flowers in the Attic* shit: the two of us raised together as siblings (we weren't), left unsupervised to explore our undeniable passion for each other (I wish).

The truth, whether you want to believe it or not, is that Heath and I were both still virgins at sixteen. Sure, we kissed, we touched each other, we slid aside clothing so we could press skin against skin. We knew how to make each other gasp and groan and shudder with pleasure. I knew he wanted to go further. So did I.

In some ways, it seemed absurd to wait. After all, we were already intimate in ways even adults in years-long relationships find difficult to comprehend. We went to school together, skated together, spent practically every waking moment together—and our sleeping moments too, when we managed to sneak past my brother.

Despite that, the upcoming trip to Nationals would be the first time the two of us were truly on our own. We still technically had a coach, though we could barely afford to pay Nicole. My father's will divided everything equally between Lee and me, including the property, but I couldn't access my half of the estate until I turned eighteen.

Nicole helped Heath and me out as much as she could—arranging part-time jobs at the rink to subsidize our ice time, assisting with choreography since hiring a professional was out of reach—but asking her to give up days of paid lessons to travel with us for free was out of the question. So we were going it alone, staying several nights in a shabby motel we'd booked because the official event accommodations were too expensive.

Any normal teenage girl would have been eager to take advantage of the lack of chaperoning. But I wasn't a normal teenage girl. I was going to be an Olympic champion, and I wasn't about to do anything stupid to jeopardize that. Like stabbing my brother, no matter how much he might deserve it. Or getting myself knocked up and having to spend our dwindling training funds on an abortion.

Everyone thinks Heath Rocha was my first love. He wasn't.

My first love was figure skating.

It started in February 1988—the Winter Olympics in Calgary. I was four years old, and up way past my bedtime, watching the last night of the ice dance competition.

Lin and Lockwood were the final couple to take the ice. As they posed in the center of the rink, awaiting the first note of their program music, the camera zoomed in—straight past Kirk, with his skintight costume and slicked-back hair, to focus on Sheila's face alone.

The skaters who'd gone before had looked as if they were swallowing their nerves, hoping and praying to whatever god they believed in that all those years of grueling work would pay off with Olympic glory.

Not Sheila Lin. A smirk played across her lips, which were painted the same ruby hue as the jewels shining in her black hair. Even as a kid with no knowledge of the sport, I was sure she would win. Sheila looked like she'd *already* won—like she had the gold medal around her neck and her blade firmly planted on the still-twitching corpse of her competition.

I didn't become a skater because I harbored some childish fantasy of wearing sequins and spinning around like a pretty little top. I became a skater because I wanted to feel like *that*.

Fierce. Confident. A warrior goddess covered in glitter. So sure of myself, I could make my dreams come true through sheer force of will.

Skating was my first love, but in the intervening years it had become so much more. It was the only thing I was good at—my best hope for survival, for escape from that dark and crumbling house, from my brother and his rages. And if I worked hard enough, if I got good enough . . . one day I might become as invulnerable as Sheila Lin.

Nationals was the first step, the beginning of everything. Soon, I told myself, staring into the shadows beyond my bedroom window, Heath and I would be free of this place.

And no matter what, we would be together.

CHAPTER 4

The sun was rising by the time I managed to sneak out of the house.

Lee lay facedown on the sofa in the parlor. The fireplace hearth was scattered with cigarette butts, and liquor bottles left rings all over the original hardwood floors. My brother's idea of a quiet night in.

Outside, the morning was crisp and calm, silent aside from the gentle lap of the waves and the crunch of my shoes on the gravel driveway. I picked up my pace, jogging past Lee's mud-spattered pickup truck to follow the path I knew Heath had taken in the dark.

My childhood home is in a far-flung Chicago suburb closer to the Wisconsin border than to the city, dubbed The Heights due to its *very* slight elevation over the pancake-flat landscape surrounding it. Most of the area was populated in the late 1800s, following the fires and labor riots that sent all the richest assholes fleeing downtown Chicago for the relative safety of Lake Michigan's northern shore. The Shaws had already been there for decades.

My some-number-of-greats-grandfather bought a big patch of lakefront property back when the area was nothing but dirt and sand and black oaks bent double by the winds that whipped across the water. A generation after him, another Shaw built a house right on the lakefront, leaving plenty of forest to block the view of future prying neighbors.

The house itself is relatively simple: a modest flagstone farmhouse with a few Gothic revival flourishes. It's the land that's valuable. Every decade or so, developers come sniffing around, offering stacks of cash, and whichever Shaw is currently in residence tells them to fuck off, sometimes with Midwestern passive-aggression, other times with the barrel of a shotgun.

You can see how I came by my winning personality.

As a girl, I hated that house. It had already fallen into cobweb-choked disrepair when my parents inherited it, and my mother passed away before she had a chance to carry out her grand redecoration plans. If I wasn't at school or at the rink, I was usually running wild out-doors—on my own at first, and then with Heath by my side. In warmer months, the lake itself was our favorite spot. We'd wade through the waves, climb on top of the rocks to watch the sailboats and freighters passing by, and build bonfires in the small strip of sand that passed for a private beach.

When the weather turned, we retreated to the stable. Everyone still referred to the building that way, though it hadn't held any horses since decades before my father was born. Made of the same gray stone as the house, it sat near our northern boundary line, right next to the family burial plot. Lee steered clear of that corner of the property; he never came to visit our parents' graves, not even on their birthdays or the an-niversaries of their deaths.

So when Lee banned Heath from the house barely an hour after our father's funeral, it seemed like the ideal hiding spot. For weeks, I smug-gled things out to him: candles, firewood, an old mattress I dragged up from the cellar, even a battery-operated boom box.

As soon as I entered the stable that morning, I could tell Heath hadn't gotten any more rest than I had. He'd pulled the mattress into the warmest stall, away from the shattered skylight that served as a makeshift chimney, and a Debussy nocturne played on the classical radio station he tuned in to when he had trouble sleeping. Last night's fire had burned down to ash, and though sunshine had begun to melt the frost crystals on the jagged remains of the glass, it was still so cold I could see my breath.

I'd brought him his warmest coat, which I draped over his shoulders before lying down beside him. He opened his eyes, and even in the dim light, I could see how bruised the right one was, a purple bloom unfurl-ing between his lashes and cheekbone.

My fingertips ghosted over the swollen skin. It must have been tender, but Heath exhaled a cloud of steam and leaned into my touch.

"I'm going to kill Lee," I said.

"It's not that bad." Heath's teeth chattered when he spoke. I slipped off my shoes and rubbed my wool socks against his cold-numbed toes. "You can cover it up for Nationals, right?"

I nodded, though I wasn't sure the watery drugstore concealer in my makeup kit was up to the task.

"I think freezing my ass off out here might've kept the swelling down." He brushed my hair back, fingers catching in a tangle. "I'm just glad he didn't hurt you."

Lee had figured out a long time ago: the best way to hurt me was to hurt Heath.

Heath always stayed stoic, brushing off every insult and injury, no matter how severe. Once Lee shoved him into a wall so hard, he lost consciousness for a few terrifying seconds, and when I shook him back awake, all he did was shrug and tell me it could've been worse.

As close as we were, I knew next to nothing about Heath's life before me. He had a birth certificate showing he was born in Michigan and shared his surname with his mother. The line that should've listed his father was blank. The name *Rocha* was Spanish in origin, or maybe Portuguese—the only solid clue he had to his heritage. Most people in the Midwest took one look at Heath's brown skin and dark hair and assumed he was either Mexican or Middle Eastern (then made other, less charitable assumptions accordingly).

Heath knew nothing more about his real parents and insisted he had no desire to search for them. I'd never set foot inside his foster home, a squat sepia bungalow by the train tracks that didn't look anywhere near large enough to hold the number of people who lived there at any given time. When Heath moved in with us the summer before eighth grade, my father gave him Lee's childhood bedroom, which he'd vacated the second he turned eighteen in favor of a filthy shared flat closer to the city. Heath had gaped at the cramped, drafty room like it was a royal palace, and I'd realized it must have been the first time he'd had space all to himself.

He didn't like to talk about his past, and I didn't want to pry. All I knew was, if life with Lee Shaw was an improvement, whatever he'd endured before must have been truly horrific.

"Murdering your brother seems a *little* extreme." Heath's shivering had slowed, so the words came out steadier. "But I could get behind slashing his tires."

"I've got a better idea," I said. "Check your pockets."

Heath rummaged through the coat until there was a metallic clink. A slow smile spread across his face as he held up the keys to Lee's truck.

I didn't have my driver's license yet. But Heath had gotten his the summer before.

"Now *he's* going to kill *us*," Heath said.

"Not if we're gone before he wakes up."

Still clutching the keys, Heath took my face in his hands and kissed me. Cold metal pressed against my cheek. "What did I tell you, Katarina Shaw?"

I smiled and kissed him back. "There's nothing I can't do."

NICOLE BRADFORD: At first, Heath seemed hopeless. Thanks to his hockey lessons, he could skate fast, but he had no finesse. Ice dance is all about maneuvering on the edges of your blades, carving into the ice with precision and control.

In a home video taken by Ms. Bradford during one of their first practices together, Katarina and Heath attempt some simple forward crossovers, skating hand in hand.

NICOLE BRADFORD: But they had this . . . connection.

Heath's skates keep getting tangled up as he tries to match Katarina's rhythm. She squeezes his hand. He stops focusing on his feet, looking at her instead. Soon, they're moving in unison.

NICOLE BRADFORD: It was like they were reading each other's minds. His technique needed a ton of work. But I've never seen anyone work as hard as Heath.

ELLIS DEAN: Imagine being down so bad you'd master a *whole Olympic sport* to spend time with someone.

NICOLE BRADFORD: By the time they turned thirteen, I was starting to think bigger: Nationals, Worlds, maybe even the Olympic Games. I never made it that far myself.

Katarina and Heath wave from the top podium step at a regional competition.

NICOLE BRADFORD: One afternoon, I found them together on a bench outside the rink. They were embracing, and I thought for a second they might be . . . (*She clears her throat.*) Anyway, it turned out they were crying. They were both so upset, I thought someone must have died.

A series of candid snapshots show young Katarina and Heath at the rink and at the Shaw house: wading in the lake, cartwheeling on the lawn, cuddled in a nest of blankets watching television.

NICOLE BRADFORD: I finally got Heath calmed down enough to tell me he was being transferred to another foster home, hours away. He had to leave in less than a week.

JANE CURRER: Mr. Rocha's departure most likely would have meant Ms. Shaw had to give up skating, unless she could find another partner. Since switching to ice dance, she'd developed a body type that was . . . less than ideal for the jumps required in the ladies singles discipline.

NICOLE BRADFORD: I was sad too. But what could I do? I thought it was over. Then the next day, in they walk, holding hands, big smiles on their faces. And Katarina says Heath isn't going anywhere after all.

A snapshot of preteen Katarina and Heath, standing on either side of Katarina's father outside the Rosemont Horizon arena after the 1996 Stars on Ice tour performance headlined by Lin and Lockwood. Mr. Shaw has his arms around their shoulders, and all three are smiling wide.

NICOLE BRADFORD: She'd convinced her father to become the boy's legal guardian.

CHAPTER 5

The heater in Lee's Chevy pickup didn't work, and frigid wind cut through the cracked window seals. Even so, my memories of that drive with Heath are drenched in warmth.

Our gloved hands entwined over the gearshift, winter sun caressing our faces as we sang along to Savage Garden and Semisonic on the radio. The prickling heat that spread across my chest, then pooled lower, every time Heath turned to smile at me.

After miles of fallow cornfields, dairy farms, and industrial smoke-stacks, Cleveland finally appeared on the horizon. We were hours earlier than we would have been if we'd had to take the bus—right on time for an open practice session on competition ice.

Walking into the arena, even with my unwashed hair in a haphazard ponytail and the burnt taste of gas station coffee on my tongue, I felt impossibly glamorous—which seems ridiculous to me now. A multipurpose sporting complex in Cleveland, Ohio, is not exactly the height of sophistication. But that day, staring up at the cresting wave of blue stadium seats, I felt like I'd finally arrived.

As we stretched out the tension of our sleepless night and all those hours in Lee's icebox of a truck, I watched—and judged—the other skaters.

Right away, I spotted last year's silver medalists, Paige Reed and Zachary Branwell, both clean-cut Nordic blonds from Minnesota. They showed enviable technique, but despite being a couple off the ice as well as on, there was about as much heat between them as two untoasted slices of white bread. Paige favored her left leg too, thanks to a preseason injury.

The other two teams, I didn't recognize. So either it was their first time at Nationals, like us, or they'd been ranked too low last year to make it into the TV broadcast. There was a skinny, flat-chested girl and a freckle-faced guy who weren't a serious threat; they had decent edges, but no flow in their movements, and they held each other at arm's length like they were at a middle-school dance.

The last pair—both sporting ponytails: his dark and tied with ribbon like a nobleman, hers platinum and pulled so tight she looked like a face-lifted divorcée—weren't half bad, but they lacked connection too. They were skating next to each other rather than *with* each other.

Heath and I could beat them, I thought, a giddy buzz growing in my chest.

Just then a big band track trumpeted over the loudspeakers, and a new team took the ice.

Instead of typical warm-up gear, they were in full costume and makeup. The girl's dress was a retro confection that sparkled like an ice blue disco ball. Her partner wore matching suspenders over a black shirt perfectly tailored to emphasize his impeccable posture. And they weren't simply warming up or running through their program. They were performing all-out, finishing off every step with a smile up to the rafters, as if the arena were full of adoring fans.

This was our *real* competition.

I twisted my ring, trying to settle my nerves. Since my very first juvenile competition, I'd worn my mother's Art Deco engagement band as a good luck charm. When I was small, it hung on a gold chain around my neck. By sixteen, the ring fit my middle finger—and I'd started keeping it on my person at all times, because I knew if Lee got his hands on it, he'd pawn the diamond and drink the proceeds.

"Don't worry about them," Heath said. He could always read my moods like a weather report. "If we do our best, that's all that matters."

I had no interest in "our best" unless it was *the* best. We'd been the best at our small-town rink for so long, it had ceased to mean anything. If we wanted to keep improving—if we wanted to become Olympic-caliber athletes—we needed to be pushed, to be challenged. Well, here was the perfect challenge, passing right by us in a blur of blue sequins.

I took Heath's hand, and we stepped onto the ice. As we completed a few circuits, the other team finished their program—then cut a path to the center of the rink. Their music started up again, and they repeated their choreography, step for step, smile for smile. They didn't even look winded.

Heath raised his eyebrows, as if to say, *Shall we?* I grinned and pulled him into a hold, not bothering to correct the way his hand drifted too low, settling into the crease of my waist.

We were off, whirling around the rink, syncing our movements to the song. This was how we stretched out our training time at home—we'd show up early and improvise to whatever music happened to be playing, whether it was the Top 40 pop they blasted during public skate sessions or the perky cartoon themes that accompanied kids' birthday parties.

Our feet followed the bombastic harmony of the horn section first, then sped up to chase the driving string bass line. We spun faster and faster, my ponytail coming undone, wild curls whipping around my face, the competition forgotten. For a few blissful moments, it was only me and him, only the ice and our blades and the beat.

And suddenly I wasn't in Heath's arms anymore.

I was sprawled facedown, my hip wrenched at a strange angle, ice burn all over my palms. Snow sprayed in my eyes as a pair of skates skidded to a stop a few inches from my nose.

"Are you okay?" a voice said from somewhere above me.

The skates were so clean, they looked brand-new—blinding white leather, carefully knotted laces. I polished my boots every night before bed, and they were never that spotless.

"Katarina." Heath's voice now. His breath at my ear. "Can you stand?"

I blinked melting snow from my eyes. Or maybe I was crying, I couldn't be sure. I kept staring at those skates, studying them. There was something engraved on the blades too. Words, in delicate, flowing text. A name.

Her name. *Isabella Lin.*

Kirk Lockwood—who we previously saw in news footage from the Sochi Olympics—takes a seat by the bay window in the parlor of his Boston home.

KIRK LOCKWOOD (Former Ice Dancer): Is it time to talk about Sheila?

JANE CURRER: To fully understand Katarina Shaw, first we have to discuss Sheila Lin.

KIRK LOCKWOOD: Sheila started training at my rink in the summer of 1980. She was between partners. I guess she'd gone through a couple different guys already—which isn't uncommon. She was so good, though. I couldn't understand why anyone would let her go. Or why I'd never met her before.

Exterior shot of the Lockwood Performance Center ice rink in the suburbs of Boston.

NARRATOR: While Sheila Lin seemed to come out of nowhere, Kirk Lockwood came from a long skating bloodline. His family founded the Lockwood Performance Center, which is known for turning out champion figure skaters—including Kirk's mother, Carol, who won silver in ladies singles at the Cortina Games.

JANE CURRER: It was quite the scandal, when Kirk left his partner for Sheila. He and Deborah Green had been together almost ten years, and they'd just won gold at Junior Worlds.

KIRK LOCKWOOD: Maybe if I was a nicer person, I'd say I regretted it. But I don't. Teaming with Sheila was the first decision I made on my own, without my parents telling me what to do.

JANE CURRER: Sheila manipulated him. He was the best, and she wanted him for herself.

KIRK LOCKWOOD: She was better than I was, and I knew she'd make me better than I could've ever been with Debbie. You had to skate up to Sheila's level, because she wasn't gonna skate down to yours.

Old, glitchy camcorder footage shows Sheila and Kirk practicing synchronized side-by-side rotations, also known as twizzles. Kirk loses his balance and falls. Sheila doesn't even slow down.

KIRK LOCKWOOD: And if you couldn't get on her level? Well, too damn bad for you.

CHAPTER 6

A hand reached down, and I took it.

I didn't realize until I was back on my feet that it belonged to the boy with the blue sequined suspenders.

If the girl was Isabella Lin, he must be her twin brother, Garrett. Their resemblance to their famous mother was unmistakable. They both had Sheila's high cheekbones, her full lips, her shampoo-commercial hair. And they'd clearly inherited her skating talent as well.

Winning two consecutive gold medals was a rare feat, but Sheila Lin had accomplished something even rarer: managing to stay competitive after motherhood. The twins were born following her first Olympics. At her second, they had front row seats.

I knew Isabella and Garrett had followed in their mother's footsteps, but I still thought of them as the little kids I'd seen on Sheila's lap during the Calgary coverage. They were younger than Heath and me, though not by much: fifteen, and already competing at the senior level, skating circles around teams a decade older. Amazing what you can accomplish when you're born with the best coach in the world.

"Are you hurt?" Heath asked, putting his arm around me.

I was still holding on to Garrett Lin's hand. I dropped it, backing up and brushing ice off my leggings. "I'm fine. Just got the wind knocked out of me."

Every skater is used to falling. I knew how to brace myself to absorb the impact and prevent injury, but I'd been too caught up in the moment, already down before I realized what was happening.

"I'm so sorry." Garrett looked more upset than I was. "I didn't—"

"Don't apologize to them."

Unlike Garrett, who was pushing six feet and still growing, his sister shared Sheila's petite stature. Isabella barely came up to my chin, yet somehow she seemed to be staring down her nose at me.

"It was their fault," she said.

Heath's fingers tensed, digging in. A dull ache radiated from my shoulder.

"You ran into *us*," he said.

Isabella crossed her arms. "Our music was playing."

"Whoever's program music is playing gets the right of way during a practice session," Garrett explained. His tone was kind, not even a hint of condescension. "But even so, we should have been paying more attention. Are you sure you're okay? If you hit your head, or—"

"She's fine." Heath steered us toward the boards. With every stroke of my skates, the ache in my back spread, rooting deeper in my spine.

I couldn't be injured. We were at the National Championships. We had three straight days of competition ahead. We'd worked so hard.

"What are you doing at *Nationals*," Isabella called after us, "if you don't even know—"

"Bella."

The voice was soft, even-toned. But both twins snapped to attention as if they'd been issued a military command. I followed their gaze, and there she was.

Sheila Lin.

She looked as stunning in person as she did in the photos on my bedroom wall. Her hair was shorter, precision-cut in a bob following the sharp line of her jaw. She wore all white: slim-fitting pants and a leather blazer as spotless as her daughter's skates.

I was only a few feet away from the woman I'd idolized for as long as I could remember. And she'd witnessed me wiping out like a total amateur, almost taking her champion children down with me.

Heath didn't even seem to notice Sheila's presence. He led me off the ice and helped me sit down on a bench, then knelt to snap my blade guards back in place.

"What do you need?" he asked. "I can get you an ice pack. Or a medic, to check you out, make sure there's no—"

"I'm fine," I repeated. My hips felt stiff, a pulsing pain settling into the right socket. Movement should help. "Let me rest for a second, and we can get back out there."

"I'm going to get the medic."

He was gone before I could stop him. I knew it would make him feel better to do something, even though I was certain my pride was more bruised than my body.

The twins were at the boards now, heads bowed, consulting with Sheila. Probably talking about the ignorant girl who'd run into them because she didn't know basic ice-sharing rules. I shut my eyes, determined to hold back the tears that threatened.

"Please tell me you did that on purpose."

I looked up. It was the ponytailed guy I'd seen earlier. Close-up, he was so skinny he looked less like a nobleman and more like a freakishly tall Victorian urchin.

"What?" I said.

"Trying to take out the Lin Twins." He plopped down next to me, a smirk twisting his pale face. "Please tell me you did it on purpose."

"It was an accident. I wasn't watching where I was going, and—"

"Too bad. You struck me as the type."

"The 'type'?" I couldn't figure out whether he was making fun of me or not.

"The type who'll do anything to win." He stuck out his hand. "Ellis Dean."

I took it. "Katarina Shaw."

"Nice to meet you, Katarina Shaw." He leaned closer, dropping his voice to a whisper. "Next time, aim for her toe pick. Then she'll be the one eating ice."

As if she'd somehow heard him from the other side of the rink, Isabella shot a glare in our direction. Ellis gave her a smile and a finger-waggling wave. She did not return either.

"Trust me," he said through his teeth. "She deserves it."

When Isabella's glare settled on me, I didn't bother with the pretense of a smile. I glared back, holding her gaze without blinking until my eyes started to burn.

Finally, she turned away, taking a sip from her Swarovski-encrusted water bottle.

My first victory over Bella Lin. I vowed it wouldn't be my last.

Garrett Lin, now in his late thirties, lounges on a leather sofa at his home in San Francisco.

GARRETT LIN (Sheila Lin's Son): If you think I'm going to spill a bunch of dirt about my mother, how mean she was to me and my sister or whatever... forget it, all right? That isn't why I agreed to do this.

A few candid Polaroids showing Sheila during her pregnancy are followed by a formal birth announcement. As infants the twins look identical, with black hair and gold swaddling.

KIRK LOCKWOOD: Sheila was the most driven, focused person I'd ever met. Then she's pregnant, with twins, at twenty-two years old? I was shocked.

ELLIS DEAN: Bella and Garrett were born *exactly* nine months after the Sarajevo Games. Sheila refused to tell anyone who the father was, but it had to be an Olympic Village hookup.

KIRK LOCKWOOD: All I know is, it wasn't me. I'm proud to be both a gold medalist and a gold-star gay man.

GARRETT LIN: I know my mother didn't plan her pregnancy, but it's almost like she did, right? We were a ready-made ice dance team, and she had us in skates as soon as we could stand.

NARRATOR: After revealing her pregnancy, Sheila Lin retreated from the public eye. Though she hadn't announced her retirement, most assumed she wouldn't return to competition.

In a series of paparazzi photos, Sheila pushes a double stroller down a city street.

KIRK LOCKWOOD: We didn't speak for months. When she finally got back in touch and said she wanted to start training for the '88 Games, I almost told her to fuck off. Excuse my language. But c'mon—she thought I was waiting around for her? Well, I guess I kind of was, but that's not the point.

Sheila laces up her skates at the Lockwood Performance Center, staring at the ice with fierce determination.

KIRK LOCKWOOD: I figured, quit while you're ahead, right? But she was so sure we could win again. And if Sheila Lin wanted something? Only an idiot would try to stand in her way.

CHAPTER 7

The next morning, the ache in my hip was worse. I told myself it was from the motel mattress springs stabbing into me as I tried to sleep through the combined noise of the highway traffic and the most definitely *not* faked cries of pleasure coming from the room next door.

I turned the shower as hot as it would go and stretched under the stream, willing my muscles to loosen. The first event started in the late morning and would be over by mid-afternoon, then I'd have the whole rest of the day to take it easy and recover.

In those days, ice dance competitions kicked off with the compulsory dance, where all teams had to perform the same exact steps—by far my least favorite event; unfortunately, the skating Powers That Be didn't do away with it until near the end of my career. The original dance, which allowed teams to put their own spin on each season's required dance style, was better, but I much preferred the final event, the free dance. There, we could choose whatever music and choreography we wanted.

After a scalding shower and lots of warm-up stretches, I made it through our compulsory Quickstep program without too much trouble. I wasn't able to swing my leg as high as usual, but Heath adjusted his turns so we still had matching lines. Not our best performance, but enough to put us in seventh place.

It wasn't until the next day, when I was getting dressed for the original, that I noticed the bruise. We didn't have the funds for fancy costumes, so Heath wore the same nondescript black shirt and trousers for all three programs, while I had one more elaborate dress I saved for the free. My costume for the compulsory and original dances was plain black velvet with spaghetti straps and a slit up the leg—a slit that perfectly framed the furious purple splotch spreading from my hip down toward my knee.

"That looks bad," Heath said.

"At least we match now," I pointed out.

I'd been able to conceal the worst of the damage to Heath's eye, but all the Cover Girl in the world wasn't going to make the mark on my leg go away. It was obvious even through my thickest tights. My free dance costume was longer—a structured bodice over a gauzy, shredded skirt; I'd DIY'd it from a thrift store prom dress—so I put that on instead, ignoring the sparks of pain that lit up my thigh every time the skirt swished.

The required style for the original dance was Latin ballroom, and our program was a Rhumba to the old standard "Perhaps Perhaps Perhaps"—a mash-up of the Desi Arnaz version and a cover by the band Cake to provide the changes in musical character and tempo the judges wanted to see from a well-balanced program.

Later in our career, the Latin dances would become something of a specialty for us, since they made such good use of our natural chemistry (and plenty of the officials thought Heath had Latin heritage, an assumption he didn't bother correcting if it boosted our scores). We weren't as polished back then, but Latin was still one of our best styles. While the Quickstep relied on sharp, controlled movements, the Rhumba required formal carriage in the upper body and more exaggerated, sensual movements in the lower.

Not an ideal combination in my condition. Seconds into our program, Heath could sense how much pain I was in—and I could sense how desperately he wanted to stop and make sure I was all right.

We couldn't stop. If we stopped, it was all over. So I let the momentum of the steps carry me, and we made it through. As we skated to the boards, Heath looped his arm around my waist, and he kept it there during the walk to the kiss and cry area to wait for our scores. He knew I wouldn't want anyone to see me limp. Especially not the Lins, who were about to take the ice as part of the final warm-up group.

By the time we made it back to the motel that night, it was snowing so hard we almost drove right past the flickering neon *Vacancy* sign. And I was in so much agony, I couldn't get out of the car without Heath's help. He had to carry me over the threshold like a bride.

While he trudged through snowdrifts to the drugstore across the street, I lay prone on the bed, listening to the wind rattle the flimsy windowpanes and silently panicking.

The sixth-place team had stumbled during their twizzle sequence, and by the end of the original dance, we found ourselves in fifth—right behind Ellis Dean and his partner, Josephine Hayworth. One more event to go, and we were within striking distance of the podium. We'd only have to advance a single spot, since they awarded a pewter medal for fourth place finishers at Nationals in addition to the usual bronze, silver, and gold.

The worst of the pain was coiled around my hip socket, but even the smallest movement sent it slithering out to attack the rest of me. My mother's ring was typically loose on my finger. Now my hands were so swollen, I couldn't get it past my knuckle.

Heath returned with snow caked on his eyelashes, bearing Tylenol, a jar of Tiger Balm, and a bag of ice. He alternated between the cold of the ice, the heat of his hands, and the balm's strange combination of both. Nothing helped.

I hated being taken care of like that, nursed like a helpless child. I'd only let Heath do it once before.

The day my father died.

He always picked us up from the rink on his way home from the college where he taught history. When he failed to show that evening, I told myself he must have forgotten, gotten distracted and lost track of time. As children, Lee and I would often find him sitting in the same place for hours, staring at the wallpaper like he hoped to see our mother's face in the pattern. It was unspeakably sad, and so we never spoke about it.

Since Heath had come to live with us, though, my father had been better. More present. He even arrived at the rink early sometimes and sat in the stands, watching us skate and chatting with the other parents—

who were all mothers rather than fathers. Those women *adored* him. I suppose he had a certain awkward, absentminded-professor charm.

Nicole let me use the phone in the back office to call him, but there was no answer at his campus number. After an hour had gone by, she gave up and drove us home herself. The house looked dark, but as we drew closer, I saw a single light burning. In my father's study.

A strange mix of anger and relief swirled through me. I'd been right, he'd forgotten about us. So when we came through the front door, instead of calling out a greeting, I glanced at Heath and laid a finger over my lips. We tiptoed down the hallway.

All we wanted was to sneak up on him, give him a little fright. A petty prank, to pay him back. He'd shout, and then he'd laugh, and we'd be even. He would fix us something to eat—frozen waffles, or macaroni and cheese from a box; my father's cooking repertoire was not extensive—and he'd let Heath pick dinner music from the record collection. We'd sit around the table talking, like a normal family.

Heath was always envious that I'd grown up with a father and brother and a house to call my own, but the truth was, my family never felt the least bit normal until Heath joined it. Maybe it was their shared affinity for music, or the rapt attention Heath paid during my father's frequent tangents. Or maybe it was simply that Heath was a child my father could dote on without being haunted by memories of his lost love. All I knew was, Heath's presence sparked a light in my father's eyes that I once feared had been snuffed out for good.

The study door had been open only a sliver. I steepled my fingers against the paneled oak and pushed. The hinges screeched, and I cringed. So much for sneaking in undetected.

But my father didn't move. He was in his favorite broken-down leather chair, facing the bay window; he liked to stare out at the lake while he was thinking. The glow of his banker's lamp reflected in the glass, showing a mirror image of his face.

Skin pallid. Mouth slack. Eyes wide and staring and empty.

Gone.

The next thing I remember was Heath's hand on my back, turning me toward him, pressing me close as if we were dancing.

Then, minutes later, or maybe hours: Heath's fingers squeezing mine as we stood together on the front porch, watching the ambulance pull away. Lights off, no siren. The thing that had been my father zipped into a black bag on the stretcher inside it.

Heath had called the paramedics. He called Lee to tell him the tragic news too, then tucked me into bed and stayed by my side until I fell asleep. When I woke up barely an hour later, sobbing and shaking, Lee still wasn't there, but Heath hadn't moved an inch.

When I reached for Heath, he didn't hesitate. He climbed in beside me under the covers, and I clung to him as if I were suspended over a yawning darkness and he was the only thing keeping me from plummeting down, down, down.

That was the first night we shared a bed. And ever since, I'd had trouble falling asleep without his arms around me. Heath Rocha was there for me when no one else was.

At the motel in Cleveland, I managed to drift off with my cheek pillowed on Heath's chest and his fingers gently stroking my hair. When I woke up in the morning, the snow had stopped—and my hip was screaming.

Heath took one look at my face and said, "Katarina, you need to see a doctor."

We both knew we couldn't afford a doctor. And we knew if we didn't skate today, it could spell the end of our skating careers. Clawing our way onto any step of the podium was the best hope we had of attracting the attention of sponsors, a better coach, *something* that would allow us to continue without begging for scraps from my brother.

I thought about Isabella and Garrett Lin, waking refreshed after eight hours cosseted in feather-down luxury at the Ritz-Carlton. Eating egg whites and fresh fruit delivered to them on a literal silver platter. Riding to the arena in a chauffeured car so the slap of the lake-effect wind couldn't touch them.

People like them didn't know how to fight. They'd never had to.

I sat up in bed. I put one foot on the grimy chartreuse carpet, then the other. As I pushed myself to standing, Heath flinched like the pain was coursing through his own body.

But he knew better than to try to stop me.

ELLIS DEAN: Kat Shaw always was a stubborn bitch. *(He takes a sip of his martini and raises his eyebrows.)* What? I meant it as a compliment. Trust me, she'd take it that way.

GARRETT LIN: Part of being an elite athlete is pushing past your limits when it counts.

JANE CURRER: We would never want a skater to compete injured. That said, it's ultimately up to the athlete and their coach. U.S. Figure Skating can't be held responsible. Or liable.

NICOLE BRADFORD: If I had been there, I would have withdrawn them and driven straight to the nearest hospital. *(She pauses, lips pursed.)* Well, I would have tried anyway.

GARRETT LIN: The thing is, when pushing your limits is all you know, when it seems normal to you . . . it's hard to remember you even *have* limits. Until you run right into them.

CHAPTER 8

I broke it down into small, manageable steps, like in training.

First, I had to make it to the shower. Next, I had to get dressed. Then walk to the car without slipping in the unsalted parking lot.

I got through the day one excruciating moment at a time, until Heath and I were by the boards, waiting for the sixth-place skaters to finish so we could take our turn.

He stood behind me, palm pressed against my stomach, and we took slow, deep breaths together until we felt our pulses beat in sync. Even with the pain, a sense of calm settled over me, the way it always did when Heath and I touched.

If this was going to be our last competitive skate, I wanted to know I'd done everything I could.

We skated to center ice, and I let it all fall away. Not just the pain—everything. The hum of the crowd. The scrape of our blades. The sound of the announcer saying our names. Everything faded, until my focus shrank to the heat of Heath's fingers intertwined with mine.

I don't remember much about that free dance. We were skating to a medley of songs from Madonna's *Ray of Light* album, anchored by "Frozen," which was all over the radio at the time. Heath had recorded it off B96 for me, and I'd worn out the cassette, playing it over and over until Lee smacked the wall and shouted to *turn that shit off*.

Here's what I do remember about our first national final: the way my body took over as soon as I heard those familiar synthesized strings. The sensation of Heath's breath against my neck as we wound ourselves around each other in a sinuous combination spin. The burning in my legs as we entered the last minute of the program, and how it felt more like pleasure than pain.

We ended with a standing spin that left us facing each other, Heath's hands around my waist. The crowd cheered as the final note faded— and cheered louder when we gave each other a quick, chaste kiss. Well, chaste compared to the way we kissed when we were older anyway.

As we made our way off the ice, I couldn't stop smiling. We'd done it. I hadn't let the pain hold me back; in fact, I could barely even feel it anymore. That was the best we'd ever skated. It had to be enough to put us into fourth. Maybe even higher.

No one had thrown flowers for us during the first two events, but now they were raining down. Heath bent to sweep up a single red rose and handed it to me.

We were the only team at Nationals without a coach in attendance, so we sat alone as we awaited our scores. I'd felt awkward about it at first, but now I was glad. I knew Nicole would have tried to stop us from skating, and she would have been wrong. We were going to stand on the national podium like I'd dreamed about since I was four years old, and this competition would be the beginning for us, not the end.

Our technical marks displayed first. No 6.0s, but several high fives. I clutched the rose with one hand, Heath's knee with the other. We almost always scored higher on the artistic side.

The technical score is scientific—especially nowadays, with the impenetrably complex scoring system the International Skating Union has implemented. But the artistic score is pure magic. That's what the crowd responds to. Your passion, your connection, the way you interpret every single note of the music with the most dramatic extensions of your limbs and the subtlest tilts of your chin. If you can make every person in the arena, from the front row to the nosebleeds, feel something real? That's how you win.

"And now, the marks for artistic impression."

I held my breath. Heath tightened his arm around my shoulders.

Then the first number appeared, and I forgot how to breathe.

ELLIS DEAN: They were robbed. I'm the one they would've knocked off the podium, and I can admit that.

JANE CURRER: Their performance was engaging, but this was Nationals, not the Ice Capades.

A clip from the 2000 U.S. Nationals broadcast of Katarina Shaw and Heath Rocha's "Frozen" program plays, slowed down and zoomed in to show their facial expressions. Even during complicated elements, they never take their eyes off each other.

NICOLE BRADFORD: I can understand why some judges might not have responded to their style. Skating to a Madonna song, the dress Kat wore—it was a little edgier than what the other teams were doing.

JANE CURRER: Presentation is important, and that includes hair, makeup, costumes. The whole package.

ELLIS DEAN: I mean, yeah, that was the ugliest effing dress I'd ever seen. But she wore it for the original dance too, and they didn't ding her then.

Katarina and Heath react to their artistic presentation scores. She looks like she wants to break something. He squeezes her hand. There are a few scattered boos from the crowd.

JANE CURRER: I would call figure skating a conservative sport, and I don't see why that's a negative thing. The young athletes who win U.S. medals go out into the world as ambassadors of our great country. We have to be sure they'll act appropriately. On *and* off the ice.

ELLIS DEAN: They looked at Kat Shaw and saw white trash, and they looked at Heath Rocha and saw a foreigner. Never mind that he was as American as any of those snobby-ass judges.

JANE CURRER: As I said, I stand by my scores, and my decisions. At 2000 Nationals, and every competition thereafter.

PRODUCER (Offscreen): What about your decision regarding th—

JANE CURRER: Next question, please.

CHAPTER 9

The best skate of our lives so far, and we slid back to sixth place.

The Lins took silver, right behind the reigning national champs Elizabeth Parry and Brian Alcona. Reed and Branwell got the bronze, Hayworth and Dean the pewter.

Heath didn't ask if I wanted to stay to watch the medal ceremony. It was just a matter of time before I lost control of the emotions I'd been holding in since our dismal artistic marks flashed across the screen, and we both wanted to be on the road home before that happened.

Home, where my brother might actually kill us for taking his truck without permission. I almost wished he would, because otherwise I somehow had to survive until my eighteenth birthday, stripped of the one thing I'd been living for this entire time.

With those scores, no one better than Nicole would want to coach us. No sponsors would look twice. No one would remember us at all.

The snow had started up again, so Heath offered to go get the truck while I waited in the lobby. My hip was shrieking in protest after everything I'd put it through, but that pain was nothing compared to the humiliation gnawing a hole in my chest. I slouched against the wall, burying my hands in my coat pockets, blinking fast to keep the tears at bay.

I wasn't a champion. I wasn't special. I was nothing.

Eventually, I looked up. And there she was again.

Sheila Lin.

For a second, I thought I was hallucinating. She was still all in white—a structured sheath dress this time—and the streetlights beyond the lobby windows made her glow like a goddess. She looked so beautiful, so flawless, I couldn't help staring at her.

But then, inexplicably, she stared back at me.

I straightened out my slumped posture, ignoring the resulting muscle spasm. I must have looked ridiculous, all sweaty and disheveled, that stupid shredded skirt poking out under my puffy winter coat. And my mouth hanging open in shock, because now Sheila Lin was not only looking at me but also *walking toward me*.

She stopped, the click of her stilettos still echoing. "Ms. Shaw."

I was so stunned Sheila Lin knew my name, I forgot how to form words.

"It is Ms. Shaw, isn't it?"

I swallowed. "Yes. Hi. I'm—Katarina. Or Kat. Most people call me 'Kat,' but I don't—"

She stuck out her hand. "I'm Sheila Lin."

I almost laughed. *The* Sheila Lin, introducing herself, to *me*? As if everyone in the world didn't know who she was. My hand trembled as I took hers, and I thought *this is it,* the peak of my career. I skated at Nationals, and I touched Sheila Lin's hand. It's all downhill from here.

"This is your first time competing at Nationals," she said.

I started to nod—then stopped, because she hadn't actually asked a question.

"I didn't see your coach with you. Where do you train?"

"At the North Shore Ice Rink, outside Chicago. With Nicole Bradford."

No point in explaining our strange coaching arrangement, or the money troubles that had led to it. Sheila wouldn't be familiar with Nicole anyway. Heath and I were the first team from North Shore to ever make it to Nationals.

"Well done today," she said. "It's rare to see a young team with so much raw power."

I sunk my front teeth into my lip, unsure how I should respond.

Sheila arched one expertly plucked eyebrow. "You don't think you skated well?"

"I could have skated better."

"You can *always* be better. But don't let that stop you from carrying yourself like a champion. If you don't believe you're the best, no one else will either. You understand?"

"Yes," I said—though I didn't. Not yet.

Heath pulled up outside and hopped out of the truck. I was already imagining myself introducing him to Sheila. It wasn't until he started to push through the revolving doors that I remembered the black eye. The bruise showed through his sweat-melted makeup; he looked like he'd been on the losing end of a bar fight.

I gave Heath a sharp look, and he stopped in the doorway, the truck's red hazard lights flashing behind him. Sheila didn't seem to notice.

"Tell me, Ms. Shaw," she said. "What are your plans for the summer?"

CHAPTER 10

Heath white-knuckled the steering wheel, trying to stop the truck from skidding onto the shoulder in the steadily intensifying snow. I knew he needed to concentrate, but I simply could not shut up about my conversation with Sheila Lin.

"Her skating school has *two* rinks, and they're *both* Olympic-sized! There are dedicated teachers for every single dance style on staff, and technical coaches, and—"

"Why us?" he asked.

"Why *not* us? I don't understand why you're not more excited about this!"

As we continued our slow progress west on I-80, I kept adding flourishes to the fairy tale narrative in my head. Yes, fine, we'd come in sixth. But Sheila saw something she liked. Something that piqued her interest enough she'd learned my name, sought me out, invited me—*personally* invited *me!*—to join the summer intensive program at the Lin Ice Academy in Los Angeles.

Before Sheila left to watch the twins receive their silver medals, she'd given me her business card. I clutched it so tight, the thick stock sliced my palm. I didn't care. Every bright sting of pain was a reminder that this was *real*.

"Did she say how much it would cost?" Heath asked.

I didn't care about that either. The chance to train with Sheila Lin was priceless.

"We'll figure it out," I told him.

✿

Lee would've put a stop to my grand plans.

Which is why I had no intention of telling him.

As soon as we got home, I fell on my sword and apologized for borrowing the truck. Lee was so taken aback—and, okay, also catatonic with booze—he took the keys without a scene and didn't even make a fuss when Heath helped me up the stairs to my bedroom.

The next day, once the hangover hit, Lee had a few choice words and a slap across the cheek for me, but I hardly registered the sting. The pain in my injured hip was fading too, and I felt invincible. A few more months, and I'd leave this place behind to step into my future.

When the Academy enrollment forms arrived, I intercepted the envelope and forged Lee's chicken-scratch signature on the Parent or Guardian line. My inheritance was tied up in legal red tape until I turned eighteen, but Heath and I managed to scrounge together enough money from our menial part-time jobs at the rink for the deposit required to hold our places in the program. We booked plane tickets too—the cheapest flights we could find, with a six-hour layover at some regional airport in Texas. But even after months of pulling as many extra shifts as we could, squirreling all our earnings behind a busted plank in the stable, we were well short of what we'd need to survive in Los Angeles for a whole summer.

Lee had already sold off everything in the house that had any value. There was only one option left, and I knew Heath would try to talk me out of it.

My mother's engagement ring was my last remaining tie to her. I'd been so young when she died, I retained only the vaguest memories: her hair tumbling down her back in wild waves like mine, the same plain brown that glinted golden in the sun. Her smooth alto soaring to the blue sky as I ran along the shoreline. Her strong arms around me in the water, keeping me tethered close as I learned to swim, then letting me go.

On our last day in Illinois, I told Heath I needed to run some errands and took the bus to the nicest jewelry store in downtown Lake Forest. The proprietor lowballed me, assuming I was a silly teenage girl with no concept of the ring's value. But I knew what I had, and what it was worth. I walked out with my purse stuffed full of cash and didn't look back.

I never really knew my mother, but I like to think she would have been proud of me.

When I returned, Heath was on the beach, building a bonfire. We'd decided to spend the night camping out there, so we could watch the sun rise over the waves one final time—and so we could avoid Lee until it would be too late for him to stop us. Our packed bags were hidden under my bed, ready for our early morning cab ride to O'Hare. I wasn't sure what my brother would think when he found us gone. But I was fairly certain he wouldn't bother coming after us.

The evening was warm and windy, an early summer storm brewing over the lake. Heath had laid out a blanket, the corners pinned down with chunks of rock so it wouldn't blow away.

I hoped he wouldn't notice, but his eyes went right to my hand.

"Katarina." He raked a hand through his hair. "What did you do?"

"It was only a ring," I said. "I'll buy myself a way better one when I'm a rich and famous Olympic gold medalist."

Darkness was falling fast, the wind picking up. I slipped my arms around Heath's waist.

"What about you?" I said. "What do you want when we're rich and famous?"

Heath frowned.

"The world's best surround sound system?" I suggested. "An obnoxious sports car?"

He shook his head. "I don't need anything."

"That's not what I asked. What do you *want*?"

He kissed me, just as the first lightning strike split the sky over the lake. Soon we were tangled on the blanket next to the bonfire. Thunder rumbled, the storm creeping closer to shore, but we were safe on our little beach.

As suddenly as he'd started, Heath stopped kissing me and pulled away. He drew my hand up between us, studying my bare finger in the firelight.

"What's wrong?" I asked.

Though he'd gone along with our preparations, the closer we got to our departure date, the more he retreated into brooding silence. I couldn't understand his lack of excitement. *I* was the one leaving the only home I'd ever known behind. He'd spent his whole childhood shuttling from place to place—what was one more move? Why couldn't he see this was the opportunity of a lifetime, the best thing that had ever happened to us?

"Your ring," he said.

I sighed. "Heath, it's done."

"It meant so much to you." He swallowed. "And you just—"

"It'll be worth it," I said. "Once we get to California, you'll see."

In the dancing light of the wind-stoked bonfire, his eyes looked pure black, troubled as the choppy water. The crashing waves nearly washed his next words away.

"I hope you're right, Katarina."

Now I look back and think: maybe if I hadn't been so caught up in my fantasies of being Sheila Lin's star pupil, I would have seen Heath's reticence for what it really was. Yes, he was used to change. He was used to loss. He was also used to anything that seemed too good to be true—anything that seemed good at all—being ripped from his grasp as soon as he touched it.

No wonder he held on to me so tightly.

"Do you know what it's like to be a retired mother of two at twenty-six years old?"

In a television clip from the late 1990s, Sheila Lin sits in a studio opposite a female interviewer.

"I had my gold medals," Sheila continues. "My endorsement deals. Kirk and I did the Stars on Ice circuit for several years. It wasn't enough. I wanted to build something lasting."

"For your children?" the interviewer asks.

Sheila answers without hesitation. "For myself."

NARRATOR: After Sarajevo, Sheila Lin was a star. After winning a second consecutive gold in Calgary, when everyone assumed her career was already over? She was a legend.

Footage from fan meet-and-greets during several different Stars on Ice tours, showing Sheila posing for pictures and signing commemorative programs.

KIRK LOCKWOOD: At the end of our last pro tour, the Lockwood Center offered Sheila a coaching job. She declined. I asked her why, and she said, "Do you really want to follow in your parents' footsteps, Kirk?"

JANE CURRER: Any of the top training centers would have been delighted to have Sheila on their staff. But she had to do things her own way.

KIRK LOCKWOOD: If Sheila hadn't asked me that question, I'd probably still be coaching. And miserable.

Back to the late '90s interview: "Do you consider yourself a role model?" the interviewer asks. "As the first Chinese-American woman to win the Olympic gold in ice dance, you—"

Sheila interrupts. "I think you mean the first American woman."

"Sorry?"

"I'm the first, and so far the only, American woman to win an Olympic gold medal in ice dance. Before Lin and Lockwood, the best any American team did was bronze." Sheila smiles. "So yes, I do consider myself a role model—for all American women."

KIRK LOCKWOOD: When she called and told me what she wanted to do next, I said she was crazy. So she hung up on me. *(He laughs.)* Anyway, I called right back and explained what I *meant* was, she was the only person crazy enough to pull something like this off, and I knew it'd be a huge success.

Archival photos show the Grange neighborhood in Los Angeles before its re-development: condemned buildings with broken windows, train tracks to nowhere.

NARRATOR: Today, the Grange boasts some of LA's most daring architecture and expensive real estate. Back in the '90s, though, the area was an industrial wasteland.

Later in the television interview, Sheila shows off a scale model of the Academy: an avant-garde glass-and-metal complex built over two abandoned warehouses, connected by an atrium.

"Construction is under way now. We'll be welcoming the first skaters next season, and launching an annual summer training intensive for promising ice dancers from around the globe."

"It sounds wonderful," the interviewer says. "But it also seems like an awfully ambitious project for a young woman without any business experience. And with two children to raise."

"I seem to recall people expressing similar concerns when I decided to compete in Calgary, and that worked out just fine." Sheila smiles. "Didn't it?"

CHAPTER 11

When we landed in Los Angeles, the sun was dipping low, covering our new city in gilded light, but I was too exhausted to appreciate the view. Lulled by the purr of the taxi engine in the stop-and-go traffic on Sepulveda, I nodded off on Heath's shoulder.

The next time I opened my eyes, we had arrived. I knew the Academy would be a step up from what Heath and I were used to. The North Shore rink was typical middle-class middle America: fluorescent lighting, shrieking children, a constant smell of hot dog water and sweat.

The Lin Ice Academy was a cathedral. We both fell silent as we entered the atrium, awestruck by all that glass glowing in the golden-hour sun. The soaring ceiling looked carved out of ice, and the steel doors on either side of the lobby shone like mirrors. The floor, which I'd originally taken for fresh concrete, was state-of-the-art blade-safe rubber. Everything was sleek and modern and brand-new.

And empty. We were later than planned thanks to a flight delay extending our already lengthy layover by several hours. As Heath checked the doors—both locked—I moved, drawn as if by a magnet, toward the brightly lit trophy case on the back wall. Inside was a small display with pictures of Sheila, as well as some of her medals—though not the Olympic golds.

The central photo, framed in carved crystal, showed Sheila and Kirk Lockwood on the top step of the podium in Calgary. I'd seen the picture before: the two of them young and gorgeous, wearing Team USA jackets, hands over their hearts. The photograph was cropped to show Sheila and Kirk only, but in the original version—the one printed in magazines and shown on the news after the 1988 Games—Sheila's Soviet nemesis Veronika Volkova glares from the silver medal step, her teased blond hair flaring out like a cobra's hood.

The guts it must have taken, for Sheila to return to competition after everyone had written her off. To prove all the skeptics so wrong, they were still talking about her decades later.

Someday, I thought as I gazed through the glass. *Someday that will be me.*

The door on the left side of the lobby swung open, letting in a burst of chilled air and the crisp, chemical scent of well-maintained ice. The day's final practice session had finished, and skaters streamed out of the main rink. A few were locals who trained in the Academy facilities year-round, but most were visiting for the summer like us.

I picked out a couple familiar faces: some fellow competitors from U.S. Nationals, plus the most recent French champs and a young British pair hailed as the heirs apparent to a legendary UK couple who'd retired a few seasons ago. There was no sign of the Lins.

A few of our new training mates shot us suspicious stares; the rest ignored us entirely. Though they were all drenched in sweat, Heath and I were the ones who looked a mess, with our rumpled secondhand clothes, the smoke from last night's bonfire clinging to our unwashed hair.

We hadn't set foot on the ice yet, but the competition was already under way. And we were losing.

Finally, someone deigned to acknowledge our presence.

"Well, well, well. Fancy meeting you here, Katarina Shaw."

It was Ellis Dean, the boy I'd met in Cleveland. The one who hoped I had run into Bella Lin on purpose. He'd cut his hair shorter in the intervening months, but it was still long enough to hang in rakish waves that skimmed his sharp jaw.

Ellis strolled toward us, skate bag slung over his shoulder, and gave Heath a once-over. "Aren't you going to introduce me to your gorgeous partner?"

"Heath, this is Ellis Dean. Ellis, Heath Rocha."

Ellis initiated a handshake. Heath accepted, but he looked uneasy. He hated to be touched by strangers—and he considered anyone who wasn't me a stranger.

"You two just got in?" Ellis asked. I nodded. "From?"

"Chicago." Close enough.

"Well, welcome."

The deep V of Ellis's T-shirt showed off his perspiration-soaked pecs. They clearly trained hard here; I couldn't remember the last time I'd broken a sweat like that. At North Shore, we had to be on constant lookout for gouges in the ice, as well as the orange traffic cones the management sometimes used to cordon them off instead of patching, so we couldn't exactly skate at top speed.

"You must want to get settled in," Ellis said. "Hey, Josie!"

Josie raised one finger, continuing her whispered conversation with Gemma Wellington, the petite redheaded girl from the UK team. Both girls kept glancing our way with narrowed eyes, so I had a pretty good guess what they were talking about.

"Well, she seems lovely."

Heath shot me a bemused look, and that's when I realized I'd made the comment out loud instead of in my head. Shit. Ellis was the only person who seemed willing to give us the time of day; I couldn't afford to alienate him before we'd even unpacked.

Ellis leaned in, the same way he had when whispering to me about Bella.

"Josephine Hayworth is a backstabbing bitch," he said. "Don't tell her anything you don't want the whole West Coast to know."

Seconds later, though, when Josie waved goodbye to Gemma and walked toward us, Ellis was all smiles. I decided I didn't trust either of them.

"Josephine, my love, would you be so kind as to show Ms. Shaw to her room?"

"Happy to," Josie said—though her expression said otherwise. "The girls' accommodations are right this—"

"Wait." Heath gripped my hand even tighter. "I thought we'd be sharing a room."

Josie laughed—then fell silent when she realized he was serious. "Boys aren't allowed in the girls' dormitory."

I hadn't given much thought to our sleeping arrangements, beyond gritting my teeth when I read the exorbitant room and board fee. I wasn't keen on being separated from Heath either.

But it was only temporary, and we'd still be together all day, every day in training. Besides, it wasn't like we had any other options; no landlord in their right mind would sign a lease with a pair of cash-strapped sixteen-year-olds.

"It's fine." I glanced at Heath, silently pleading with him not to make a scene.

The dormitories were on the second level: boys in the north building, girls in the south. I followed Josie to the stairwell, while Heath reluctantly trailed after Ellis. Josie took the steps two at a time, then stood on the landing toying with her gold cross necklace while I dragged my suitcase over the stair treads.

"Wake-up is at five forty-five," she told me as I struggled to keep up with her quick pace down the corridor. "Breakfast at six. Training starts at seven."

The Academy's housing seemed more like a luxury resort than an athletic training center. We each had our own private rooms, and the shared bathrooms boasted steam showers, plush linens, and a Sephora's worth of beauty products generously provided by Sheila's brand partners.

"All free for everyone to use," Josie informed me with a pointed sniff. "In case you want to . . . freshen up."

It was abundantly clear she thought I didn't deserve to be there. As if her opinion mattered. The only gold Josephine Hayworth would ever wear around her neck was that gaudy cross her rich daddy had bought her.

Soon enough I'd show her—and everyone else—*exactly* what I deserved.

CHAPTER 12

Our first night in California, I was more exhausted than I'd ever been before in my life.

And I couldn't fall asleep.

It wasn't only Heath's absence that kept me up. The dorm rooms were well-appointed, but they were also stark, modern boxes, all blinding white walls and sharp angles. Even with my eyes closed, the space felt too bright.

I tossed and turned for hours, tangling the Egyptian cotton sheets— also pure white—around my legs. Los Angeles sounded different too: the call of car horns on the freeway, the constant drone of the air-conditioning, the distant yelps of what I would later learn were coyotes roaming the city's canyons.

So I was already on edge when, sometime after midnight, a sudden tapping at the window startled me right out of bed.

From outside my window—my *second-floor* window—Heath smiled and waved.

"Let me in," he whispered.

I tugged the sash open. Heath was balanced on the sill, his grip on a slender drainpipe the only thing between him and a bone-crushing fall to the concrete below.

"What are you *doing*? If someone catches you here—"

"You want me to leave?" Heath gave me a mischievous grin and let go with one hand. My heart lurched into my throat.

"Not that way! Get in here before you break your neck."

He scaled the windowsill, landing softly in the narrow space between the twin bed and the minimalist white dresser. I shut the window against the sultry night air and drew the shade.

"I didn't wake you up, did I?" he asked.

I shook my head. "I couldn't fall asleep."

"Me either."

He wound his arms around my waist and pulled me in for a kiss. I melted into him, and we stumbled back until my legs hit the edge of the mattress.

"If you're going to stay," I said, "we have to sleep."

He kissed my neck and slid his hand under the waistband of my pajama pants.

"Actually sleep," I clarified.

"Okay, Katarina." His freshly shaved face was smooth against my throat. "We'll sleep."

I lay down on the narrow bed, back pressed against the wall. Heath climbed in facing me and pulled the covers over us both. He ran his fingers through my clean hair and inhaled.

I had *freshened up* with the free products in the bathroom—though I'd waited until Josie left, so she wouldn't have the satisfaction of knowing I took her suggestion. They all smelled sweet and expensive, like confections at a fancy bakery. My skin had never been so soft.

Heath smelled the same as always: generic 2-in-1 shampoo and woodsy aftershave. My father was the one who taught him to shave, and Heath still used the same brand.

Los Angeles was the farthest I'd ever been from home. Part of me still couldn't believe we were really there. It all felt too good to be true, like if I was to drift off, I'd wake up in my bed back in Illinois, Lee pounding on the door.

Maybe that's why, even with Heath beside me, I couldn't rest that night. Sometime around two in the morning, I gave up and broke my own rule, rousing him with my teeth on his earlobe and my nails on his back.

Afterward, I finally managed a few hours of fitful sleep. When my alarm went off at 5:45 sharp, Heath was already gone.

JANE CURRER: I never understood what all the fuss was about with the Lin Ice Academy. It was just a gussied-up ice rink.

KIRK LOCKWOOD: It was so much more than an ice rink. The Academy is Sheila's legacy.

Francesca Gaskell, a friendly-looking freckled blonde who still seems girlish despite being in her mid-thirties, sits in a glass greenhouse filled with blooming winter roses.

FRANCESCA GASKELL (Former Ice Dancer): When I was a little girl, I *dreamed* of becoming a Lin Academy skater one day.

GARRETT LIN: I realize how lucky my sister and I were. We were tremendously privileged.

A video of fifteen-year-old Bella and Garrett training alone at the Lin Ice Academy.

GARRETT LIN: We were also under a tremendous amount of pressure.

Garrett stumbles. Bella reaches for him, and they both hit the ice.

GARRETT LIN: Everyone was looking to us—to be examples, to set the standard.

KIRK LOCKWOOD: Before the twins were even born, the press referred to them as the "Lin Dynasty," which was . . . well, less than culturally sensitive. Let's leave it at that.

JANE CURRER: The top team in the country was in their late twenties, and everyone assumed they would retire after the 2002 Games. Isabella and Garrett were the future of U.S. ice dance.

GARRETT LIN: It might seem strange, training alongside our competitors. But if every day felt like a competition, real competitions would feel like a regular day.

KIRK LOCKWOOD: Sheila wanted to train her kids in her own way, on her own terms.

GARRETT LIN: That was the whole idea for the summer intensive. My mother wanted to motivate us, to surround us with world-class skaters and coaches and specialists, to give us everything we needed to become the best.

Sheila watches her children fall, then turns her back to the ice and walks away.

GARRETT LIN: But she also wanted to remind us how easily we could be replaced.

CHAPTER 13

Here's what it was really like at Sheila Lin's elite skating school.

Eyes on us all the time—coaches and choreographers and dance instructors and personal trainers and photographers and reporters and most of all our fellow athletes, always watching, waiting for us to fall, to fail. Every moment a competition. Every day a series of victories and defeats, highs and heartbreaks.

So many hours on the ice, walking on solid ground felt unnatural. Running noses, chapped lips, cracked heels, bleeding toenails. My body aching like one big bruise. Feeling sunshine on my skin only through panes of glass, because we started before dawn and ended well after dusk. Passing out the moment my head hit the pillow at night.

A gnawing, constant hunger—not only because of the nutritionist-controlled portions of organic greens, lean proteins, and probiotic smoothies, but because I was closer than ever to the thing I wanted most, and I longed to finally sink my teeth into it. To savor the taste—and to clench my jaw so tight it could never escape.

No days off. No breaks. No excuses. Some days, I thought I might not make it through.

But every day, I felt happier than ever before in my life.

Unfortunately, Heath didn't feel the same.

He did his best to hide it, but I knew him too well. I knew he was putting up with all of this—the rigid schedule and the constant scrutiny and the endless list of seemingly arbitrary rules and unspoken expectations—because he loved me. I knew the only times he wasn't miserable were the middle-of-the-night hours we managed to steal together, whenever his legs weren't too spent to make the climb up to my window.

It wasn't that I didn't care he was unhappy. I just thought he would get over it. Once we started winning, he'd see all the long days and hard work and sacrifice had been worth it.

As for me, I had only one complaint about the Lin Ice Academy.

Sheila Lin was hardly ever there.

One day, she'd be standing steps from the ice, analyzing our every move. The next, she was walking in a runway show in Seoul or filming a champagne commercial in Paris or waving from the step-and-repeat at a Manhattan movie premiere.

We were in good hands with the rest of the coaching staff. But I'd come to California to work with Sheila, and after more than a month, the closest I'd come to her was passing by the trophy case in the entryway. Even when she was present, she spent most of her time working with the twins. Feedback for the rest of us was passed through a telephone game with the other coaches and technical specialists.

I said no days off, but they did give us a single day off that summer: the Fourth of July. Though there would be no formal practice sessions on the holiday, the facilities remained open for anyone who wanted to train. It felt like a test. Who among us was dedicated enough to forgo the patriotic pleasures of day-drinking and fireworks in favor of extra ice time?

Heath wanted to spend the day at the beach. He'd been talking about it for a week already: swimming in the Pacific, watching the sun set over the water. *A whole day, just us.*

It sounded lovely. It also sounded like a waste of our already limited time.

Despite our lackluster training regimen back in Illinois, we were managing to keep up with the other skaters. Heath and I weren't the best—not yet—but we weren't the worst either. An extra day of practice might not give us an edge. Skipping it, though, could leave an opening for some other team to surpass us. There weren't official rankings at the Academy, but we all knew exactly where we stood in the pecking order.

And Bella and Garrett Lin were at the top. During the final practice session before the Fourth, most of the skaters had gone a little distracted and delirious, counting down the minutes until that precious twenty-four hours of freedom. The twins, though, were laser-focused as ever.

They spent a full hour fine-tuning the twizzle sequence for their original dance, then took over the rink for a punishing series of program run-throughs. They both wore white spandex, the crisscross back of Bella's top showing off her toned shoulders. She always had her hair up in a complicated crown of braids, and even after skating all day, not a strand was out of place. Meanwhile, my own topknot had gone from artfully messy to mushroom cloud, and Heath and I had sweated through our clothes hours ago.

We waited our turn, completing an off-ice session with Sigrid, the Academy's Cirque du Soleil–trained lift specialist, on a crash pad set up next to the rink. The Academy didn't have to share rinks with hockey players or speed skaters, so the facilities had been designed especially for figure skating—no boards, only a pristine white expanse that seemed to flow into the horizon like an infinity pool.

"Engage your core!" Sigrid kept shouting at us, her harsh Scandinavian accent slashing through the Lins' smooth jazz program music. "Again!"

Up to that point in our career, we'd stuck to relatively basic lifts. If we wanted to be competitive at the international level, though, we needed to step it up—which meant Heath had to do far more than simply pick me up and put me down again without falling.

The lift we were practicing that day involved me performing a backbend while standing on Heath's thighs. Doing it on solid ground was hard enough; pulling it off while moving at breakneck speeds across the ice seemed almost impossible. The longer we worked, the more Heath's hands kept slipping against my sweat-soaked leggings. Every time I came crashing down, his noble efforts to catch me ended with both of us on our asses.

But I was determined. And having the Lins sailing through their foxtrot a few feet away only motivated me more. I couldn't understand how they made it look so goddamn easy. They were somehow fast and slow at the same time, the staccato scrape of their blades picking up every pluck of the strings, while they flowed over the ice in time with the languorous vocals. When they finished their program, I had to curl my hands into fists to keep from applauding.

Then it was our turn. Our original dance, created by one of the resident choreographers, was set to a Cole Porter medley. The concept had us playing celebrities at a Golden Age Hollywood soirée. Heath hated it—all that fussy footwork and formal posture, with little space for our natural chemistry to shine through. We were used to selecting our own music, spending hours sprawled on the floor listening to song after song until we heard a beat that made us want to get up and move. But that wasn't how things were done here.

Whenever he grumbled, I told him to trust Sheila. Nothing happened at the Academy without her approval, and she knew what she was doing. I hoped it would be easier to get into character once our costumes were finished. Heath's was a tux with tails, rendered in a movement-friendly fabric, while mine was a knee-length gown with a high halter neck. Even in the muslin mock-up I'd tried on for the Academy's in-house designer, I felt like a movie star—until the sizable down payment reminded me I was a middle-class Midwestern nobody.

As we took the ice, I tried to imagine how we'd look in competition: Heath, the sharp lapels of his tuxedo setting off the line of his jaw. Me, wearing lipstick the same color as the sequins on my dress, my hair swept up into a sophisticated twist. We assumed our starting positions— facing each other, my hand pressed to his chest as if I were torn between pushing him away and dragging him closer—and met each other's eyes. Focused, calm, ready.

Our music started, and the fantasy fell away. We were an exhausted, wrung-out mess, behind the beat for the first few measures, nearly tripping over each other as we rushed to catch up. We made it through the foxtrot pattern without disaster—though my knees were too stiff, and Heath kept looking down at our fast-moving feet. Then came the lift.

I knew we were in trouble from the moment my blade touched Heath's leg. He didn't have a solid grip on me, and I couldn't stand up in time to execute the backbend properly. My knees started to buckle. I engaged my core, squeezed my calves, clenched my teeth—anything I could think of to save it. But it was too late. I was going down.

Heath bailed out of the lift, skidding to a halt with his arms lashed around my waist. I braced myself for us both to slam into the ice, but miraculously we stayed upright.

"Are you okay?" His breaths came fast and shallow. "I'm so sorry, I thought I—"

"Why did you stop?"

Sheila. She was there. Standing right beside the rink, watching us.

CHAPTER 14

I hadn't known Sheila was on the premises. No one else had either, judging by the uneasy hush in the space after our music cut out.

"I asked you a question, Mr. Rocha."

She folded her hands, waiting for his answer. Some coaches yell at their athletes, but Sheila Lin's silences were more harrowing than any scream.

Heath swallowed. "I thought she might be hurt."

"She's fine," Sheila said. "Aren't you, Ms. Shaw?"

I nodded. Heath's hand fell away from my waist, though I could still feel his heart against my back, beating faster.

"I just wanted to make sure," he said. "What if—"

"What if you were at the World Championships? The Olympic Games? Would you take a nice little rest in the middle of your program then, Mr. Rocha?"

Heath was smart enough to keep his mouth shut that time.

"You have to keep going," Sheila said. "No matter what. Every skater makes errors, but the best skaters fight through their mistakes to continue the program. Now do it again. And this time"—she looked directly at Heath—"do not stop."

Heath was practically vibrating with rage as we moved back to our starting positions. I pressed my hand to his chest harder than usual, trying to soothe him.

"It's okay," I whispered.

He took a deep, shuddering inhale. "I don't want to hurt you."

"You won't."

Heath looked uncertain. But when the music started up again, he was with me.

We were perfectly in sync. Shoulder shimmies with each thump of the solo tom-tom that started the song. Moving smoothly into the promenade step as the horn section came in, gliding through the rest of the foxtrot as Ella Fitzgerald crooned *you are the one.*

And then the lift. Heath's grip around my ankle, pulling my blade against the crease of his hip. His hands finding purchase on the back of my knee, sliding higher as I pushed myself to standing and swung my other leg into position.

I was up! My skates balanced on either side of his waist, my body tall and proud, a beautiful flower stretching its petals toward the sun. He deepened the bend of his knees and held on to my thighs to provide enough counterweight for the final pose: my back arched, my arms flung out behind me, as we covered the ice in a graceful curve.

We had it. We finally had it. We—

Lost it.

Heath's feet wobbled. My hips pitched too far forward. We didn't fall, but my exit from the lift was a clumsy tangle of limbs that left us several steps behind in the choreography.

The music revved into the quicker tempo of "Too Darn Hot," and we chased it until we caught it. We battled through every measure, fought for every move. It wasn't pretty. It wasn't good. But we didn't stop.

By the end, we were panting, shaking, dripping with sweat. The second the final note faded, Heath let go of me and bent at the waist. I didn't realize until he straightened up again that he was dripping with blood too.

My blade must have caught his thigh during that travesty of a dismount. It had shredded his pant leg and sliced into the skin below, leaving an angry red gash.

"Shit," I said. "Are you okay?"

"We finished. That's the important thing." He glared toward Sheila. "Isn't it?"

Her back was to the rink as she gave some instruction to the French team, Arielle Moreau and Lucien Beck. We'd given everything to our performance, and she wasn't even watching.

Heath didn't wait for permission—or for me—to leave the ice. By the time I looked away from Sheila, he was already seated on one of the benches against the wall, examining his cut.

I skated over, trying to figure out what to say. Garrett Lin beat me to it.

"She got you, huh?" Garrett held out a first aid kit. "Used to happen to us constantly. I lost count of how many pairs of my pants Bella destroyed."

The Lins could afford to go through endless items of clothing in pursuit of the perfect lift. Heath only had two decent pairs of practice pants, and I'd just ruined one of them.

Heath hadn't moved to accept the first aid supplies, so I took the box instead, placing it gently beside him. He'd been so worried about hurting me, but I hadn't even noticed when I hurt him.

"Don't feel bad," Garrett said. "The key's to make sure you're balanced right on the center of your blade, and—it's probably easier if I show you. Do you mind?"

Even without looking at Heath, I could tell he very *much* minded. But Garrett had asked me, not him. I moved into position for the lift entry, extending my leg.

Garrett's grip was lighter than Heath's. He moved so fast, I didn't have time to think. I was on the floor, and suddenly I was in the air.

As I leaned into the backbend, I wasn't some delicate flower on display. I was a goddess carved on the prow of a ship, the sea parting to get the hell out of my way. I'd never felt like that before. Effortless and powerful all at once. I could have stayed up there for hours.

Garrett initiated a more difficult dismount—flipping me so my hips rolled over his shoulders on the way down, something I'd seen him do with Bella.

I looked over at Heath. His jaw twitched, and he was gripping the first aid kit hard enough to crack the plastic.

"That was great!" Garrett said. "And see: no cuts."

My blades had left small creases in his white pants, but no injuries. Except perhaps to Heath's pride.

"Thanks," I said.

"Sure." Garrett grinned. "Always happy to help."

He meant it. Garrett never seemed to get caught up in—or even take notice of—the petty rivalries and power plays at the Academy. Everyone liked him.

Well, almost everyone.

Heath finished tending to his cut and came to stand beside me, putting a possessive hand on my back. Garrett kept right on grinning.

"So," he said, "what do you two have planned for the holiday?"

"We've been talking about—" Heath started, but I cut in.

"No definite plans," I said. "Why?"

"My mom throws a little party for the Fourth every year," Garrett said. "No problem if you've got something else going on, but we'd love to see you there."

I highly doubted that "we" included Bella—who was on the other side of the rink doing a series of cool-down stretches, studiously ignoring our entire interaction with her brother.

I had nothing to wear either. In the Midwest, a "little party" means a backyard cookout with brats and beer and maybe some s'mores if you're feeling fancy, all the guests in cutoff shorts and flip-flops. Whatever the Lins had planned, it was bound to be more formal.

If it gave me a chance to spend more time with Sheila, though . . .

"We'll think about it," Heath said.

"I'll be there," I told Garrett.

ELLIS DEAN: Ah yes, Sheila Lin's Red, White, and Gold Party. So nicknamed because, unless you were one of Sheila's students, you had to have a gold medal to get invited.

KIRK LOCKWOOD: Not true. There were silver medalists there too. In fact, back in '94 a certain *very* famous figure skater got blitzed and barfed in the flower bed.

Inez Acton, a thirty-something woman sporting a messy bun with a pen stuck through it, sits in the Brooklyn offices of feminist blog TheKilljoy.com.

INEZ ACTON (Staff Writer, The Killjoy): I'm a hardcore skating fan. But sometimes it's tough to reconcile with my politics. Being a competitive figure skater costs upwards of $40k a year. Unless you have rich parents, you're pretty much fucked.

ELLIS DEAN: Josie's parents were rich. The Lins were *royalty.*

KIRK LOCKWOOD: That party was the ultimate networking opportunity. In skating, doing the right thing on the ice is important, obviously. But knowing the right people can't hurt.

ELLIS DEAN: The Red, White, and Gold Party represented everything wrong with the sport. Skating is elitist enough.

PRODUCER (Offscreen): So I take it you never attended?

ELLIS DEAN: Are you kidding? I wouldn't have missed it for the world.

CHAPTER 15

The afternoon heat broke right on time for the party, as if Sheila had negotiated with the weather itself to ensure conditions would be ideal.

A snow-white convertible, the top lowered to reveal an interior the color of raw meat, idled in front of the building. Ellis Dean leaned against the car with his bare ankles crossed, bouncing the toes of his woven leather loafers.

Until he saw me approaching. Then he stood and pushed his sunglasses down.

"Well, look at *you*."

Arielle had offered to let me borrow something from her closet full of effortlessly chic French designer clothes. Which quickly turned into a full-fledged emergency makeover. Everything I had on, from the clips holding my updo in place to the lipstick that matched the rose pattern on the dress, belonged to her.

I'd felt glamorous when she showed me the finished product in the mirror. But I was already second-guessing. The dress had such thin straps, it was impossible to conceal a bra under it; but when I tried going braless, I looked obscene, especially with the slit on the skirt already displaying so much bare leg.

Until the Academy, I'd never spent much time thinking about my body aside from what it could do. When I was ten, another girl at North Shore told me I had thighs like tree trunks, and I genuinely didn't get the insult. Trees were tall and strong and beautiful. Why *wouldn't* I want to resemble one?

Ice dancers didn't have to be petite little pixies like the pairs girls, or as prepubescently slim as the singles skaters. But my curves and muscular legs stood out, as did the fact that I was almost the same height as my partner. Surrounded by teams with more conventional body types and size differences, it was hard not to be self-conscious.

I tugged at the straps of my borrowed dress. "Is this okay?" I asked Ellis. "I wasn't sure about the dress code."

"Are you kidding? You look *hot*. Heath's gonna lose his mind. Where is that man of yours anyway?"

I hadn't seen Heath since practice the day before—the longest stretch of time we'd spent apart in years. Still, I couldn't imagine him standing me up.

"He'll be here any minute," I assured Ellis.

"Good. Cause the later we leave, the worse the 10's gonna get."

Finally the glass doors swung open, and Heath emerged.

Whatever had delayed him, it certainly wasn't primping for the party. He hadn't shaved, and he was wearing a plain black T-shirt over broken-in jeans. Though neither of us owned many dressy clothes in those days, I knew he'd packed nicer things than *that*.

"Hey." I reached for his hand; he kept it stuck in his pocket. "Ready to head out?"

Heath nodded without looking at me and climbed into the cramped backseat. His sneakers left a dusty smudge on the passenger door; I swiped it away before taking shotgun.

"Nice car, by the way," I told Ellis. The sunbaked leather was hot enough to sear my skin, but even so, I couldn't help caressing its buttery softness.

"Isn't it?" Ellis stroked the steering wheel. "Josie's Sweet Sixteen present. By her eighteenth birthday, she was sick of the color, so her parents bought her a blue BMW and gave me this one."

"What does she get when she turns twenty-one?" Heath muttered. "A private jet?"

"I believe the traditional twenty-first birthday gift in Orange County is a penthouse with Pacific Ocean views. But what do I know, I'm mere Florida Panhandle trash."

I wouldn't have guessed Ellis was from Florida. For one thing, he was so pale he was almost translucent. And there was his accent—flat, generic American like mine, not a trace of Southern twang. It took me longer than it should have to see how much about Ellis Dean was a performance. Like all the best figure skaters, he made hard work appear effortless.

Ellis spun through the radio frequencies until he found a song worth turning up—"Try Again" by Aaliyah—and peeled away from the curb.

We'd been in Los Angeles for weeks, but hadn't seen anything much beyond the airport and the Academy. After so much time in those sterile surroundings, the view from the car seemed almost too vivid to be real. Green palm tree fronds burst against the blue sky, and the violent magenta of bougainvillea blooms rambled over the red rock walls lining the road. The closer we got to the ocean, the cooler the breeze became.

After a few miles curving along the Pacific Coast Highway, Ellis switched on his turn signal. At first it looked like we were about to steer into a cliff—but then I saw the gate.

A uniformed security guard took our names and the license plate number before waving us through. On the other side, a white paver driveway wound up the side of a steep hill. It took a few more turns before Sheila Lin's house loomed above us.

"Welcome to the Ice Palace," Ellis said.

CHAPTER 16

I had expected harsh, angular modern architecture like the Ice Academy complex. Instead, Sheila Lin's house was pure Hollywood glamour.

The facade was all white: painted brick, custom-glazed terra-cotta roof tiles, arched window casings. Fluted columns flanked the front door, which could only be reached via a steep imperial staircase. I'd grown up marveling at the Gilded Age mansions on Chicago's North Shore, but the Ice Palace put them all to shame. It looked fit for a movie star. Or a queen.

Ellis tossed his keys to the valet—who was dressed much better than Heath—and we ascended the staircase. I picked up my feet like a trotting horse, but Arielle's trendy platform sandals kept catching on the steps. Heath put a hand on my waist to steady me and kept it there as we made our way inside.

The interior was white too: the floors, the walls, the furniture, the marble mantelpiece in the two-story living room. The only hint of color came from Sheila's Olympic gold medals, hung above the fireplace like hunting trophies.

I didn't see Sheila herself, but the space was already packed full of other athletic luminaries. In the center of the room, Sheila's old partner, Kirk Lockwood, held court, leaning against the back of a sculptural chair with the sort of haughty I-belong-here ease Heath and I struggled to cultivate in our Cole Porter program. Since retiring, Kirk had started doing commentary for skating competitions, and it was strange to hear his smooth baritone voice live and in person instead of through my television speakers.

The rest of the crowd was similarly impressive. In addition to the many Olympic medalists, there were movie stars, rock stars, fashion designers, fashion models, and politicians—including Josie Hayworth's senator father and his fake-blond second wife.

All three Hayworths stood by the massive sliding doors that opened to the backyard, talking to Garrett Lin. Josie kept touching Garrett's arm and laughing so loud I could hear her over the jazz combo playing out on the patio.

"What do you think?" Ellis said. "Food first, or should we rescue Garrett before Josie unhinges her jaw and swallows him whole?"

"Why do you skate with her anyway?" I asked. Ellis wasn't the most talented skater, but he was decent enough—and male ice dancers were in such demand, even the mediocre ones had their pick of partners.

He shrugged. "Her parents paid the best."

"They *pay* you?" Heath said.

"They pay for everything. Training, housing, equipment, costumes, travel. It's the only way they can get anyone to put up with their darling daughter for more than a season. I'm her third partner. Or is it fourth? I always forget."

Across the room, Garrett edged away from Josie, bumping into the doorjamb. Instead of taking the hint, she stepped closer, squeezing his bicep.

"Looks like she's gunning to make Garrett Lin number five," I said.

"In her dreams. He's too rich to be bought, and too nice to ever leave his sister."

Garrett noticed us looking his way. His face lit up with a smile. He excused himself from his conversation with the Hayworths—leaving both Josie and her stepmother with sour-lemon expressions—and crossed the room to greet us.

"Hey! You made it." Garrett bent down and kissed my cheek. Heath's grip on my hand tightened. "Are you hungry? Can I get you a drink, or—"

"We're good," Heath said.

Garrett glossed right over Heath's attempt to speak for me. "Kat?"

"Water would be great," I told him. "Thank you."

"Come on, it's a party! The bartender makes these incredible pomegranate daiquiris." He grinned. "Virgin, of course."

"Okay, I'll take one of those." I couldn't help smiling back; even at fifteen, Garrett's charm was infectious.

"Me too," Ellis said.

Garrett mimed writing down our orders. "Two daiquiris, coming right up. You sure I can't get you anything, Rocha?"

Heath shook his head, mouth set in a sullen line. As soon as Garrett headed toward the bar, I leaned over to whisper in Heath's ear. "He's just trying to be nice."

"Trust me," Heath said. "I've noticed how *nice* Garrett Lin is to you."

He didn't bother with whispering—and Ellis didn't bother to conceal his delight at the obvious tension brewing between us.

I tugged on Heath's hand. "Come on, let's get something to eat."

He stood back with his hands in his pockets while I loaded up a plate with enough for both of us. To anyone else, his expression looked blank, but I knew him well enough to pick up on the disgust in his eyes.

Wealth like the kind the Lins had seemed incomprehensible to me, so I could only imagine how appalling it was to someone with Heath's background. That enormous house for only three residents, more money than plenty of people made in a year blown on a single party, piles of gourmet food that would probably be tossed in a dumpster at the end of the evening.

Still, we were guests. There was no need to be rude.

"Hey." I set the plate down and took Heath's face in my hands, forcing him to look at me. "Don't be like this."

"Like what?"

"Cranky." I kissed him. His mouth stayed stiff and unyielding. "Broody."

"You knew I didn't want to come here, Katarina."

I dropped my hands. "Then you shouldn't have come. No one forced you."

I was no longer sure whether we were talking about the party, or about Los Angeles in general. Either way, I'd had about enough of his bad attitude.

Garrett reappeared with a crimson drink in a sugared-rim cocktail glass. "Virgin daiquiri for the lady." He produced a small bottle from his jacket pocket and held it out to Heath. "And I grabbed you a water, just in case. Hope sparkling's okay."

For a moment, I felt sure Heath was going to dash the bottle against the floor. Instead, he took it with a toothy, sarcastic grin. I'd never seen him look that way at anyone but my brother.

"Sparkling is splendid, thank you *ever* so much."

Garrett's friendly smile faltered. "Well, uh, let me know if I can get you anything else."

As soon as Garrett was out of earshot, I dug my nails into Heath's wrist. "What's the *matter* with you?"

"What's the matter with *you*? The Katarina I know would be making fun of all these stuck-up assholes, not sucking up to them."

"You're the one who's being an asshole right now, not Garrett. He can't help his upbringing any more than you can help yours."

I knew that would hit a nerve, and I said it anyway. Heath wrenched out of my grip and slammed his sparkling water down on the nearest table.

"Heath."

He turned, the heels of his sneakers squeaking against the polished floor, and stalked out into the yard.

"Heath."

I'd raised my voice loud enough that two women—actresses I vaguely recognized from a prime-time drama—turned to stare at me. I dipped my head toward my drink to hide the flush spreading across my face.

"Where's he off to in such a hurry?"

Ellis Dean sidled up, holding his own cocktail. Heath was so far away now he looked like a smudge against the sky. I wasn't sure whether he was going to cool off and come back, or leave the party—and I told myself I didn't give a damn either way. He could walk back to the Grange for all I cared.

"He's . . . not feeling well," I told Ellis.

"Sure." Ellis held out his elbow. "Shall we mingle?"

I linked my arm through his, and for the next hour, we made the rounds together. Ellis was fearless in a crowd the way I was on the ice. As he insinuated himself into conversations with famous strangers, I watched and learned—and clutched my drink close, terrified I might spill sticky red slush all over Sheila Lin's immaculate decor.

Around sunset, I finally spotted her—and Bella. They stood side by side on the patio, backlit with burnished light. Sheila wore a white gown with an intricately twisted Grecian goddess neckline, while Bella's dress was pale blue with delicate white embroidery, in a similar bias-cut slip style to the one I'd borrowed from Arielle. On her, though, the fabric skimmed over her body instead of clinging. She and her mother looked so alike. Not only their features, but their gestures, their posture, their practiced smiles.

I thought about nudging Ellis in that direction—approaching Sheila seemed less nerve-wracking with him as a conversational wingman—but the Lin women were already occupied, talking to an older lady with tightly coiled red hair.

"Who's that?" I asked. She looked familiar, but I couldn't place her.

"Jane Currer," Ellis said.

"The judge?"

Jane was the official whose harsh artistic score cost Heath and me a medal at Nationals. And now there she was, laughing with the Lins like they were old friends.

"Don't tell me you thought this sport was *fair*," Ellis said. "That's adorable."

He pointed out a few other guests. "She's a judge too. And him. And that guy's the current second in command at the U.S. Figure Skating Association, but if Sheila has her way, he'll have the top job by the start of the season."

"How do you know all this?"

"I pay attention." He raised his glass in a sweeping gesture. "You want to win on the ice, you have to win here first."

I didn't want to believe him. I thought my talent and hard work would be enough.

That's how young and foolish I was.

✿

As the sun faded and the temperature fell, all the partygoers who'd been on the patio retreated indoors. The doors were pulled shut against the night air, and what had been a pleasant hum of small talk and soft music became a cacophony, ricocheting off the vaulted ceiling.

Still no sign of Heath. A headache brewed behind my eyes, from the noise and the too sweet mocktail and all that smiling, so I left Ellis trading Parisian nightlife tales with Arielle's partner, Lucien, and slipped into the backyard alone.

The night might have felt freezing to the Californians, but it was balmy to me. And quiet, despite the distant thunder of fireworks displays farther down the coast. I slipped off my shoes and let my feet sink into the grass.

I didn't miss my house. I certainly didn't miss my brother. But I had missed that feeling. Breeze on my skin, blades of grass between my toes, waves crashing in the distance. I shut my eyes for a moment, savoring the calm, steeling myself to go back inside.

When I opened them again, I saw her.

Bella Lin. She perched on the stone wall bordering the in-ground swimming pool. Her hair was down, tumbling past her shoulders—the first time I'd seen it loose.

She hadn't spotted me yet. I weighed my options. If I was quick, I could sneak back inside before she noticed my presence.

Too late. Bella looked up, and I braced myself for another scathing glare.

It never came. Her eyes were softer than I'd ever seen them, and her usually ballet-perfect posture was slumped. But it wasn't simply weariness.

Bella Lin looked lonely.

I took a step toward her. She'd removed her shoes too, and her bare feet dangled over the water, her shiny pedicure reflecting the eerie blue of the pool lights.

"What are you doing out here all alone?" I asked.

"Well, I'm not alone now, am I." Her voice was flat, impassive.

There I was, trying to be nice—okay, maybe not *nice*, but civil, at least. And she was throwing it back in my face. The longer I let her animosity go unchallenged, the more power she'd have over me. Better to get it all out in the open.

"Look." I folded my arms. "I know you don't like me. I ran into you at Nationals—which *was* an accident, by the way—and you don't want me here. At this party, or at the Academy."

Bella stared at me. It was the same unreadable expression Sheila wore during training.

"But I'm not going anywhere," I continued. "So we're going to have to learn to get along, or at least to—"

"You're wrong."

"Excuse me?"

"I *do* want you here," Bella said.

I scoffed. "Really."

"Yes, really." She lifted her chin. "I'm the one who asked my mother to invite you."

GARRETT LIN: Figure skating, especially at the elite level, is a small world.

ELLIS DEAN: Skating's incestuous. Everyone knows everyone, everyone knows your business.

GARRETT LIN: No one outside the sport understands your life. And everyone in the sport is your teammate. Or your competition.

ELLIS DEAN: You know the saying about keeping your friends close, but your enemies closer?

FRANCESCA GASKELL: Of course it's possible to be friends with your fellow competitors!

Teenaged Katarina and Bella pose for a photo backstage at a competition. They're in full makeup, wearing matching Lin Ice Academy warm-up jackets, arms around each other.

ELLIS DEAN: That's what Bella Lin was doing: keeping her enemy as close as possible. Exactly like her mother taught her.

FRANCESCA GASKELL: It might not be *easy*. But it is possible.

INEZ ACTON: The whole Katarina versus Bella narrative is so reductive. These women were competing for gold medals, not catfighting over petty bullshit.

GARRETT LIN: Katarina Shaw was the best friend my sister ever had.

The same image of Katarina and Bella again, slowly zooming in on Katarina's hand. She's clutching Bella's sleeve, digging her nails in. The screen darkens, ominous music playing.

GARRETT LIN: Until . . . well, we'll get to that, I suppose.

CHAPTER 17

I blinked at Bella. "*You* told her to ask me? Why?"

"Because you're good."

The way she said this, it didn't sound like flattery. She was simply stating a fact: grass was green, water was wet, and I was a good skater.

"Not as good as me," she continued. "But you could be."

"Thank you?"

"You're welcome." She slid off the wall, walking toward the pool. Even barefoot, she moved as if she were balanced on blades.

"So you wanted me here . . . to be your rival?"

Bella nodded. "You push me, I'll push you, we'll both get better."

"Like your mother and Veronika Volkova."

"I'd rather you refrain from sticking razor blades in my skates, but otherwise, yeah."

"That actually happened?"

"Oh, that's the least of it," Bella said. "The stories I could tell you . . ."

In the lead-up to the 1988 Games, the press had made the most of the Lin vs. Volkova rivalry, turning it into a full-blown spectacle with feverish speculation about sabotage attempts and secret love affairs. I'd assumed most of the reports were media spin, the usual obsession with pitting powerful women against each other.

Since her retirement, Veronika had trained ice dancers for Russia— and *only* Russia. Unlike most top coaches, she refused to take on international skaters, no matter how deep their parents' pocketbooks. Her star pupil was her niece, Yelena, who skated with the eldest son of Veronika's former partner. People were already salivating over when Yelena and Bella would meet in competition, hoping for a next-generation Battle of the Ice Queens to bring high drama (and high television ratings) back to ice dance.

Maybe Bella saw competition with me as a lesser battle to help prepare her for that all-out war. I didn't care. All I heard was: *you could be as good as me.*

That wouldn't be enough, of course. I'd have to be even better. Better than Yelena Volkova too. But it was a place to start.

Bella sat by the edge of the pool, and I lowered myself beside her.

"So." She folded her hands on her knee, like she was interviewing me for a talk show. "Tell me your goal."

"My goal?"

"The thing that, when you achieve it, will make all this worth it."

"Well . . ." I knew my answer, but I felt foolish saying it out loud. Then again, a few months earlier, I would have considered training with Sheila Lin to be a pipe dream too, and there I was in her backyard. "I want to go to the Olympics. I know Salt Lake's a long shot, but Torino in 2006 maybe."

"That's all?"

For her and Garrett, making it to the Olympic Games wasn't a lofty goal. It was the bare minimum expected of them.

"No," I said. "That's not all. I want to be national champion, and world champion, and I want an Olympic gold medal."

Bella smirked, and for a second I thought she was going to laugh at me—that this had all been a trick, to get me to confess my delusions of grandeur so she could knock me back down to the bottom where I belonged.

But then she said, "Of course you do. You wouldn't be here otherwise."

No one had ever spoken to me like that before. My father, even at his most supportive, seemed to consider skating a childish pastime I'd eventually outgrow. As for my brother, he took my ambition as a personal attack.

Arrogant bitch. You think you're better than me? You're worthless. You're nothing.

"What about you?" I asked Bella. "What's your goal?"

"Me? I want all that too—except why stop at one Olympic gold?"

"You want two, like your mother?"

"I want my mother to be a footnote on my page in the record books."

If someone had called Bella an arrogant bitch—to her face, that is; plenty of people called her that and worse behind her back—she would have smiled and said *You're damn right*.

And if she wanted me to push her, I'd push her.

"Want to go for a swim?" I asked.

"Are you serious?"

I stared at her, unblinking, a spark of challenge in my eyes.

"It's freezing," she said.

"You think this is freezing? Where I come from, we consider this bikini weather."

The wind had picked up, and it actually was a little chilly so close to the ocean. But I wasn't going to back down now.

Neither was Bella. She stood up and pulled her dress off over her head, revealing a strapless bra and underwear in a matching eggshell hue. Then she turned and dove into the water, so smooth she hardly made a splash.

She flipped her hair back like a mermaid. "All right, your turn, Shaw."

I removed my dress the opposite way, shimmying it past my hips. Bella watched me the whole time, and I couldn't help feeling embarrassed by my less glam undergarments: a cheap black push-up bra and cotton panties grayed from too much washing.

I dove in headfirst too, but not with nearly as much grace as Bella had.

As soon as I'd gotten over the shock of it, though, I realized.

"It's heated?"

Bella laughed. I heaved some water at her head, and she ducked under the surface, so she was a shimmering shape drifting among the pool lights.

Of course the swimming pool was heated. Only the best for the Lins.

She emerged again, and we floated in silence for a few moments. The pool was relatively shallow, so the tips of my toes skimmed the bottom.

"Why didn't you say anything?" I asked. "Before tonight?"

"No offense, but you're not the most approachable. You've barely said a word to anyone besides Heath since you got here."

I wanted to argue, but she was right. We were so used to only having each other.

"How long have you two been together?" Bella asked.

I wasn't sure whether she meant our skating partnership or our relationship. We met when we were ten, and started skating together shortly thereafter, but as far as our romance . . . there wasn't a clear demarcation, an obvious before and after. Even our first kiss had been on the ice: a brush of the lips during a choreographed position change, the contact so fleeting I thought it might have been accidental—until we did it again during the next run-through, lingering long enough that we botched the beginning of a diagonal step sequence. I loved Heath Rocha before I knew what love was.

"We've been skating together for about six years." That seemed like the simplest answer. Six years. It felt like forever, and like no time at all.

Our coach Nicole thought I was oblivious to Heath's presence when he'd started staying after hockey practice. But from the first day, I'd felt his eyes on me and a pull between us, even if I didn't understand what it meant.

I kept expecting him to come talk to me—to say hello, at the very least. Finally, I got impatient. The next afternoon, I waited by the doors, intercepting him before he had a chance to retreat to his usual seat at the back of the stands.

"Why are you always sitting up there watching me?" I demanded.

He didn't answer right away. He looked a bit frightened of me. We were about the same height even then, but in my skates and blade guards I had a couple of inches on him.

"Your music," he said finally. "It sounds like . . . like a thunderstorm or something."

I shrugged. "I guess."

The piece was a section of "Summer" from *The Four Seasons*—chosen by Nicole, after she'd rejected my suggestion of skating to Paula Abdul. Despite my father's attempts to educate me, all classical sounded the same to my young ears. Heath was the one who eventually taught me to appreciate the endless shades and textures of emotion an orchestra could evoke. I liked how fast I got to skate, though, my footwork timed to match Vivaldi's vigorous strings.

"Well," Heath said, "you're really good."

I tossed my hair—which must have looked ridiculous. I used to wear it in pigtails for practice, one always bigger than the other, pieces falling out.

"Yeah, I know," I told him. "So if you're gonna watch me, at least get a better seat."

Heath had smiled—and then sat down in the front row.

"You two are super cute together," Bella said. "But a word of advice? You might want to be a little more discreet."

I opened my mouth to protest, but Bella stopped me with an arch of her eyebrow.

"Your room is right next to Gemma's. And Gemma's best friends with Josie."

Well, shit. "So everyone knows?"

Bella nodded.

"Does your mother know?"

"I find it best to assume my mother knows everything."

"Do you think . . ." I didn't even want to say it.

"Oh, don't worry. She's not going to kick you out. Not for that. If it were to start affecting your skating, though—"

"It won't." At the time, I couldn't see how our connection could be anything other than an asset on the ice.

"So are you *in love*?" Bella's voice went all gooey and mocking. "Or just fucking?"

I was so taken aback by her bluntness, I didn't know what to say. I should have told her Heath was my boyfriend; that was true enough. But the word *boyfriend* seemed insufficient to describe our relationship. No matter how annoyed I was with him for running off in a sulk, he was my best friend, my family, my favorite person in the world.

"It's complicated," I said.

Bella laughed—less dignified this time, with a little snort that made me like her even more. "Yeah, I bet. Be careful, though."

"What do you mean?"

"Mixing skating and romance can be tricky."

"You have a lot of experience with that?"

This fucking fifteen-year-old, dragging me about my relationship, trying to give me sage advice. She'd probably never even been kissed. She certainly couldn't fathom what Heath and I felt for each other. We were soul mates.

"No. Ew." Bella sounded exactly her age for once. The pool water had started to wash away her makeup, making her look even younger. "I don't have time for boys. I'm going to be an Olympic gold medalist by the time I'm twenty-two; I can't afford distractions."

"I guess that's one good thing about skating with your brother."

"Believe me, it comes with its own set of problems."

I couldn't imagine what they were. I was jealous of Bella, but not because of the money or the mansion or even her talent on the ice. What I envied was her *confidence*—the firm belief she'd been born with that, yes, she deserved the best, and she was destined to be the best.

There was a sound from the shadows at the side of the house. Footsteps. Bella and I both whirled around in the water.

"Katarina?" Heath called out.

CHAPTER 18

I wasn't certain how much Heath had overheard. He looked per-
plexed, but it might have been by the sight of me and my sworn
enemy, Bella Lin, treading water in our underwear.

"I was looking for you," he said.

"She's been right here with me." Even soaking wet, Bella managed
to seem imperious. "So you couldn't have been looking that hard."

His jaw twitched, the same way it had after Garrett lifted me. Well,
I was annoyed with Heath too. He'd disappeared to God knows where
for who knows how long, and I was fairly certain he'd been drinking.
Despite the chlorine and the night-blooming flowers, I could smell it
on him. He smelled like Lee.

"Ellis is heading out," Heath said. "So if we want a ride back . . ."

"Already?" I'd lost track of the hour while talking to Bella. We had
ice time scheduled bright and early in the morning, same as always.
Though training would be a shitshow if my partner was hungover.

"Stay," Bella told me. "Someone else can give you a ride."

I could tell Heath expected me to jump out of the pool, to go with
him without hesitation, despite how he'd treated me all night.

That's what made my mind up. "I'm gonna stay," I said. "I'll see you
later."

He didn't budge at first. Bella waved at him, flicking water onto his
jeans.

"Have a good night. Thanks for coming."

Heath stalked off into the dark, shoulders bunched tighter than ever.

"Jeez, possessive much?" Bella said. "Is he always like that?"

"He has a hard time with new people," I replied weakly.

"Well, I'm glad you stayed," Bella said, "because I actually wanted to ask you something. What are your plans for next season?"

I'd been trying not to think about anything beyond the end of the intensive in August.

"I don't know," I said. "I guess we'll go back to Illinois. Keep going to school and training. Hopefully make it to Nationals again."

We'd be lucky if my brother let us back in the house. We'd be even luckier if he didn't fly into a drunken rage and break Heath's legs while I watched, as punishment for running away in the first place. It was possible Nicole would let us stay with her, but that wasn't a long-term solution. And we still had no money.

"What if you didn't go back to Illinois?" Bella asked. "What if you stayed here?"

My stomach flipped. She was messing with me. This couldn't be real.

"Garrett and I have been looking for dedicated training partners for a while," she continued. "But we haven't found the right match yet."

"And you think Heath and I—"

"Like I said, you push me, I'll push you. I know Heath and Garrett aren't exactly BFFs, but give Garrett long enough, he can win anyone over."

I highly doubted he could win over Heath. But maybe it wouldn't matter. They didn't have to get along for us to train together. Maybe Heath's loathing toward the Lins would make him work even harder.

"I don't know if . . ." I swallowed. This was humiliating. "It might be tough for us to come up with enough money."

I didn't even have a concept of how much a full season of training at the Academy might cost. It would be more than a year before I could access my inheritance, and I didn't have any more family heirlooms to sell off.

Bella waved her hand. "Oh, don't worry about the money. We'll work something out."

There was that confidence again. The idea of worrying about something so mundane as *money* was alien to Bella Lin.

When I was a little girl in messy pigtails, demanding to be watched from the front row, I'd had that sort of unshakable, semi-delusional confidence too. But after years of losses, disappointments, scraping by, holding on tight to Heath because he was all I had, I'd shoved that little girl aside, locked her up in some small box inside of me.

That night in the pool, it felt like Bella was handing me the key.

"I'll talk to Heath," I said.

Bella winked, a bead of water sparkling on her eyelashes. "I'm sure you can find some way to convince him."

Bella ended up inviting me to sleep over. *We've got plenty of room,* she said.

A staggering understatement; the Lin house had at least a dozen bedrooms, though some had already been claimed for the night by Sheila's gold-medal-winning guests from out of town.

I'd tried to imagine it: waking up under the same roof as Sheila Lin. Sitting at the breakfast table with her and her children. Riding with them to the rink. The look on Josie's and Gemma's faces when I emerged from the Lins' chauffeured town car.

Then I had imagined Heath, tossing and turning in his twin bed. More comfortable, certainly, than he'd been in the stable back home. But just as alone. Just as abandoned.

Besides, Bella's offer was burning in my chest. I had to tell him. I had to make him see what an incredible chance this was. Maybe our *only* chance, to become the athletes I knew we could be.

I splurged on a cab back to the Academy, but I didn't go to my room. Instead, I snuck around to the north side of the building.

There wasn't a drainpipe next to Heath's window, but there was a small tree, the roots surrounded by concrete. Shoes in hand, I shimmied up the trunk, cringing every time the bark snagged Arielle's dress. Once I was high enough, I tapped one shoe heel against the glass.

Heath slid the pane up. "Katarina? What the hell are you—"

"You make this look a whole lot easier than it is." I rucked up my skirt, rustling the branches. "Are you going to let me in?"

"It's late." He'd showered and brushed his teeth, so he didn't smell like alcohol anymore.

It was late. But there was no way I could wait until morning to tell him. The words were buzzing on my tongue, like a whole hive of bees trapped in my mouth.

So I heaved myself up onto the windowsill. Heath relented, gripping my wrists to help me get safely inside—though not without some under-the-breath grumbling.

"Listen," I started as soon as I was on solid ground. "I was talking to Bella, and—"

His lips twisted. "So you two are friends now?"

"So what if we are?"

"You can't trust her," he said.

"You don't even know her."

"Neither do you. You thought she hated you, and now all of a sudden y—"

"She wants us to stay."

"Stay?" Heath took a step back. "What do you mean?"

"Stay here, in Los Angeles. Skate at the Academy. We'd be their training partners."

I didn't want to let him get a word in edgewise. I had to get this out, defuse all his arguments before he could make them.

"Bella said the money wouldn't be a problem, we'd work something out. We wouldn't have to worry about school, either; we'd be tutored a few hours a day, like she and Garrett are, and the rest of the time we could train."

Heath opened his mouth. I kept barreling ahead.

"We wouldn't have to see my brother ever again. We'd be free."

"I don't know, Kat."

I took his hand. I led him toward his unmade bed. I drew him down beside me.

"We could be together," I told him. "Like we've always wanted."

He stared at me, eyes shining in the glow of the streetlights outside the window.

Bella's words rang in my head. *Convince him.*

"Unless . . ." I leaned closer. One of the flimsy straps of Arielle's dress slid off my shoulder. "Unless that's *not* what you want."

Heath slid a finger under the strap, like he was going to tug it back into place. Instead, he twisted it around his knuckle.

"Of course I want to be together." His voice was hoarse, breathing gone ragged. "But—"

I pushed him back onto the bed, straddling his waist like we were about to perform a lift. His eyes widened with surprise when I raised the dress over my head and tossed it onto the floor.

"You're sure?" he said. "You're sure this is—"

"Yes."

I wanted it all. California and gold medals and Bella Lin's unshakable confidence. I wanted so much skill and fame and money that we'd never have to worry about anything, ever again.

And him. I wanted Heath so much. I was tired of waiting.

I wanted it all, and I would have it.

"I'm sure," I said. "About everything. But if you . . ."

I knew Heath wanted me—but did he want the same future I did? I needed to hear him say it, before I could go through with this.

"I realize it's a lot to ask. Living in California long-term."

"Katarina."

"It's a lot of money, and we're a long way from home, and—"

"*Katarina.*"

I fell silent. Heath sat up and pulled me against him, so close I couldn't tell his heartbeat from my own.

"*You're* my home," he said.

PART II

The Rivals

Katarina Shaw and Heath Rocha stand on the second step of the podium at the 2001 Nebelhorn Trophy competition in Germany. Katarina leans down to receive her silver medal. Her ponytail gets caught in the ribbon, and Heath gently tugs it free.

KIRK LOCKWOOD: After a year at the Academy, Katarina Shaw and Heath Rocha had improved tremendously.

The Lins smile from the top step of the Nebelhorn podium, gold medals around their necks.

GARRETT LIN: Kat and Heath were nipping at our heels. Which was the plan all along.

Katarina and Bella grin at each other as "The Star-Spangled Banner" plays.

GARRETT LIN: My sister thrived on the pressure. The closer their scores got to ours, the more it motivated her.

FRANCESCA GASKELL: It was inspiring, seeing skaters not that much older than I was accomplishing so much. Watching Kat and Bella made me think: maybe I could do that too.

ELLIS DEAN: The rest of us felt like, what's the point? We all knew we were never going to beat the Lin Twins. Now we have to fight Shaw and Rocha for podium spots too?

KIRK LOCKWOOD: They still had a long way to go, though. Especially Rocha.

Competition footage from the 2001–2002 season shows Katarina and Heath performing a tango in the original dance event.

KIRK LOCKWOOD: Rocha's edges weren't deep enough. His transitions were sloppy.

The video zooms in on Heath's skates, showing the difference between his technique and Katarina's, then cuts to the judging panel, where Jane Currer peers sternly over her glasses.

GARRETT LIN: Heath had so much passion when he skated, but he struggled with the details. I offered to give him some pointers, several times. He wasn't interested.

Back to the Nebelhorn medal ceremony, as Katarina hugs Bella, then Garrett.

GARRETT LIN: The guy barely spoke, except to Kat. Bella complained all the time about how he wasn't good enough for Kat, on the ice or off. I thought maybe he was ... I suppose *shy* isn't quite the right word. Proud, maybe? Stubborn?

While Katarina embraces the Lins, Heath stands off to the side, glowering.

GARRETT LIN: After a while, I stopped trying.

CHAPTER 19

You never forget your first time.

For Heath and me, it was Skate America 2001. The day before I turned eighteen.

We weren't even supposed to be there. We were alternates—until Parry and Alcona pulled out due to injury, and Reed and Branwell withdrew, citing concerns about travel safety. The event was only six weeks after the September 11 attacks, and everyone was on edge. At LAX, Heath was pulled for a supposedly random search, the TSA agents' eyes flicking with suspicion between his ethnically ambiguous features and his Illinois ID.

As I stood on the other side of the barricade, watching Heath get patted down, I grew more and more furious. He was a teenage boy and an American citizen—en route to represent his country in a major athletic event, no less. How dare they treat him that way? Heath endured this with his typical impassivity, but once they released him, his hand trembled in mine until well after we'd boarded our flight.

In any case, we made it to Colorado Springs—a few days early so we'd have time to acclimate to the higher altitude. By the final day of competition, we were in second place behind Olivia Pelletier and Paul McClory from Canada. Sheila's pre-skate pep talk was all about holding off the Italian team to stay in silver-medal position.

The choreography and concept of our free dance were deceptively simple, modern Fosse-esque moves to a new arrangement of the classic torch song "Fever." Sheila claimed the program was the perfect showcase for our chemistry, but to me it felt forced, like Heath and I were trying to playact what had always come so naturally to us. The costumes seemed on the nose too: black velvet and mesh with bedazzled flames curling up our torsos.

From our first synchronized hip isolations to the hypnotic bass line, though, I realized Sheila had been right. The audience was spellbound by every articulation of our bodies, every moment of sizzling eye contact we shared. Heath and I skated with the controlled power of banked embers that might burst into a conflagration at any second, and they loved it. They loved us. All my nerves burned off, leaving nothing but determination and desire. Desire for the gold, for the adulation of the audience, for Heath—it all felt the same, flaring bright inside me.

When we hit our final pose, the crowd in the Broadmoor World Arena cheered so loud Heath had to shout in my ear.

"I think we might win," he told me.

As we headed to the kiss and cry, the applause made me even dizzier than the oxygen-starved atmosphere. Our scores were a personal best, by far, but we had to wait until the Canadians finished their skate to find out if we'd clinched the gold.

I sat backstage between Sheila and Heath, my knee jiggling against the cool silk of her trousers. The twins were back home in Los Angeles, getting ready for the Sparkassen Cup, which would be their first Grand Prix event of the season. So for once, we were Sheila's main focus.

When the final scores were displayed, Heath hugged me so hard my blades lifted off the floor. Sheila gave me a gentle pat on the shoulder and said, "Well done, Katarina." Winning my first senior-level gold medal was great, but those words felt like the ultimate prize.

When we walked into the Academy for our first practice following Skate America, I felt like a celebrity couple. People approached to congratulate us on our win, all warm smiles and eyes frozen solid with envy. Finally, *they* were jealous of *us*.

Except of course for the Lins, who were jealous of no one.

"There's the gold medal–winning birthday girl!" Bella called out when she saw me. She crossed the lobby to wrap me in a one-armed hug, her other hand behind her back.

"Congrats," Garrett said. "So well deserved, both of you. How was your birthday, Kat?"

Most of the day following our gold medal win had been consumed with press interviews, performing in the exhibition gala event, and attending the skating association's formal banquet afterward. Sheila stayed by our side the entire time, fielding everyone's flattering comments with a sense of calm, confident entitlement I wished I could inject straight into my veins. It was the most uninterrupted time I'd ever gotten to spend in her presence.

For our final night in Colorado Springs, Heath had talked his assigned roommates into making themselves scarce so he and I could have the hotel room to ourselves. I filled the twins in on everything he'd done to make the standard-issue Sheraton accommodations seem romantic: candles lining the particleboard dresser, artificial rose petals scattered across the comforter, Portishead in the CD player. He even got a frosted devil's food sheet cake like the ones my father used to buy for my childhood birthdays.

"That's so sweet," Bella said. "I got you something too."

"You didn't have to get me anything," I protested.

Bella rolled her eyes. "Stop being so Midwestern. Here in California, when someone gives us a gift, we say 'thank you.'"

She revealed what she'd been holding behind her back: a small, professionally wrapped box. Heath watched over my shoulder as I carefully removed the metallic paper. Inside was a red plastic rectangle, covered in buttons. A cellphone.

"It's the same as mine, see?" Bella held up her phone—blue to my red, but otherwise identical. "You can't even get these in the United States yet. They play music files and everything; I've got our program music on mine so I can listen to it while we're traveling."

"Thank you." I turned the device over in my hands. "I've never had my own phone."

"Yeah, I know. Figured it was time you joined us in the twenty-first century."

I pressed one of the buttons, and the digital screen lit up. Bella had already programmed her number into the contacts list, as well as Garrett's.

"We should do dinner too," Bella said. "I'll text you the deets. Don't forget to switch silent mode on, though; if that thing goes off during training, my mom *will* confiscate it."

"Are you sure dinner out is a good idea?" Heath asked as soon as the twins were gone. "We haven't gotten the prize money yet, and—"

"It'll be fine. I can access my inheritance now, remember?"

The sum my father had left me in his will wasn't anything approaching a fortune, but it would be enough to keep us afloat for a while. For the past year, Heath and I had made ends meet by working the various evening and weekend events held at the Academy. Some months, we were flush with tips from the affluent attendees who frequented the skating exhibitions and fashion shows and charity fundraisers Sheila hosted; other times we were left scrounging for wrinkled dollar bills and begging for extensions on our training fees. I was grateful for the gig, but it soon started to chafe. How could we ever hope to beat the Lins when we spent our off-ice hours standing in the corner in cater-waiter uniforms, watching them mingle with the Los Angeles elite?

The Lins moved through the world with such ease, getting whatever they wanted without having to struggle or strive or even ask. When I was with them, I felt caught in a slipstream. Sticking close would take me where I wanted to go.

As long as I stayed a step behind.

On our lunch break, I took my new phone and ducked into one of the locker rooms to call the bank back in Illinois. The device felt strange in my hand, like a child's plastic toy—but I felt extremely adult as I introduced myself to the teller and explained why I was calling.

"Happy belated birthday, Ms. Shaw," she replied. "Let me check on that for you."

I gave her the account details and listened to her crisp keystrokes as she input the information. Everything was going according to plan. Heath and I were gaining on our competition. We had our first gold medals. If we performed well at our second Grand Prix event in St. Petersburg, we might make it to the Grand Prix Final—which would be great preparation for Nationals. If we maintained our trajectory, we could even qualify for Worlds in the spring.

And then, surely, the sponsorship opportunities would come rolling in. Unless you were an Olympic champion, endorsement deals weren't going to make you rich. But combined with the inheritance money, they'd give us breathing room. No more sweating over a single dinner out. Maybe we could even move out of the dorms and into a home of our own. Most likely a single-room studio apartment in a semi-scary part of town, but it would be ours.

"Thank you for your patience, Ms. Shaw. You were granted access to the account in question as of your eighteenth birthday. However, there aren't any funds allocated at present."

I gripped the phone tighter. "What?"

"The account balance is zero. Well, technically the balance is negative, since several overdraft fees were charged recently. Would you like to resolve that today?"

As a professional athlete, you're taught to visualize the exact future you want. Every step of a flawless program. The view from the top of the podium. The weight of an Olympic medal around your neck. But all it takes is a second—a slip of your blade, a lapse in your concentration, a spark of doubt in your mind—and everything falls apart.

"Who withdrew the funds?" I tried to maintain my poise, but my voice was trembling. It must have been a mistake. My father's lawyer moved the money to another account, or—

"The primary account holder," the teller told me. "Leland Shaw."

CHAPTER 20

I couldn't tell Heath about the money. He would've been furious enough to blow our last dollar flying back to Illinois just to punch Lee in the teeth.

Lee was my brother. My problem. I was determined to fix the situation myself.

So I punched my childhood number into my brand-new cellphone. It rang over and over, so many times I almost gave up and disconnected.

Finally, someone answered. "Hello?" A woman's voice, scratchy and sultry.

"Hi." I tried to keep the rage from seeping into my tone. Whoever she was, this situation wasn't her fault. "Is Lee there?"

"Who's calling?"

Even through the haze of whatever substances she was on, the edge of jealousy was obvious. How my idiot brother got all these women to give him the time of day, let alone compete over him, was beyond me.

"Katarina," I said. "His sister."

Shuffling sounds as she handed the phone over.

"Yeah?" Lee said, and from that word alone, I could tell he was wasted. Later in life, I acknowledged Lee's addiction as the illness it was. But at eighteen, all I knew was that my shitty older brother was screwing me over yet again.

"Where is it, Lee?"

"Katie? Is that really y—"

"What did you do with my money?"

"*Your* money?" He laughed. Halfway through, it turned into a hacking cough. "Are you fucking serious?"

"Dad left that money for me. I'm eighteen now, so—"

"So what? We both know you've gotten way more than your fair share."

"What the hell is that supposed to mean?"

"All those ice twirling lessons and pretty little dresses add up, princess. You know what Dad left me when he died? A big damn mess."

I shook my head. "No. You're lying. You blew it all on drugs, or—"

"He took out loans so you and that freeloading little creep could keep competing. Hate to break it to you, sis, but half of nothing is nothing."

I knew skating was an expensive sport, and that our family wasn't wealthy. But my father never complained, never hinted at any money troubles. He just kept writing checks.

If Lee needed to drain my trust to cover our father's debts, the least he could have done was discuss it with me first. Not that I'd made myself easy to reach over the last couple of years, but as far as I knew he hadn't even tried to find me.

"If you're so strapped for cash," I said, "let's sell the house."

"We are *not* selling the house," Lee snapped, all the slur vanished from his voice.

"Why not?"

"Our ancestors built this house with their bare hands, Katie, it's—"

"Stop calling me 'Katie.'"

"Our parents are buried here."

"And you've never even visited their graves, *Leland.*"

"What do you care?" he said. "You left. You left me here all alone."

It was the closest my brother would ever come to saying he missed me.

The line went silent.

"Lee?" I dug my nails into the phone, scratching the satin finish. "*Lee.*"

He'd hung up on me.

With a frustrated scream, I snapped the phone shut.

"Everything all right?"

I looked up to find the locker room door open, and Garrett Lin on the threshold. Great.

Another thing I'd learned at the Lin Ice Academy: how to appear calm and composed when I was anything but. I took a deep breath, willing my pulse to slow. Gold medalists don't scream, and they only cry pretty, photogenic tears.

"I'm fine," I told him. "Just got some . . . bad news."

Garrett's brows knitted with concern. "I'm sorry. Anything I can help with?"

"No, no. It was more of a miscommunication. My older brother spent some money that was supposed to be for next month's training fees."

And last month's, and every damn month from now until Nationals.

"I didn't know you had a brother." Garrett leaned against the door-frame. I could've sworn he was taller every time I saw him; he had almost a foot on Bella. "He lives in Illinois?"

I nodded. Despite the increasing amount of time I'd been spending with the Lins, we rarely talked about anything besides skating. No one at the Academy knew anything about my past life. The only part of it worth bringing with me was Heath.

"Well, I'd be happy to talk to my mom," Garrett said. "I'm sure she'll have no problem with you paying a little later."

I didn't want to tell him his mother had already allowed us several generous extensions. The Grand Prix money might be enough to get out of that hole, but without the inheritance, we'd fall right back into debt. There was little chance of repeating our victory at the next competition, where we'd be facing off against both the Lins and the Russians.

"That's okay," I said. "I'll handle it."

"Maybe I can help," Garrett said.

"That's really nice, Garrett." If he'd pitied me, I could have hated him, but Garrett was so goddamn sweet and earnest. I wondered what it would have been like to have a brother like him, instead of the dead-beat I'd been stuck with. "But I can't take money from you."

"That's not what I meant." He stepped forward, letting the door swing shut behind him. "What are you doing next Saturday? I might be able to hook you up with a job."

An ad campaign photo shoot, Garrett explained, for an athleisure brand. Bella would be there too. The company was on the smaller side, popular mostly in Asian markets, but they were always looking for spokesmodels who could move well in front of the camera.

"It doesn't pay that much," he said. "The designer's an old acquaintance of my mother, though, and if he likes you, he might book you again in the future."

"I appreciate the offer." I hesitated, chewing on my lip.

"But?" Garrett prompted.

"I mean, I'm not exactly . . . a model."

"What are you talking about?" He smiled. "You're gorgeous."

He's just trying to be nice. That's what I'd said to Heath at the Fourth of July party, and as I stood in that locker room with Garrett Lin gazing into my eyes, I told myself the same thing.

Heath wouldn't like this. But Heath didn't have to know—about the modeling job, the missing inheritance money, any of it. I'd take care of everything myself, and we would keep going, on to the next gold medal.

"Thank you," I told Garrett. "I'll be there."

GARRETT LIN: I won't pretend my sister and I didn't grow up with certain advantages. We also had a lot to live up to.

KIRK LOCKWOOD: The Lins had a stellar season. Shaw and Rocha did well too, but their Skate America gold was definitely the high point.

At the 2002 U.S. National Championships in Los Angeles, Bella and Garrett Lin receive silver medals for the third year in a row. Katarina Shaw and Heath Rocha are on the podium as well, in the fourth-place pewter medal spot.

GARRETT LIN: We were basically still kids, but because we were *Sheila Lin's* kids, it wasn't enough to compete. We were expected to win.

JANE CURRER: Some people thought we made a mistake, making the Lins alternates for Salt Lake instead of putting them on the Olympic team.

GARRETT LIN: I was fine with being an alternate. It wasn't our time yet. My sister, on the other hand . . .

KIRK LOCKWOOD: Right after the Games is the perfect time for a new generation of skaters to step it up and stake their claim for the next Olympic cycle.

JANE CURRER: The World Championships take place a few weeks after the Olympics, so many skaters who competed at the Games sit out Worlds. Or they announce plans to retire.

At the 2002 Winter Olympics in Salt Lake City, Utah, previous top American ice dance team Elizabeth Parry and Brian Alcona give a disappointing, error-riddled performance. At a post-Olympics press conference, they confirm their immediate retirement.

KIRK LOCKWOOD: In an Olympic year, the World Championships are a golden opportunity.

JANE CURRER: With Parry and Alcona retired, and Reed and Branwell opting to skip Worlds, some of the lower-ranked teams were given the chance to compete.

GARRETT LIN: The 2002 World team was me and Bella, Kat and Heath, and Josie and Ellis.

ELLIS DEAN: No one thought Josie and I were medal threats. Well, maybe Josie's dad, but he thought Ronald Reagan was our greatest president, so.

Split-screen images: Katarina and Heath on top of the podium at Skate America, Bella and Garrett collecting their own Grand Prix golds at the 2001 Cup of Russia.

ELLIS DEAN: No, it was all about Lin and Lin versus Shaw and Rocha. And that competition did turn into quite a showdown. Just not in the way any of us anticipated.

CHAPTER 21

When I woke up the morning of the 2002 World Championships final, I was sure it would be the best day of my life.

The free dance wasn't until the evening, so Bella suggested we spend the day pampering ourselves. She'd invited her brother and Heath too. Garrett declined in favor of touring some local Shinto shrines with a group of other skaters. Heath simply declined.

"How much does this spa cost anyway?" he'd asked me as I dressed in the gray morning light. He was sprawled across the thin futon bed on the floor; to wrangle a room to ourselves at the official event hotel, we'd had to settle for the Japanese-style accommodations none of the other Westerners wanted.

"I don't know. Bella's paying for it." I was already late to meet her, and my phone kept buzzing with her texts.

"Of course she is." He leaned back against the buckwheat pillows and picked up his Walkman. Nine Inch Nails bled through the headphones. "Better get going. Wouldn't want to keep Her Royal Highness waiting."

The Lins were staying at a four-star establishment a few blocks away. I met Bella in the library hush of the lobby, and she snuck me into the breakfast buffet so I could fill my plate with fresh soba noodles and Shinshu apples. Then a private car whisked us to a hot spring spa in the countryside, where we spent several hours cycling between chilled and steaming pools that left my muscles supple and my skin luminous.

"You have a real chance at the bronze," Bella told me on our way back to Nagano City. We were tucked together in the backseat, both smelling of the spa's signature blend of seasonal plant essences hand-picked in the same mountain ranges that blurred past our tinted windows.

"You think so?"

She nodded. "Maybe even silver, if the Russians screw up again."

Heath and I were in fourth after the original dance, a scant point behind the French, and well ahead of the Canadian couple we'd beat at Skate America. The Russians had come into the championship expecting to dominate the podium the way they had at the Olympics, but a few uncharacteristic errors knocked one team out of the running and left Yelena Volkova and her partner—fresh off a bronze medal in Salt Lake and favored to take the world title—in second place below the Lins.

"Arielle and Lucien have been struggling with their combination lift all season," Bella said. "Plus they have *zero* chemistry, which'll be even more obvious when they skate right after you and Heath. You skate clean, you can beat them."

At the time, I was flattered. Looking back, though, I understand what she was really telling me: Heath and I might have a chance at a medal, but the gold was out of our reach. Because there was no way in hell we were going to beat her and Garrett.

In fairness, we never had before. Heath couldn't understand why it bothered me so much. He enjoyed winning, but he didn't feel the same gnawing ache of ambition, the bottomless pit inside me that got exactly what it wanted and then demanded more, more, more.

With Bella, I didn't have to explain. She felt the exact same ache. And that meant she knew me in a way Heath, despite all our history, never could.

Bella had made post-spa lunch reservations at a restaurant famous for their tender cuts of beef from cows fed on the same sweet local apples we'd enjoyed for breakfast. Heath had—grudgingly—agreed to join us.

When the car dropped Bella and me off near the Zenkoji Temple, Heath was already waiting at the curb, hunched against the wind. I barely sensed the cold. I felt like I had a small sun trapped inside my core, suffusing my whole body with a warm glow.

"How was the spa?" Heath asked, reaching for me.

"Amazing!" I kissed him; his lips felt like cold marble. "They had all these pools filled with special minerals, and—"

"I'm *starving*," Bella groaned. "I swear I could eat a whole cow."

She linked her arm with mine and dragged me away. Heath fell in step behind us. The restaurant was on a side street off the main tourist drag leading up to the temple gate. Nagano was a strange mishmash of ancient and modern, steel-and-glass office blocks and fast fashion stores intermingled with pagoda-roofed shrines and carefully cultivated meditation gardens. There was even a traditional Zen garden tucked right behind our hotel, the entrance guarded by smiling stone lions. Heath had been eager to explore it, but I told him we should wait until after we'd finished competing.

Bella picked up speed, weaving around the slow-moving sightseers, and I let her pull me along at the same pace—until I spotted something that made me stop, mouth agape.

"What?" she said. Then she saw it too.

A billboard, on the side of a building ahead of us, featuring a towering photo of two models posing together in skintight black clothing.

Garrett Lin. And me.

When Garrett told me the clothing brand was more popular in Asia, I had imagined our ad printed in the glossy pages of South Korean fashion magazines, maybe plastered at a bus stop or two in Beijing. Nothing like *this*.

"Bitch!" Bella gave me a playful backhand on the bicep. "You look *hot*."

Heath's footsteps behind us had been hurried, trying to catch up. Suddenly, they stopped.

"What the hell is that?" he hissed through his teeth.

CHAPTER 22

The day of the photo shoot with Garrett was a blur in my memory. Bright lights and pulsing electronic music and the photographer shouting to *arch your back, tilt your head, more, yes yes just like that, hold it, don't you dare move.* The space had been freezing, and it took all my concentration to keep from flinching whenever Garrett's cold hands brushed against my skin. The experience felt bizarre, awkward. Not the least bit sexy.

But you'd never have guessed that from the finished product. On the billboard, Garrett was shirtless, his pants so snug they may as well have been ballet tights, while I wore shorts and a strappy crop top that barely contained my cleavage. My leg was hitched up around his hip, his hand gripping my bare thigh, and we were gazing into each other's eyes.

Except we hadn't been—I distinctly remembered focusing on his ear, or the lock of hair across his forehead, because looking right at him felt too uncomfortable. Despite that, the photographer had somehow made it seem as though I was looking not into Garrett's eyes, but into his very soul.

And now Heath wouldn't look at me at all.

"I'm not hungry anymore," he muttered, turning back the way we'd come.

I started to follow him. Bella caught my arm.

"Let him go. He's being a dick."

"But we have to skate tonight."

"So what, you're gonna beg for his forgiveness? Screw that. You did nothing wrong."

I had lied to him—by omission, at least. Because I knew exactly how he would react.

My first instinct was to soothe his hurt feelings the way I usually did. But staring up at the billboard, I didn't want to be my usual self. I wanted to be the fierce, confident woman I saw in the photograph. That woman wouldn't apologize or grovel or explain.

"You're right." I looped my elbow through Bella's again. "Let's eat."

I didn't see Heath again until it was time to leave for the competition. The shuttle bus was so full, he had to take the seat next to mine, but it was clear he was still stewing. As the other skaters chatted amongst themselves or sang along with the J-pop on the radio, he remained stubbornly taciturn the whole way to the M-Wave Arena.

The arena's ridged structure was supposedly designed to echo Nagano's mountainous landscape. It looked more like an armadillo crouched in the frostbitten grass. The first time we'd crossed the threshold, though, it had given me a heart-pounding thrill to know I stood in one of the venues from the 1998 Olympics. Heath and I had watched them on TV when we were fourteen, and four years later, there we were, about to compete in our first World Championships final.

About to compete, and giving each other the silent treatment. We went through our pre-skate routine separately. I stretched alone, using the cinder-block walls instead of Heath's hands to get the necessary support and resistance.

I hoped once we were on the ice, muscle memory—or plain old habit—would take over. But Heath wouldn't even take my hand during the group warm-up. After doing my own makeup, I usually applied his eyeliner—a subtle smudge along his lashes, enough to make his expressions show to the back of the stands—but he decided to do that by himself too. The black line was so messy, it made him look slightly feral. We stayed close to the sides of the rink, stiff and awkward with a wide space between us as our competitors spun and stroked past in perfect sync.

By the boards, our coaches looked on. The Canadian coaching team stood between Sheila and Veronika Volkova, as if they sensed a buffer was necessary. Veronika's hair was bleached even blonder than it had been back in her skating days, and she wore a sable coat with a dramatic collar that set off the steep angles of her features. She was one of the only women in ice dance taller than I was—though her partner Mikhail had been well over six foot even out of his skates.

Yelena Volkova had the same pale hair and narrow, feline eyes as her aunt, but otherwise the two women were nothing alike. Yelena had only just turned sixteen, and she was so small and fragile-looking she could've passed for younger. Her partner—Nikita Zolotov, Mikhail's son—was well into his twenties, which made her seem even more like a little girl out on the ice.

With two minutes left in the warm-up, Sheila waved Heath and me over to her. I steeled myself for the worst—but if she could shake Heath out of his funk, it would be worth it.

As soon as he'd snapped his blade guards on, though, Heath stalked away, leaving me to face Sheila alone.

"I'm sorry." The words I refused to say to Heath fell right out of my mouth when faced with our coach's intimidating stare. "Heath's mad at me, because I—"

Sheila put a hand up. "I don't care. You're on in five minutes. Make up with him."

"Why should *I* be the one to have to apologize?"

Even as the words spilled out, I wanted to stuff them back down my throat. No one spoke to Sheila Lin like that.

To my surprise, she softened. "I know how you feel, believe me. But what do you care about more, Ms. Shaw—your performance or your pride?"

I didn't see why I should have to choose. This was the World Championships, though, and we were on the brink of a bronze medal.

So I went in search of Heath, ready to say or do whatever it took to get him to forgive me—at least until the end of the free dance. My training at the Academy had improved my skating, but it had also taught me how to perform under pressure. Whether you're miserable or in pain or so pissed off you want to scream, you have to keep a smile on your face. And you have to convince everyone watching—the audience, the judges, even your partner—that it's genuine.

I'd made it all of two steps into the backstage area when Garrett intercepted me.

"Hey," he said. "Everything okay?"

"Everything's fine." I tried to peer around him, but his broad shoulders blocked my view. He still had his oversized Team USA jacket zipped over the gauzy gray costume he wore for the twins' somber orchestral piece in tribute to the 9/11 victims. The choreography had been completed months before the attacks, but their mother knew a PR opportunity when she saw one. "Have you seen—"

"Bella told me about the billboard. She said Heath was upset." Garrett leaned closer. "I could talk to him if you want? Make sure he knows nothing . . . happened, or—"

"I appreciate the offer. But I've got it under control."

Or I would, if I could get to Heath in time. The fifth-place couple from Japan had already started their program, so the clock was ticking.

"Gotcha," Garrett said. "Well, good luck out there. You two have been *killing* it."

"You too." I smiled up at him. "See you on the podium?"

"See you on the podium."

Garrett walked away, giving me a quick shoulder squeeze on his way past. The Japanese team's music shifted into the slow, lyrical section signaling the halfway point of their free dance. I had to find Heath.

But he had already found me.

Before, he'd been freezing me out. Now he was blazing with fury. Even at a distance, I could sense the heat of it, like I was standing too close to an open flame.

"Sorry," he said. Exactly what I wanted to hear, but not at all the way I wanted to hear it. "Did you two want to be alone?"

"Stop it." I pulled him behind the bank of monitors, which showed the Japanese skaters whirling in an intricate combination spin. "Garrett was just—"

"He was touching you."

"He *squeezed my shoulder.*"

"I see the way he looks at you. Not only on that fucking billboard either."

"That 'fucking billboard' is the only reason we're here."

Heath furrowed his brow. "What?"

"Without the money I made with the photo shoot, we would've had to quit the Academy months ago." It turned out "not much" to Garrett was more money than I'd ever seen at one time, enough to cover our costs for the rest of the season.

"What about your inheritance?" Heath asked.

"Lee spent it. All of it. And if it weren't for Garrett getting me that job—"

"I don't want to hear—"

"*If it weren't for Garrett,* we would never have made it to Worlds in the first place. You should be thanking him."

Heath was silent for a moment, and I expected the next words out of his mouth to be something like *Why didn't you tell me?* Or even *I'm going to kill him*—referring to Lee, or Garrett, or both.

Instead he said, "Are you attracted to him?"

I rolled my eyes. "Come on."

"Are you or aren't you?"

The space rumbled with applause as the Japanese team took their bows. We should've been out there already, prepared to step onto the ice as soon as they sat down in the kiss and cry.

"It was just a photo shoot," I said. "Now let's get going, we have to—"

"It's a simple question, Katarina. Yes or no."

An insulting question, and it deserved an insulting answer.

"Of course I'm attracted to Garrett. He's attractive."

Heath opened his mouth to retort, but I barreled ahead.

"If you trust me, it shouldn't matter."

"Trust you?" Heath scoffed. "How can I, when you're lying to me? Keeping secrets, running around behind my back with—"

"Because I knew you'd react this way! I'm allowed to have other friends, Heath."

More applause. The scores had been posted. We'd missed our entire solo warm-up.

"You're like a different person around them," he said. "I hardly recognize you."

I thought that was why we'd come to the Academy: To become different. Better. The best possible versions of ourselves. He was right, I had changed.

The problem was, he hadn't changed at all. He was the same boy I'd known for nearly a decade, wounded and stubborn and so lonely, he'd made me his whole world.

Heath had a bottomless pit inside him too, but it had nothing to do with ambition. No matter how much love I gave him, it would never be enough. He wanted to be everything to me, the way I was everything to him.

And I would always want more.

"Next to skate, representing the United States of America, Katarina Shaw and Heath Rocha!"

"It's our turn." I held out my hand. "We have to go."

The crowd buzzed with confusion at the delay. If we didn't take the ice within two minutes after our names were announced, we'd be disqualified.

"Heath, please. We've made it this far. This is our dream, our—"

"No, Katarina." He sighed and slipped his hand into mine. "It's *your* dream."

Katarina Shaw and Heath Rocha take the ice at the 2002 World Champion-
ships in Nagano.

KIRK LOCKWOOD: You could tell from the moment they came out, something was off.

The video zooms in on Katarina's face, then Heath's. Both are set in grim
masks, glaring at each other. "Fever" starts to play.

ELLIS DEAN: That program was the most passive-aggressive shit I'd ever
seen—and I'm from the South, honey.

More clips of Shaw and Rocha's free dance. They're simply going through the
motions—not connected, not looking at each other. During the twizzle se-
quence, Katarina is a full rotation ahead of Heath, and he stumbles on the
final turn.

KIRK LOCKWOOD: It was like all the heat between them sputtered out.

JANE CURRER: It was unfortunate, but that's the downside of relying
on . . . chemistry.

Another moment, later in the program: Katarina reaches for Heath, but
they're farther apart than they should be. Their fingertips brush without
grasping.

GARRETT LIN: I felt awful. They were fighting because of me.

Cut to Veronika Volkova, sitting with ramrod straight posture on a red velvet
settee in her Moscow flat. She's in her sixties now, her hair turned fully white.

VERONIKA VOLKOVA: Such childish soap operatics would not be toler-
ated in Russia.

Katarina and Heath reach the end of the program. As soon as the music
stops, they break their final pose, as though they can't stand to touch each
other for a second longer.

VERONIKA VOLKOVA: Personal feelings have no place on the ice. Many days Mikhail and I could hardly stand the sight of each other, but when we were skating, could you tell? No. Because we were professionals.

GARRETT LIN: I shouldn't have watched them. Seeing them like that . . . it got in my head.

KIRK LOCKWOOD: The Lins didn't skate up to their usual standard that day either.

During the Lins' free dance at the 2002 World Championships, Garrett momentarily loses his balance coming out of a stationary lift, nearly dropping Bella. He manages to save it at the last second, but Bella shoots him a glare before regaining her composure.

GARRETT LIN: It was my fault. And it felt like the end of the world. Years later, I would still lie awake at night thinking about that skate. I'd failed my mother and my sister and myself, and I couldn't think of anything worse. Funny how little imagination I had at seventeen, huh?

CHAPTER 23

"*In first place, and world ice dance champions for 2002 . . .*"

Camera flashbulbs lit up the arena, a barrage of small explosions.

"*Yelena Volkova and Nikita Zolotov, from Russia!*"

Yelena and Nikita skated out hand in hand, their artfully tattered costumes fluttering behind them, and stepped onto the red carpet unfurled across the ice.

"*Winners of the silver medal, Arielle Moreau and Lucien Beck, from France!*"

The solemn woodwind music set my teeth on edge. As Arielle and Lucien took their places on the podium, I kept applauding, kept smiling. I wouldn't be a sore loser.

Heath sat beside me with his hands in his lap. He didn't seem angry anymore, only weary. Defeated. It was strange to be so close without touching him.

I couldn't even look at him. If I did, I'd scream.

"*Third, and winners of the bronze medal, Isabella Lin and Garrett Lin, from the United States of America!*"

The medal that would have been a crowning achievement for Heath and me was a consolation prize for Bella and Garrett. When Bella bent to receive her bronze, she tensed as if the official was about to string her from a gallows.

You ungrateful bitch, I thought. But I kept smiling.

"*Please rise for the national anthem of the champions.*"

We stood. Heath brushed my knuckles, and I curled my hand into a fist. We should have been on that podium, the American flag ascending above us. Not sitting in the stands, watching.

He cupped his hand around my clenched fingers, leaning close so I could hear him over the triumphant strains of the Russian anthem. "We'll do better next time."

I jerked away. He flinched like I'd struck him.

"What makes you think there'll be a next time?" I said.

Coming into the championships, we'd been on the rise, a team to watch. Now we were a joke. Sheila hadn't said a word to us since our dismal scores flashed on the screen; if she agreed to train us for another season, it would be a miracle. Or charity, which was worse. With a lesser coach—and as far as I was concerned, every coach was lesser when compared to Sheila Lin—we'd have no chance of clawing ourselves back to relevance.

Maybe that was what Heath wanted, consciously or not. Leaving the Ice Academy would have meant leaving California. Leaving the Lins. He would have me all to himself again.

"Ladies and gentlemen, your 2002 world medalists!"

The skaters squeezed onto the top platform for official photos, then began their victory lap around the rink. I descended the steps, not waiting to see whether Heath would follow.

By the time I reached Bella and Garrett, I'd stretched my smile even wider, jaw aching from the effort.

"Congratulations!"

Bella was closer, so I embraced her first. But I made sure to hold on longer to Garrett. I knew Heath was watching. I knew it would hurt him. I wanted it to hurt.

"Thanks." Bella wrapped the medal ribbon around her wrist. "Sorry about—"

I waved off her condolences. "It's fine. We should celebrate."

At that, Bella's eyes lit up. "Wanna eat some carbs?"

"Absolutely. Where should we go?"

"Katarina."

Heath had caught up to us. I turned to face him but stayed between the twins—battle lines drawn. Garrett shifted uncomfortably beside me.

"Can we go somewhere and talk?" Heath asked.

"We're going out." My voice was so cold, I felt as if a layer of frost had settled over me.

"When you get back, then."

"I don't know when I'll be back."

"Katarina, please, I—"

"Don't wait up."

CHAPTER 24

"*Why* is it so damn cold?" Bella complained as we closed the short distance between the car and the restaurant entrance. "It's almost cherry blossom season, for God's sake."

I resisted the urge to roll my eyes. The temperature had dropped since our spa outing, but it wasn't even cold enough to snow. Moisture hung in the air, caught somewhere between rain and mist. It made me think of early spring mornings on Lake Michigan—sitting cross-legged on the shore with Heath, watching the whitecaps through a scrim of fog.

He'd gone back to the hotel to sulk, I assumed. Garrett had opted for a room service dinner, so Bella and I were on our own again.

The restaurant was cozy and welcoming, with multicolored paper lanterns strung above low wooden tables. A Japanese skater had recommended it, and most of the patrons looked to be locals—though the place was still accustomed enough to tourists that the waiter laid a fork and spoon beside my place setting without asking. For Bella, he brought ebony chopsticks with delicate gold designs inlaid on the handles.

She kept her coat on and huddled close to me for warmth as we perused the menu. I could feel every knot in the floorboards through the thin cushion, and my hips ached so much I couldn't believe I'd had a massage that morning. How much could change in a single day.

Heath and I had never fought like that before. I had no idea what a breakup felt like; I'd never experienced one.

Bella ordered for both of us in overly confident Japanese. Thanks to their globetrotting childhood, she and Garrett spoke fragments of about a dozen languages.

I had no idea what we were eating until the plates started to arrive, heaped with noodles, pickled root vegetables soaked in savory miso broth, and delicately folded dumplings with fresh wasabi root grated over the top. I should have been starving after the competition, but I felt too queasy to do more than push the food around my plate.

Between bites, Bella dissected the results of the free dance, speculating about biased judges and backroom dealings that kept her and Garrett in third place.

"I mean, I know we screwed up our twizzles. But Nikita did a *major* balance check during the last choreographic sequence—like, are the judges blind?"

By the time the dessert course arrived—a chestnut cream cake frosted to look like a snow-topped mountain—I couldn't take it anymore.

"You're only seventeen," I pointed out.

"So?" Bella took a big bite of cake.

"You're seventeen, and the third best in the *world.* You know that's good, right?"

"We could have won. We should have at least gotten silver."

"But Heath and I would have been *so lucky* to get the bronze, right?" I stabbed my fork through the frosting, triggering an avalanche of candied chestnuts.

"I didn't mean it like that." Bella laid her hand over mine before I could do any more damage to our dessert. "What happened between you two tonight anyway? That couldn't have all been about the stupid billboard."

"He thinks there's something going on between me and your brother."

Bella arched a brow. "Is there?"

I knew Bella wasn't Heath's biggest fan, but her question sounded a little *too* hopeful.

"Of course not. Heath and I—"

"Have been dating for like half your lives. This isn't Victorian times; you're allowed to speak to other guys." She took another bite and smiled, icing stuck between her teeth. "He's right, though. Garrett likes you."

"Garrett likes everyone."

"He doesn't. Trust me." She balanced her chopsticks on the edge of the plate. "Can I tell you something?"

"Okay."

"You have to swear not to tell anyone else."

With Heath and me hardly on speaking terms, I had no one to tell. "I swear."

Bella leaned in and lowered her voice, even though the only people close enough to overhear were two old Japanese women with wispy gray hair and owlish glasses.

"My mother's finally going to let me and Garrett switch partners next season."

"What?" I said. "Why?"

I'd always been jealous Bella was born with a skating partner. Garrett wasn't showy like some male ice dance stars, but he was solid, a steady backdrop against which Bella could glitter.

But it was never enough for her. That's why we were friends: nothing was ever enough for either of us.

"Did you know," she said, "a sibling ice dance team has never won Olympic gold?"

"So you two could be the first. You're amazing together."

"Sure, I mean, we have the technical skills. But we're so limited in the choreo we can do without it looking creepy. And the height difference has been a problem ever since he had that insane growth spurt."

"Who are you going to skate with?"

Male skaters were a rare commodity in the ice dance world. Ones of Garrett's caliber were even rarer. Since Ellis's revelation that the Hayworths were paying him to skate with Josie, I'd heard far wilder stories of the lengths women went to in order to find partners. Bribes, blackmail, under-the-table deals with other figure skating federations that bordered on human trafficking.

Bella wouldn't have to resort to such unseemly methods. She'd have them lining up like dating show contestants, willing to renounce their citizenships, abandon their current partners, do whatever it took for the chance to skate with Sheila Lin's only daughter.

"I'm considering my options," she said. "Zack Branwell has expressed interest."

"Isn't he still with Paige Reed?"

Reed and Branwell finished in the top ten in Salt Lake but had to sit out Worlds due to some unspecified injury. Everyone expected them to return for the next Olympic quad, though, and to try for the Torino Games in 2006.

"You didn't hear this from me, but . . ." Bella leaned closer, eyes gleaming in the lantern light. "Paige isn't injured. She's *pregnant.*"

That explained a lot. Though her parents must have had her on serious lockdown in their Minnesota hometown to avoid that rumor churning through the mill.

"Is it his?" I asked.

Bella shrugged. "Not my problem. But she'll be out all next season, at least. And once he's skated with me, no way is he going back. Paige is mediocre at best."

Though his self-consciously masculine skating style wasn't my cup of tea, Zack had always been the star of the pair. He was several inches shorter than Garrett too, which would make him a better physical match for Bella. For all his flyover country blandness, on the ice the guy came across like an honest-to-God *Tiger Beat* pinup, golden hair and a strong jawline and full, kissable lips. Bella was beautiful on her own; with Zack at her side, she'd look like a princess and a movie star, all rolled into one.

"And what about Garrett?" I said. "Who's he going to skate with?"

He'd have his pick, that was for sure. Every female ice dancer in the world would crawl across shattered glass to skate with a partner like Garrett Lin.

"That's the best part." Bella reached across the table and took my hands in hers. "*You* can skate with Garrett."

INEZ ACTON: Figure skating is a strange sport, because it depends so much on image and narrative. You have to kill it on the ice, but you also have to look the part and have a compelling story. What better way to add a plot twist than switching partners?

KIRK LOCKWOOD: It's pretty common for ice dancers to change partners, especially if they paired up when they were children.

In a home video, three-year-old Bella and Garrett toddle around the ice together. Garrett wears a pint-sized tuxedo and has a serious expression on his face, while Bella beams and waves, swirling the full skirt of her glittery dress.

KIRK LOCKWOOD: And the start of a new Olympic cycle is the perfect time to do it.

GARRETT LIN: I could understand why Bella wanted a change.

VERONIKA VOLKOVA: It is rare for sibling teams to be competitive at the elite level. No matter how talented, they are painting with only a few shades of the palette.

JANE CURRER: Ice dance needn't involve romantic undertones. Brother/sister teams can perform a variety of programs. The implication that they're disadvantaged is, frankly, insulting.

INEZ ACTON: Of all the skating disciplines, ice dance is the most invested in traditional gender roles. Even skaters who are clearly queer are expected to pretend like they're into their partners—on the ice, and sometimes off the ice too. Audiences love a love story.

ELLIS DEAN: Of *course* ice dance is all about sex! If you can't picture the skaters banging, truly what is the point?

VERONIKA VOLKOVA: I was not shocked in the least when I heard about Isabella and Garrett. For Sheila, it was a win-win scenario.

KIRK LOCKWOOD: Splitting up the twins was a shame, but it made sense, I suppose. Now Sheila had two opportunities for her kids to take the gold.

VERONIKA VOLKOVA: By pairing her children with some of their top com-petitors, she neutralized the threat of those other teams. And she would be able to drive the twins to greater heights by pitting them against each other—in training, and in competition.

GARRETT LIN: I just wanted my sister to be happy. I wasn't thinking about myself.

VERONIKA VOLKOVA: It is precisely what I would have done myself in her position.

GARRETT LIN: The truth is, I didn't know what I wanted. But Bella did. She always had.

CHAPTER 25

"Me, skate with *Garrett*? You're not serious."

"You two looked incredible together in that picture," Bella said. "And you're tall enough. His height wouldn't be an issue the way it is with me. You'd balance each other out."

Heath and I were fiery and passionate—but as we'd shown in our awful free dance, the fire could snuff out as quickly as it flared. Garrett was the total opposite: steady, calm. Too calm sometimes. I could bring out his passion, he could temper mine. I knew Bella was right. Her brother and I would be an ideal match on the ice.

I also knew Heath would never forgive me.

"Your mother knows about this?" I asked.

After my failure at Worlds, I couldn't imagine Sheila would want to keep working with me at all, let alone allow me to skate with her prized, perfect son.

Bella nodded. "She knows you and Heath have been having problems."

Heath and I were unraveling. We had been ever since we moved to LA, and I couldn't deny it any longer. For better *and* worse, we were incapable of keeping our personal feelings off the ice. If we broke up, that would be the end of our athletic partnership too. Heath didn't love skating. He loved me.

But on the ice, he couldn't keep up with me. I was skating down to his level, instead of pushing myself to new heights.

"You can still date Heath," Bella said, "if you're skating with Garrett.

It might even be better—separate the skating and the romance, you know?"

I shook my head. "He'll be devastated."

"He'll get over it."

He wouldn't. People had abandoned Heath all his life. Now I was considering doing the same.

Except, I told myself, I wouldn't *really* be abandoning him. We could be together off the ice, like Bella said. We could get our own apartment, the way we'd always talked about.

In a sport like figure skating, there are no sure bets. But skating with a partner like Garrett Lin? That's about as close as you can get. The endorsement opportunities alone meant I wouldn't have to worry about money anymore. And neither would Heath. I could follow my dreams, while giving him the time and support he needed to figure out his own.

"Can I think about it?" I said.

"Sure," Bella told me. "Just make sure you're thinking about what's best for *you*, okay?"

After dinner, Bella took the car back to the hotel. I told her I'd rather walk.

"Suit yourself," she said. "Don't freeze to death!"

The mist had given way to soft rainfall, cold enough to be bracing even for someone used to Midwest winters. I took a slow, circuitous route through the hushed streets of Nagano City, hands buried in my coat pockets.

I tried to think—about what *I* wanted, regardless of my relationship with Heath—but my head was roiling. Back home, when I felt like this, I would go to the lake and look out at the water until everything became clear. In landlocked Nagano, I had to settle for the next best thing.

I knew the garden was near the hotel, but it still took me a few tries to find the stone lions in the dark. When I stepped past them, I felt like I'd fallen through a portal into another world. My shoulders relaxed as I made my way down the rain-slick stone path to the edge of the pond in the center. Water rushed under a miniature wooden bridge, and I shut my eyes, savoring the sound. It wasn't Lake Michigan, but it would have to do.

"Excuse me, this is *my* moping spot."

I spun around. Ellis Dean sat in the shadows under the arbor, smoking.

"Ellis." I stepped closer. The cigarette smoke stung my eyes. "You know if Sheila catches you with those—"

"You gonna tell her?" He took another drag, the glow of the cherry carving out the hollows of his cheeks.

No, I wasn't. If he wanted to wreck his lung capacity, that made one less competitor for me to worry about.

I sat down on the other end of the bench. "Sorry about you and Josie."

Hayworth and Dean had barely qualified for the free dance, and ended up in twenty-second place overall. As disappointed as I was in our result, it could have been much worse.

"Eh, there's always next season," he said. "Unless she trades me in for a newer model. What about you, where's your other half? I heard there was trouble in paradise."

"Something like that."

"Wanna talk about it?"

I hesitated, pressing my hands into the cold stone.

"You can trust me," Ellis said.

That, I didn't believe for a second. But I needed to talk to someone, and I wasn't ready to face Heath yet. Not until I figured out how I felt on my own, without all our history and heat clouding my judgment.

"The Lins are looking for new partners," I told him.

"Shit, really?" He blew out a long stream of smoke. "Don't tell Josie, she'll cream her chastity belt. Any idea who they're going with?"

I bit my lip. Ellis stared at me.

"They want you to skate with Garrett." He stubbed out his cigarette and turned to face me. "So what are you going to do?"

"I don't know."

Ellis pursed his lips. "Yes you do."

"I have to—"

"You'd have to be a fucking idiot to turn down the chance to skate with Garrett Lin. And you're a lot of things, Kat Shaw, but you are not an idiot."

"But . . ." I swallowed, heartbeat fluttering in my chest. "What about Heath?"

"Boyfriends are easy to come by. Skating partners like Garrett, not so much."

Especially for women like me—with my body type, my above-average height. If I turned this opportunity down, Garrett would have a hundred girls begging to skate with him by morning. Creating yet another high-performing team for Heath and me to compete against.

If Heath even still wanted to skate with me. Maybe all this soul-searching was a moot point. I might go back to the hotel and find him ready to break things off for good.

"Look, Kat." Ellis dropped the smug look. Without it, the angles of his face softened; I might even have called him handsome. "I like you."

I scoffed. "Really."

"I've always liked you. You're scrappy. Most of the other girls in this sport are spoiled little bitches like Josie. You may be a bitch, but you aren't spoiled."

"Wow, thanks." I rolled my eyes, but I knew that was high praise coming from Ellis.

"You want to be a champion, right?"

"Of course. Don't you?"

Ellis shrugged. "When I started out, I did. But at some point, you've got to be realistic. So here's my question for you: do you think you can get to that level skating with Heath?"

I could have hesitated. Pretended to consider. I could even have lied.

Instead I looked Ellis right in the eyes, and I told the truth.

"No. I can't."

It was such a relief to say it out loud. I exhaled, breath clouding the chilly air. The rain was coming down harder now, turning the pond into a tessellation of ripples.

"He's holding me back," I said. "He's been holding me back for years."

"Well." Ellis smiled and shook another cigarette free of the pack. "There you go."

He wasn't looking at me anymore. He was looking behind me, toward the garden entrance. I started to turn, to see for myself. But a part of me already knew.

Someone stood between the stone lions. It was too dark to make out his features, but I could see the outline of his body, the hunch of his shoulders, and that was enough.

"Heath." His name came out in a horrified whisper.

I shot a panicked glance over at Ellis. He lifted the smoldering cigarette to his lips, but it wasn't enough to conceal his smirk.

He'd known all along Heath was listening. He had wanted him to hear.

I stood. "Heath, wait!"

Heath turned, disappearing behind a curtain of raindrops. I ran after him. My shoes slipped on the wet stone, and I went down, gravel biting into my knees.

By the time I'd scrambled to my feet again, he was out of sight. I kept running, calling his name until my throat was raw. The few people out in the torrent gave me strange looks, but I didn't stop. I couldn't. I had to find him. I had to explain.

Finally, I spotted him a few blocks ahead—head bowed, leaning into the driving rain.

"*Heath!*" I screamed.

He froze for a moment. But he didn't turn back.

That's when I knew I'd lost him.

GARRETT LIN: I wish I knew what happened that night.

ELLIS DEAN: Oh, I know *exactly* what happened that night.

GARRETT LIN: If there was something I could have done to stop it . . . but by the time I found out, it was too late.

ELLIS DEAN: I figured Kat would catch up with him, and they'd have some big romantic screaming match in the rain and go back to their hotel for makeup sex. I honestly thought I was doing them both a favor, getting everything out in the open so they could get the hell over it and move on.

GARRETT LIN: I know I'm biased, but Kat didn't deserve that.

ELLIS DEAN: How was I supposed to know he'd react that way? I swear Heath Rocha was the most dramatic straight boy I ever met.

GARRETT LIN: Kat deserved . . . well, she deserved better.

CHAPTER 26

When we left Japan, I was still in denial.

I don't know how long I stayed out searching for Heath. Long enough for the freezing rain to soak through my thin jacket and the sweater underneath, down to my skin.

Eventually, I gave up and returned to our hotel, but I didn't want to get in the shower—what if he came back, came looking for me, and I missed him?—so I lay under the covers, sleepless and shivering until dawn.

Later that morning, as I dragged my bags to the bullet train alone, I told myself he would be waiting at the station. Or at the airport. Or back in California. I imagined throwing my arms around his neck and kissing him until I couldn't breathe. I imagined choking the life out of him.

No one knew what to say. The other skaters on our flight avoided me, as if my failure and heartbreak might be catching. After takeoff, Garrett insisted on switching seats so I could sit next to his sister—my first time in first class. Bella split her headphones with me and queued up a terrible movie on the seat-back screen, tactfully pretending not to notice the tears running down my face.

Somewhere below the Bering Strait, I managed to fall into a fitful sleep. I dreamed of ice shattering under my feet, cold water rushing into my lungs when I tried to scream.

By the time we got back to Los Angeles, I was burning with fever.

The twins offered to let me come home with them and stay in one of the guest suites. But I wanted to be alone, so I went back to the dorm. For days, I stayed in bed—sweating, shaking, the only indication of time passing the light shifting over my closed eyelids.

Bella brought me food and medicine—not the usual chicken noodle soup or Sudafed, but extremely LA cure-alls: green juices, organic bone broths, packets of herbs labeled only with handwritten Chinese characters.

Nothing helped. I hadn't been so sick since I was a child. And that time, Heath had been by my side, as miserable as I was.

It was February 1994—the first time the Olympic Winter Games were held in a different year than the Summer Games, and the first year of my friendship with Heath.

People talk about Great Lakes winters as though they're hell frozen over from Thanksgiving to Easter, but it's February you've got to look out for. After weeks of bitter temperatures, several feet of snow fell overnight, and even in the Midwest, they have to cancel school for that.

I knew Heath would be miserable trapped in that tiny house with his foster family all day, and I didn't relish the thought of spending hours cooped up with my brother shouting at his Sega Genesis either. So I suggested we go to the lake.

At least once every winter, the lake iced over—though you didn't have to venture out far before the surface became dangerously thin. My father had taught me what to watch out for: clear ice with a blue tinge is the strongest. If the ice is milky-white, tread carefully. If it's gray or slushy, don't even think about it. And if it starts to break apart under your feet?

Don't run. You'll only make it worse.

The high winds had cleared away the snowdrifts closest to the shore, leaving us with our own private rink surrounded by sky. I'd unearthed two pairs of old hockey boots from the depths of the basement, because Heath didn't own skates yet, and I knew better than to let my pricey blades touch anything other than pristine indoor ice.

We were both awkward, tottering and sliding like baby deer on the dull, rust-speckled runners. Within a few minutes, though, we'd worked out a rhythm, and soon we were gliding across the lake's surface, mittened fingers clasped, faces stretched into giddy grins.

Heath had been watching me skate for months by then, but that was the first time we ever skated together. He started spinning me around in a simple waltz step, and I shut my eyes and imagined we were skating to victory in front of an adoring crowd.

Sometimes I think my entire career was an attempt to recapture the elation I felt that winter day, with the wind on my cheeks and Heath's hand in mine, moving so fast we were almost flying. I had no idea how long we'd stayed on the lake, or how far out we'd gone.

Until I heard the crack.

It only hurt for a second. Then I went numb. My legs were submerged in the lake. Shards of ice scraped my waist, but I was too shocked to scream. Luckily, Heath wasn't.

"Katarina!"

Everyone always called me "Kat" as a kid, Heath included. Until that moment. He kept shouting my full name, over and over, like somehow the extra syllables would help close the distance between us.

"Katarina, give me your hand!"

When I tried, I only slipped in deeper, frigid water soaking my coat, weighing me down. Heath lunged forward and grabbed me by the shoulders. But I was sliding back, faster and faster. Dragging him with me through the hole we'd made in the ice.

"Katarina, *please.*"

He pulled, and I heaved myself up. I wouldn't fully understand how we'd managed it until years later when we started doing dance lifts, achieving seemingly impossible feats through counterbalance and adrenaline and pure trust. All I knew was that I was out of the water.

I collapsed on top of him. The ice groaned under our weight.

My hat had come off somewhere in the struggle, and my hair tumbled free, curtaining around our faces. We needed to get up, off the lake, back to the safety of solid ground. But we were frozen in place, staring into each other's wide, startled eyes.

Eventually we caught our breath and trudged back to the house to warm up by the fireplace. By nightfall, we were both wracked with chills and coughs, and Heath ended up staying over for days, until we were both on the mend. I thought his foster parents might object, but they seemed relieved not to have to take care of a sick kid. The two of us curled up together on the sofa in a nest of blankets, watching hours of skating competitions I'd videotaped, and I was so grateful for the feverish flush on my face, because it kept Heath from seeing how I blushed every time he looked at me. Every time I thought about how close we'd been.

Eight days following our flight out of Nagano, my fever finally broke. I'd still heard nothing from Heath.

After so much time spent prone, my body was strung tight with anxiety and restlessness. I needed to move.

I needed to skate.

It was nearly midnight. I had no idea whether I'd be able to gain access to either of the Academy rinks at that hour, but I decided to try my luck anyway. I pulled on some ratty leggings and my old Stars on Ice shirt, slung my skate bag over my shoulder, and went downstairs, my deconditioned leg muscles protesting every step.

The door to the main rink was shut, but light leaked around the edges. Not the bright white banks of overheads, but the soft blue-tinted spotlights they used for ice shows and exhibitions. There was music playing too—though the volume was so low I couldn't pick out the song until I went inside.

"The Good Fight" by Dashboard Confessional. And there, whirling across the ice in time with Chris Carrabba's wailing vocals, was Garrett Lin.

Instead of his usual perfectly fitted, designer-branded workout gear, Garrett was in loose-fitting sweatpants and a tank top that showed off his well-developed shoulders. Sweat glistened all over his arms and chest, streaming below the neckline of his shirt as he leaned into a layback spin. He'd clearly been at this for hours.

Another song started; I didn't recognize this one, but it had the same angsty, emo vibes. Despite his casual attire and the intensity of the music, Garrett's every move was impeccable, a masterclass in technique.

He was mesmerizing. I didn't realize how long I'd stood there watching from the shadows like a creep until Garrett stopped skating and looked at me.

He seemed startled for a second. Then he smiled and gave me a little wave, like we'd bumped into each other on the street.

"Kat." He was winded, and my name came out in a gasp. "You should be in bed."

The rise and fall of his chest pulled his sweat-soaked shirt taut, revealing every muscle underneath. Off the ice, Garrett sometimes seemed like an awkward teen boy, uncomfortable in his body, unsure of himself.

But on the ice? He looked like a man. And an artist. Garrett wasn't just some reliable backdrop to show off Bella's talent. He was a star too, and he'd been holding himself back so he wouldn't outshine her.

"I'm feeling much better," I told him—though if I'd known I was going to have company, I would have bothered to shower or at least brush my hair.

He skated over to the boards and picked up his water bottle. "If you're better, you must have thrown out that disgusting green juice Bella brought you."

"Of course not." I smiled. "I poured it down the drain."

Garrett laughed. "Very wise."

"Is that what your mother used to bring you, when you were sick as kids?"

"No. Our nanny." He tipped his head back to down the last of the water; a bead of sweat slid over his Adam's apple. "I'm glad you're feeling better, but what are you doing up so late?"

"I could ask you the same thing."

"Jet lag. It always screws me up for a couple weeks. By the time I get back on track, it's usually time to fly somewhere else."

"Your mother doesn't mind you coming here in the middle of the night?"

"Not as long as I'm practicing." He set the bottle down. "I'm glad you're here, actually. I've been hoping to talk to you, but I wanted to wait until you recovered."

"Oh? About what?"

"About what Bella told you in Japan."

My stomach sank. He was going to tell me it had all been a big misunderstanding. Why would Garrett Lin want to skate with *me*, when he could have anyone? And now that I'd blown up my relationship with Heath, I had no partner, and I'd never make it to the Olympics, and—

"I never would have asked her to talk to you," Garrett said, "if I'd thought it'd lead to—"

"You asked Bella to talk to me?"

"Yeah. Why, what did she say?"

"Only that you two were splitting up. Looking for new partners for the next quad."

"I honestly wasn't trying to mess things up with you and Heath. But I could see how much you two had been struggling lately. And when we did the photo shoot together—well, I thought . . . I mean, it might just have been me."

"It wasn't just you."

That was the first time I'd admitted, to myself or anyone else, that I felt something during the shoot. It wasn't attraction, exactly, beautiful as Garrett was. More like compatibility. We'd shifted from pose to pose so seamlessly, I couldn't help wondering what it would be like to skate with him.

Garrett's playlist faded into the next track, and a thunderclap of memory rattled me.

I'll be your dream, I'll be your wish, I'll be your fantasy.

Heath and me at sixteen, driving to Cleveland, belting those lyrics over the whine of the car engine, thinking we'd love each other forever. And now I didn't even know what continent he was on. I had no idea whether I'd ever see him again.

"You okay?" Garrett asked.

"Yeah, I . . ." I swallowed. "I love this song."

"Me too." He held out his hand. "Care to join me?"

I hesitated. If simply posing with Garrett had been a betrayal, what would this be? I'd never skated with anyone except Heath.

"I understand that you two . . ." Garrett shook his head. "Well, okay, I don't understand you two at all. But I know there's a lot of history there."

Heath knew me when I was a gangly little girl with bloody kneecaps and prairie grass in my hair. He'd seen me sobbing and weak and shaking with helpless rage. He knew my pressure points. He knew how to provoke me.

Garrett had never known me as Kat Shaw from Nowhere, Illinois. I could leave her behind, as abruptly and heartlessly as Heath had left me. With Heath, I could be myself. But with Garrett, I could be someone better.

And if Heath wanted to see me again? He could watch me on television, winning goddamn gold medals with Garrett Lin.

PART III

The Champions

In front of the Lin Ice Academy's glass atrium, Katarina Shaw and Garrett Lin pose for photos next to Bella Lin and Zachary Branwell as their new partnerships are announced in spring 2002.

JANE CURRER: New skating teams typically take a while to gel.

GARRETT LIN: Kat and I worked well together from the start.

Both teams hold hands and beam at the cameras as if they're on homecoming court. Katarina has a new look: blond hair, professional makeup, clothing chosen to coordinate with Garrett.

ELLIS DEAN: From Hot Mess to Ice Princess. Incredible what a makeover can do, isn't it?

JANE CURRER: I didn't see Ms. Shaw's potential until her partnership with Mr. Lin.

A clip of Shaw and Lin's original dance for the 2002–2003 season: a smooth waltz to the song "Kiss from a Rose" by Seal. They spin across the ice in perfect sync, Katarina's skirt—layered to evoke rose petals—swirling around her legs with each turn.

JANE CURRER: Katarina Shaw grew into a lovely young lady during those years.

INEZ ACTON: They made her look like fucking Figure Skater Barbie. It was some bullshit.

GARRETT LIN: Kat and I brought out the best in each other. Everyone talks about her like she was so difficult, but that wasn't my experience at all. She made everything easier for me.

KIRK LOCKWOOD: Shaw and Lin were unstoppable. They won the U.S. title the first year of their partnership, which is practically unheard of.

FRANCESCA GASKELL: People used to call them "24 Karrett," cause they always got gold.

A video montage shows Katarina and Garrett standing on podium after podium: collecting gold at three consecutive U.S. National Championships, silver at two World Championships.

VERONIKA VOLKOVA: They were good together, I will admit. But not good enough to take the world title from Yelena and Nikita.

FRANCESCA GASKELL: Bella and Zack, though—they had a tougher go of it.

A clip of Lin and Branwell's free dance for the 2002–2003 season: they skate to selections from the score of the popular film Titanic, *in Jack and Rose-inspired costumes.*

INEZ ACTON: It made sense Bella would want to do more romantic programs, since she'd been skating with her brother for so long. But this was ... not it.

In a closeup of some steamy choreography from the Titanic *program, Bella tries her best to connect. Zachary barely makes eye contact with her.*

ELLIS DEAN: She had more chemistry with her brother.

Paparazzi shots show Bella and Zachary out on the town in Los Angeles, wearing party clothes and bored expressions. Katarina and Garrett walk a few steps behind them, arm in arm.

ELLIS DEAN: After their first season, Bella gave up on trying to convince everyone she and Zack were a couple. No one was buying that shit. Everyone knew he was still hung up on Paige.

GARRETT LIN: It was hard for Zack, being away from his family. Especially when he was doing all that rehab for his injured knee.

ELLIS DEAN: Sometimes I wonder if he hurt his knee on purpose, to have an exit strategy. It was some real old Hollywood shit, the way the Lins insisted on hushing up Zack's love child.

JANE CURRER: I don't particularly like this metaphor, but people often say an Olympic cycle is like a political campaign.

In a photo montage spanning the first few years of Katarina and Garrett's partnership, they greet fans, sign autographs, and pose for pictures.

JANE CURRER: There are years of preparation required, then an intense push to the finish. And it takes far more than athletic prowess to be successful.

GARRETT LIN: There was so much pressure on Kat and me going into the 2005 World Championships. In our three years together, world champion was the one title we hadn't won yet. And we were competing in Moscow—home turf for our biggest rivals. Not to mention this was one of the first major events using the new scoring system.

KIRK LOCKWOOD: In the 2004–2005 season, the International Skating Union introduced a revamped scoring system. The goal was to make skating fairer and less subjective.

A graphic explains the new metrics: levels from one to four assigned to each element based on its difficulty, then a base value that can increase or decrease with the "Grade of Execution"—that is, how well the team performs the element.

JANE CURRER: It was an adjustment, certainly, but it was necessary. *I* always judged objectively, but the old system was rife with opportunities for corruption and collusion.

VERONIKA VOLKOVA: The Americans could not defeat us, so they changed the rules.

ELLIS DEAN: The new scoring system was a pain in the ass. I knew how to work a crowd and put on a good show, but all this "level" and "GOE" shit? Hard pass. Josie and I had become a total afterthought anyway, ever since our shit-tastic showing in Nagano. Sheila kept taking our money, but she never showed the slightest interest in our progress.

GARRETT LIN: People think my mom put all this pressure on us, to win or to be perfect or . . . but the truth is, she didn't need to. I pressured myself. I knew it wasn't normal. But I told myself *we* weren't normal. We were Lins. We were supposed to be extraordinary. And with Bella and Zack struggling so much, it was all up to me. I had to win.

CHAPTER 27

"*O*ur final skaters, from the United States of America: Katarina Shaw and Garrett Lin!*"

Hand in hand, Garrett and I glided to the center of the ice. We hadn't watched Yelena and Nikita's free dance, but based on the collective gasp the crowd in the Luzhniki Palace of Sports had let out halfway through their *Swan Lake* program, I knew our rivals had made at least one obvious mistake.

Garrett and I had taken the lead after our flawless Midnight Blues compulsory, and we'd extended it with a season's best performance of our energetic original dance to selections from the musical *42nd Street*. Now all that stood between us and our first world title was the four minutes of the free dance. Skate clean, and we'd be heading into the upcoming Olympic season as reigning world champions.

Our free was set to a Tchaikovsky piece too: his symphony inspired by the Shakespeare play *The Tempest*. This was Sheila's idea of subtle psychological warfare: showing up our competition by outskating them to music by the same composer (and a Russian legend, no less).

Garrett's costume was dyed with a delicate oceanic swirl, while mine had bedazzled lightning cutting across the chest. We were meant to be the sea and the storm, colliding in a passionate clash of raw, natural power. The conceptual elements seemed a bit over the top to me. But in comparison, Volkova and Zolotov's traditional balletic choreography seemed downright tired. We'd already bested them at the Grand Prix Final in Beijing.

And our other biggest rivals were already out of the running. I hadn't spoken to Bella since the night before, when she and Zack officially withdrew after a lackluster original dance that left him limping off the ice. They'd already had to simplify their programs significantly to accommodate his worsening knee issues; even if they had been able to finish the competition, they wouldn't have medaled. He was scheduled for knee surgery after Worlds, and his doctor thought he should be able to return to the ice by the fall. But there was no guarantee.

I assumed my starting position: embracing Garrett, my head tilted to rest on his shoulder. After three seasons of skating together, I still felt as if I barely knew Garrett Lin, but I knew this: he was petrified when we took the ice, every time. From a distance, he came across as serene and confident, but close up I could smell his sweat, feel his quickened pulse against my temple. Somehow his panic made me calmer, as if we were a pendulum swinging into stillness.

I took a deep breath, waiting for the first note of the sedate string and brass melody that underscored our opening choreographic sequence.

That's when I saw him.

He stood on the steps leading up into the stands, to the left of the judges' table. He wore a black wool coat, and his dark hair was shaved close to his scalp.

He looked entirely different from the Heath Rocha I'd known and loved. And yet recognition struck my heart like a bell.

"What's wrong?" Garrett whispered. Without realizing it, I'd lifted my head, drawing my body bowstring-taut in his arms.

But it was too late to explain. Our music started, and we were off—a beat too late, but Garrett skillfully caught us up without missing a step.

Skating with Heath, I always felt right on the edge of control, swept away. With Garrett, everything was precise. Correct. Controlled. All the things that came so naturally with Heath had to be manufactured. I had to remind myself to smile, to gaze into Garrett's eyes, to reach for him at the right moments, with the right amount of passion and yearning. It became part of the choreography, one more thing to learn along with the steps and spins and lifts.

The artifice had bothered me initially. That day, though, I was grateful for it. By the time we reached our first set of twizzles—coinciding with the shower of woodwind flourishes that signaled the approaching musical storm—muscle memory had taken over, and I was performing impeccably as ever.

As I exited the final spin, though, I couldn't help sneaking another look at the steps.

He was gone.

I told myself I was imagining things. Letting my nerves get the better of me. I'd stopped searching for Heath years before—after the authorities told me he was an adult who had left of his own volition and so couldn't be considered a missing person, after the twins' skating-world contacts turned up zero hints as to his whereabouts, after Sheila gave me a talking to about how I needed to let it go and focus on the present, because my personal preoccupations had no place on the ice with her son.

I'd stopped searching, but I'd never stopped looking. How many times over the past three years had I worked myself up with the worry that Heath would appear in the stands at a competition? How many times had I mistaken a dark-haired stranger for him—walking in city crowds, or waiting in line to board a plane or buy a coffee?

That's all this was. Another phantom, conjured by my anger and heartbreak and the unspeakable fear that Heath was truly gone for good.

I didn't have time for fear. I had a title to win. So I threw myself into the dance, picking up speed as Tchaikovsky's tempest intensified with a thunderous timpani roll. As we reached the climax of the piece, turbulent strings and cymbals crashing like waves against rocks, Garrett swung me up into our most dramatic lift. I balanced with a single skate against his leg and spread my arms wide like a sorceress casting a spell, skirt whipping behind me as we shot across the ice with so much power it was as if we'd created our own gale, until—

There he was again. Closer now, watching from right behind the boards.

Heath. It couldn't be. But it was.

My leg started to quake. Garrett dug his fingers in, trying to save the lift. As I was about to come crashing down, he improvised, catching me in his arms and bouncing me off his hip like we were doing a clumsy Lindy Hop. His quick thinking saved us from a fall, but it was ugly and took far too long.

I tried to do the math in my head, figure out what my error had cost us. The new rules meant we'd be docked at least a point for going over the time limit on our lift. Our awkward dismount position would cost us even more. We had a decent lead over the Russians, but any further mistakes, and it might not be enough.

I barely remember skating the rest of the program. My eyes were open, but all I could see was Heath, that hateful expression under his harsh new haircut. The next thing I knew, the crowd was cheering, and Garrett was hugging me.

As we made our way to the kiss and cry, Garrett scooped up one of the stuffed animals tossed onto the ice—a puppy with shaggy golden fur—and handed it to me. I held it in my lap as we awaited our scores, clutching its plush throat like I was trying to throttle it.

When our scores flashed on the monitor, I was still scanning the stands for Heath. I didn't realize we'd won until Garrett lifted me off my feet with a victorious whoop. Sheila wrapped her arms around both of us, beaming like she'd gotten the gold herself.

I'm world champion was my first dazed thought.

My second was: *Bella is going to hate me.*

Garrett and I were hustled straight from the kiss and cry to a flurry of interviews—microphones and cameras stuck in our faces, overlapping voices asking questions in a dizzying array of languages. He did most of the talking, while I held fast to his arm.

Smile, I kept repeating to myself. *This is the best day of your life.*

I thought perhaps it would sink in once the medal was around my neck. But even as I waved to the crowd from the top step of the podium, I felt numb. As the national anthem played, I rested one hand over my heart and the other over the medal, trying to ground myself through deep breaths and the cool sensation of the gold against my palm.

Not real gold, only plated silver. Scratch it hard enough, the finish would come right off.

Tears glittered in Garrett's eyes as he sang along to "The Star-Spangled Banner." My lips moved too, but no sound came out.

Then, there he was again. Under the flag, where he could be sure I would see him. Nearly everything about Heath had changed since three years earlier in Nagano, but his eyes—they were the same. Heavy-lidded, long-lashed, so dark the irises blended into the pupils. So intense, they held me in place sure as a hand around my throat. I would have recognized those eyes anywhere.

We were supposed to stay on the podium for official photos, and then take our lap around the rink. Medal ceremonies had become so routine, I knew the procedure.

But as soon as the anthem ended, I pressed my bouquet into Garrett's hands. He gave me a bewildered look, but I was already stepping off the gold medal platform, heading for the exit.

I thought I'd lost Heath. When I reached the lobby, though, I spotted the back of his dark coat as he pushed through the glass doors leading to the parking lot. I ran after him as fast as I could still wearing my skates. I hadn't even stopped to grab my guards; the blades would be ruined. I had custom ones now, like Bella's and Garrett's, with my name engraved in cursive.

The weather had been arctic all week, and it was snowing—white eddies swirling across the pavement, splinters of ice stinging my eyes. My blood had thinned after so many years in Los Angeles, but I hardly noticed the chill. I held my breath as I scanned the lot, from the dormant fountain in the center to the stand of cedar trees marking the edge. Heath had disappeared.

If he'd even been there in the first place.

"Kat!" Garrett caught up with me. "What are you—"

"What the hell do you think you're doing?" Sheila was only a few steps behind her son, and while he seemed genuinely concerned about my erratic behavior, she was furious.

"Give her a minute," Garrett said.

Sheila turned her glare on him. He shrunk from her, looking like a timid little boy instead of a twenty-year-old champion athlete.

"I'm sorry." My legs shook, rocking on the curved blades like I stood on the deck of a pitching ship. I'd been so sure it was him, but I was already doubting myself. "I—"

"You're a world champion now," Sheila snapped. "So act like it."

She turned on her heel and strode back inside.

"Come on." Garrett draped his Team USA jacket around my shoulders. "Everyone's waiting for us."

I'd sacrificed so much for this moment. So much I could never get back, even if I wanted to. And it had all been worth it, hadn't it? Garrett and I were world champions. We would be the gold medal favorites at the next Olympics.

So act like it.

GARRETT LIN: In Moscow, it seemed like Kat had seen a ghost.

A closeup of Katarina Shaw during the medal ceremony at the 2005 World Figure Skating Championships. Her eyes widen with shock, and Garrett and the other medalists watch, confused, as she leaves the podium.

GARRETT LIN: She didn't tell me what happened, and I didn't want to pry.

At the 2005 Worlds post-event press conference, the medal-winning teams sit at a long table with name placards and microphones in front of them, taking questions from reporters.

"Why did you take off so abruptly during the medal ceremony, Katarina?"

Katarina turns to the reporter with a stiff, too-wide smile.

"It's always been my dream to win Worlds," she says. "Standing up there, listening to the anthem, I suppose I was . . . overcome with emotion."

The answer sounds overly rehearsed, as fake as her smile. Garrett puts his arm around her shoulders and shines a disarming grin over the whole room.

"She didn't want anyone to see her cry," he says. "Even though I was already up there blubbering like a baby!"

He laughs, and so do the reporters. Katarina relaxes a bit, leaning into Garrett's side.

ELLIS DEAN: Yeah, no one believed that sad attempt at spin. Not Sheila's best work.

JANE CURRER: Ms. Shaw's behavior was poor sportsmanship, plain and simple.

VERONIKA VOLKOVA: Extremely disrespectful. My Yelena would never dream of doing such a thing.

GARRETT LIN: It never feels like you imagine it will, when you achieve a milestone like that. I wasn't in a celebratory mood either, because of how upset my sister was.

Bella Lin and Zack Branwell watch from the back of the stands during the 2005 Worlds free dance. Bella holds an American flag crumpled in her lap and wears a sullen expression. When she realizes the camera is focused on her, though, she brightens up and starts waving the flag, elbowing Zack until he does the same.

GARRETT LIN: Bella wanted to go to the Olympics more than anything in the world. It was unfortunate, what happened with Zack, but I knew she'd still find a way to make it to Torino. My sister always got what she wanted. No matter what.

CHAPTER 28

On our last day in Russia, Sheila took us all out for brunch at a restaurant with starched white tablecloths and stunning views of Red Square. Bella showed up late—and alone.

She hadn't spoken to me since Worlds ended, beyond a perfunctory *Congratulations* far less convincing than the one I'd mustered for her bronze medal back in 2002. After teaming up with Garrett, I'd moved in with the Lins, staying in a spare bedroom down the hall from the twins' side-by-side suites, and at first it had felt like a never-ending slumber party with the sister I never had. The more Bella and Zack struggled, though, the more she withdrew.

I waited patiently through several courses of savory breakfast pastries and caviar served on ornate silver dishes before asking about her partner's absence.

"Zack's fine," Bella said. "He flew home early."

"To Los Angeles?"

"To Minnesota. He's going to stay with his parents for a while."

Which meant staying with his ex-partner—and supposed ex-girlfriend—Paige. Their kid was a toddler by then, and Paige had been living with the Branwells since she gave birth. Zack went home to visit them any chance he got—one of the many points of contention between him and Bella, since it cut into their training time.

Bella had been so certain she and Zack would become the golden team, with Garrett and me safely in their shadow. Now she was facing the possibility of an Olympic season without a partner, while her brother and I had established ourselves as the ones to beat.

"What are you going to do?" I asked.

She took a sip of her Russian Caravan tea, skimming her nails over the gilded holder enclosing the glass. "Don't worry about me. I'll figure it out."

I was relieved to see her so calm, given the circumstances.

I should have asked myself why.

After our almost thirteen-hour flight from Moscow back to LA, Sheila told us we could sleep in—but only for an hour. No days off, even for world champions.

My room at the Lin house was luxurious but plain: white walls, white bedding, white enameled furniture straight out of an appointment-only showroom. We traveled so much, I hadn't bothered to decorate, or even fully unpack. The space felt about as much like home as the endless string of hotels we stayed in during the competition season.

The bed was like a cloud, though—layers of memory foam, bedding laundered every other day by Sheila's housekeeper. Even so, I couldn't sleep. I'd stayed wide awake on the plane too, despite the lie-flat seats, lavender-scented silk eye masks, and other comforts of first class.

I hadn't had such bad insomnia since the months right after Heath left. I used to toss and turn and try to imagine where he was, what he was doing. Was he in bed too, or was he in some faraway time zone where the day was just beginning? Was he alone? I hated to think of him alone, but I hated even more to think of him with someone else.

Had that been him in Moscow, or was I losing my mind?

A little after five, I gave up on getting any rest and decided to head to the rink early. Garrett had given me standing permission to borrow his Audi SUV, and I sped down the blissfully clear Pacific Coast Highway with the windows lowered, savoring the cool ocean breeze on my face as the sun rose over the fan palms.

Maybe some time alone, just me and the ice, was exactly what I needed. No spectators, no competition, no pressure.

Though I didn't expect to encounter anyone until closer to the seven a.m. training session, I'd taken the time to do my hair and makeup. Sheila impressed upon us the importance of always looking put together; you never knew who might be watching and judging.

I walked into the main rink a few minutes before six, only to find I didn't have the place to myself after all. Another skater had beaten me to the fresh ice.

Dressed in skin-tight black, he was a blurred shadow against the walls. There wasn't any music playing, but somehow I could hear the rhythm—in the scrape of his blades over the smooth ice, the subtle movement of his hips, even the extension of his fingertips.

This guy was good. *Really* good. Changing directions, he leaned so deep into his edges I feared he might tip over, but he maintained complete control.

He skidded to a stop at center ice, skates sending up a glittering arc of snow. Then he looked right at me, as if he'd been watching me too.

I staggered back like I'd been struck.

Heath Rocha parted his lips, flushed crimson with exertion. The same way he used to look after he'd spent hours kissing me.

"Hello, Katarina," he said.

CHAPTER 29

K atarina.

    Heath was the only one who ever called me that, besides journalists and commentators. In the past, when he'd used my full name, he pronounced it like he was taking pleasure in every syllable, like it was his favorite word in the whole world.

Now he hurled it like an insult.

"Congrats on the world title," Heath said, and he made that sound taunting too.

It had been three years, almost to the day, since he'd run from me in the freezing rain in Nagano, and he looked like a different person. His posture was straighter, shoulders back like a ballet dancer. His features were almost gaunt—all softness carved away, leaving a face that was angular to the point of severity. That lush forest of curls razed to the roots. A small white scar cut across his left cheekbone, emphasizing the flintiness of his stare.

But he was still so beautiful to me. That might have been the worst part.

I could tell he was cataloging the ways I'd changed too. During our time apart, I'd done my best to tame every unruly thing about myself into submission: bleaching and blowing out my hair, submitting to whitening and waxing and whatever other beauty treatments Bella and her mother recommended, even losing weight so my body looked less womanly.

My new look had made me feel professional, put together, like a real elite skater who deserved to stand next to golden boy Garrett Lin. But under Heath's hard gaze, I felt ridiculous, a little girl in an ill-fitting costume.

He saw through all of it, down to my core. He always could.

I had so many questions for him—*where have you been, why did you leave me, how could you be so cruel*—but the only one I managed was, "What are you doing here?"

"I was invited," he said.

"By who?"

The lobby door burst open, and Bella ran into the rink, Garrett right behind her.

They'd both dressed in a hurry. Bella's hair was up in a sloppy bun rather than her usual crown of braids, and she hadn't even applied lip balm.

They must have woken up and realized I'd gone to the rink early. Realized what I would find when I got there, and rushed to intercept me.

The threads started to weave together in my mind. Heath showing up in Moscow. Bella's uncharacteristic calm about Zack's departure. The frantic, guilty look in her eyes as she glanced from me to Heath and back again.

She didn't need a new partner, because she'd already found one.

Heath hadn't come back for me. He'd come back for *her.*

"Look," Bella said. "This isn't how I wanted you to find out. But we all know Zack's not going to be competition-ready for a long time, if he ever is again, and—"

"And you're *Bella Lin*! You could have any partner you want!"

"You know it's not that simple."

"Bullshit. Get your mother to pull a few strings, ship some poor guy over from—"

"It's too late for that. The Olympics are in less than a year."

There wasn't sufficient time to clear the citizenship hurdles required to partner with a skater from another federation. But even limiting the pool to American citizens, even with how she'd tumbled in the rankings during her seasons with Zack, Bella had options.

Heath stood off to the side, watching our argument play out as if it were an exhibition program performed solely for his pleasure.

"Bella never thought you were good enough for me," I said to him. "Now suddenly you're good enough for her?"

Heath's only response was a smile—but it was nothing like how he used to smile at me. It was the way he used to smile at my brother, when he was trying to get a rise out of him.

"Kat." Garrett put his hand on my shoulder. "Why don't we all take a deep breath and—"

I whirled around, shirking his grip. "Did you know about this?"

"Not until this morning."

"If you'd known, would you have told me?"

Garrett hesitated, eyes cutting toward his sister. There was my answer. And obviously Sheila was well aware. I recalled Bella's words, that night by the pool: *I find it best to assume my mother knows everything.* For all I knew, the entire thing was Sheila's idea.

At the time, I told myself I was only angry because they hadn't been honest with me. Now I can admit that wasn't true. There was no circumstance in which I could have accepted Heath and Bella skating together.

Her betrayal stung, but his was worse. Because Heath hadn't simply improved since leaving me—he'd *transformed.* He wasn't the same skater he'd been when we were together. He was the skater I'd always dreamed of him becoming.

His love for me hadn't been motivation enough to reach his full potential. His hatred, though? That made him capable of anything.

ELLIS DEAN: So for three whole years, this motherfucker dropped off the face of the earth. And then, out of nowhere, he shows up? Tell me that's not some epic daytime soap-opera shit! You can't. I wish I'd been there to see Kat's face.

GARRETT LIN: After Nagano, I was afraid Heath might have . . . hurt himself. I never said so to Kat. But I imagine it must have crossed her mind too.

Video of a Lin Ice Academy practice session in summer 2005. Heath warms up, improvising some choreography to match the song another team is performing to across the rink. Several skaters stop what they're doing to watch him, but he seems oblivious to their attention.

FRANCESCA GASKELL: He'd always been good at the expression and performance parts of skating. But now he had the technique to back it up. Heath could, like, *become* the music.

KIRK LOCKWOOD: It's not impossible for a skater to improve so much in such a brief time. But it is unlikely.

ELLIS DEAN: I mean, he had to be on 'roids or something, right?

GARRETT LIN: He wasn't taking anything. Doping isn't all that prevalent in ice dance—mostly because it wouldn't help much. You could improve your stamina, sure, but ice dance is all about artistry. There's no magic pill for that.

JANE CURRER: The U.S. Figure Skating Association has a zero-tolerance policy for performance-enhancing drugs. That's all I have to say on the matter.

ELLIS DEAN: The boy was always cute and all, but he did *not* have those muscles before.

GARRETT LIN: My mother made everyone at the Academy drug test weekly—and yes, I mean everyone, her own children included. If Heath was on something, she would have caught him and kicked him out.

ELLIS DEAN: Kat must have been kicking herself for letting him go. Everyone was talking about it—skaters from Canada to China had betting pools going about how long it would take before Kat Shaw and Bella Lin clawed each other's eyes out.

GARRETT LIN: You think my mother would have stood for that sort of petty infighting? We all wanted the same thing: to go to the Olympics. We didn't have time for anything else.

Sheila coaches Katarina and Garrett, while Bella and Heath skate by in the background.

GARRETT LIN: Honestly, Bella and Kat avoided each other for the most part. It was sad, after they'd been such close friends for so long. But anyone who knew Bella knew she'd always choose skating over everything—and everyone—else. And if their positions were reversed? I'm sure Kat would've done the same.

CHAPTER 30

I was determined to ignore Heath and Bella. I couldn't afford to waste my energy on them—not if I was going to become an Olympic gold medalist.

But they didn't make it easy. Every time I turned around, there they were: wound around each other on the ice or sitting shoulder to shoulder in the stands. If Heath saw me looking, he'd lean closer, find excuses to touch her—and Bella didn't exactly discourage him.

It pained me to admit it, but they were good together. Heath had improved so much, he made every style from the polka to the mambo look easy. The combination of Bella's petite stature and the muscle Heath had put on during his mysterious absence meant they could perform lifts and tricks out of reach for most other ice dance teams.

Plenty of rumors flew about where Heath had been training—after all, there were only so many elite ice dance instructors out there, and even fewer who could compete with the likes of Sheila Lin. A couple of coaches tried to take credit for his transformation, but Heath refused to confirm or deny. All anyone knew was that he'd somehow gone from serviceable to world-class in a few short years.

Meanwhile, Garrett and I were struggling. For our free dance that season, we skated to a medley of R&B tracks. Our choreography was meant to be a steamy slow burn, with lots of longing looks and lifts where my legs wrapped around Garrett's waist. We'd done romantic programs before; nothing so overtly sexy, though. We could execute the technical requirements, but the whole thing felt awkward and forced—

especially with the only man I'd ever loved watching from the other side of the ice.

I couldn't avoid seeing Heath at the Academy. But I'd started taking some of my off-ice training elsewhere. I wasn't *running away,* I reasoned. I just needed some fresh air. A change of scenery, a new challenge.

Yeah, even back then I knew I was full of shit.

My favorite workout spot was in a canyon near the Lins' house: hundreds of concrete steps winding up a steep hillside. In mild weather, it would have been a challenging workout. In the scorching heat of Los Angeles summer, it was pure torture—more than enough pain to keep my mind off the true source of my suffering.

By the fall, I was escaping to the canyon three days a week, sometimes more if I could fit it in between all our ice sessions and dance lessons and promotional commitments. It was quiet there: nothing but the calls of birds, the pounding of my shoes against the concrete, and my breaths turning from steady to panting the closer I got to the top.

Until one early October afternoon, when my solitude was shattered by the sound of footfalls coming up fast behind me.

I encountered casual hikers on occasion, but most of them started at the top of the hill and took the stairs down. It was rare to see someone else run the stairs—rarer still that they could do it fast enough to catch me.

The footsteps sped up, closing the distance, until the other runner passed on my right side, almost slamming me into the rusted railing.

I was about to shout a protest. Then I saw who it was.

Heath. In running shorts that made his sculpted thighs impossible to ignore.

I stopped, huffing out a sigh of frustration. "What, you're following me now?"

Heath paused to glance down from several stairs above. His hair had grown back long enough to show a hint of wave, and the sunlight made it gleam.

"Looks like you're following me," he said.

He started off again, taking the next few steps two at a time to increase his lead. Not even breathing hard, the bastard.

I never let him win when we raced along the lakeshore as kids, and I wasn't about to start. So I poured on the gas, chasing after him.

The higher we climbed, the less shade there was. Sweat poured down my back, and my leg muscles burned like I was in the final measures of a free dance, but I was gaining on Heath.

The staircase narrowed into a switchback, a burnt-out tree trunk stretching across the path, and I saw my opportunity to overtake him. I bounded forward, brushing past so close our hips skimmed together, and then I was ahead, only a few steps remaining before the summit, Heath's breath on the nape of my neck—

Until the toe of my sneaker caught a crack at the edge of the top step, and I sprawled into the sunbaked dirt, pain searing down my shins.

Before I could get my bearings, Heath had grabbed me by the shoulders and hauled me back onto my feet. The first time he'd touched me since that night in Nagano—though he let go just as quickly, jumping back as if he'd been singed. I hated myself for the way I bent toward him, like a flower yearning for the light.

He watched, arms crossed, as I limped over to sit on a graffiti-covered rock. Scrapes painted both of my legs red from knee to ankle, bits of gravel embedded in the burning skin. I started trying to brush them off, but my hands were raw and grimy too.

Heath sighed. "Stop that. You're making it worse."

He unclipped a small bottle from his belt and knelt in front of me. So close I could feel the heat radiating off him. The scar under his eye looked fainter. Like I could reach out with my fingertips and brush it away.

I gripped the rock, nails scraping the rough surface. On a clear day, the overlook revealed a stunning vista from the Santa Monica Mountains to the Pacific, but that afternoon, a layer of smog smudged the view into a watercolor blur. As Heath rinsed my wounds with sun-warmed water, fingertips grazing my calf in a way that could have been accidental, I forced myself to keep focusing on the gray haze. Anything was better than looking at him.

No wonder I'd been having so much trouble connecting with Garrett on the ice: Heath's return reminded me what real desire felt like.

Heath stood and pulled the hem of his shirt up to wipe the sweat off his brow. I braced myself, determined not to stare at his abs or his tapered waist or—

His scars. Heath's entire back was covered in scars, much more prominent than the one marring his cheek. I sucked in a breath.

"What happened to you?"

Heath tugged the shirt back into place. "Nothing."

The scars were all different shapes and sizes, scattered seemingly at random, no pattern or symmetry I could identify. The damage was long healed, but I could all too easily imagine the marks fresh, throbbing and tender like my scraped-up legs.

I wanted to envelop him in my arms and ensure nothing could hurt him ever again. I wanted to find whoever had done this and make *them* bleed.

But when I reached for him, he jerked away.

"Heath," I said, cringing at the softness that snuck into my voice.

"Oh, *now* you care."

"Of course I—"

"You want to know what happened to me?" he spat. "*You* did. You left me, and—"

"I didn't leave you!" Was that what he'd been telling himself all these years, when I was the one who'd chased him through the streets, screaming his name? "*You* left *me*."

"Please. I heard everything you said to Ellis that night."

"I was only *talking*. I hadn't made any decisions yet."

"You said I was holding you back. I wasn't good enough. You'd never win, skating with me. And we both know that's all you care about."

"Well, you decided for both of us, didn't you? So I guess we'll never know now."

"I guess not." He turned toward the staircase. All the care he'd shown a few moments before had burned away, leaving nothing but cold disdain in its place. "Enjoy the rest of your run, Katarina. Try not to break anything on the way back."

He started down the steps—faster now, too fast for me to catch up even if I'd wanted to.

I stood on the hilltop fuming, the salt of my sweat making my shins burn again. The injuries were nothing serious, but they could have been. I could have snapped a bone, compacted my wrists when I braced my fall.

All those years of training, and I almost threw it away chasing Heath up a hill like we were still a couple of half-feral children.

It was *my* year. *My* Olympic season. No one was going to ruin it for me.

Not even Heath Rocha.

KIRK LOCKWOOD: Everyone expected Torino to be a rematch between the Americans and the Russians—the one they'd all been waiting for since Sheila and I battled it out with the original Volkova and Zolotov back in Calgary.

During their medal ceremony at the 1988 Winter Olympics, Sheila Lin and Kirk Lockwood smile on top of the podium, while Veronika Volkova and Mikhail Zolotov glower from the step below.

KIRK LOCKWOOD: But as any skating fan knows, it doesn't always go the way you expect.

In a news clip from Russian state television, an anchorman delivers a breaking report, with English translation dubbed over his voice.

"Nikita Zolotov, son of decorated Olympic ice dancer Mikhail Zolotov, officially announced his retirement from the sport today. The younger Zolotov has been struggling with injury since the World Championships earlier this year in Moscow, where he and his partner, Yelena Volkova, suffered a shocking defeat to Americans Katarina Shaw and Garrett Lin.

"Volkova and Zolotov were widely expected to triumph at the ice dance competition during the twentieth Winter Olympiad in Torino, Italy, but now Volkova has been left without a partner only a few months before the Games."

VERONIKA VOLKOVA: Yelena was heartbroken.

ELLIS DEAN: Yelena was probably relieved. I mean, I don't know her, but I always thought she seemed scared of Nikita. And of her aunt.

VERONIKA VOLKOVA: She was still young. That is what I told her. She would go to the Olympics in four years' time, with a new partner. A better partner. Another four years, and I was certain that no one would even recall who Katarina Shaw was.

KIRK LOCKWOOD: With Volkova and Zolotov out of the picture, Shaw and Lin were the indisputable ones to beat. Coming off a world title, teams typically get a big confidence boost. They carry themselves differently. They skate like champions.

Katarina Shaw and Garrett Lin perform their 2005–2006 season free dance, to the music of British R&B singer Sade. Katarina's costume is pure white, with a gauzy skirt and crystal-encrusted bodice. Garrett wears all black, with the same crystals decorating his shoulders.

KIRK LOCKWOOD: We all expected Kat and Garrett to sail to the top of every podium that season, then collect gold in Torino as their victory lap. But like I said, figure skating is full of surprises. And the surprise that year was Lin and Rocha.

At their first-ever competition together, the 2005 Nebelhorn Trophy, Bella and Heath skate to selections from the soundtrack of the 1998 film Great Expectations. *Bella wears a green dress with a flowing skirt. Heath's costume is an exquisitely tailored satin tuxedo.*

From the commentary booth, Kirk Lockwood remarks, "Seems like these two have been together a lot longer than a few months, doesn't it? The way they're skating, the gold medal is theirs."

GARRETT LIN: Kat and I didn't do any of the early season events, and we were assigned to different Grand Prix events than Bella and Heath. So we wouldn't compete against them directly until the Grand Prix Final in December, if we both qualified.

ELLIS DEAN: It was almost like Sheila planned it that way—keeping them apart to build up anticipation for the big showdown.

GARRETT LIN: I was relieved—not so much for me, but for Kat. I knew she was having a tough time, especially with our free dance. But we still won both of our Grand Prixs.

Katarina and Garrett wave from the top step of the podium at Skate America in Atlantic City, then the Trophée Éric Bompard in Paris.

KIRK LOCKWOOD: Even with as well as they were doing, it was a shock when Lin and Rocha took the silver at Skate Canada—only their second competition together, and their first with stiff international competition. Then they took gold in Japan.

Bella Lin and Heath Rocha keep a close watch on the scoreboard at the NHK Trophy in Osaka. When their winning marks appear, they smile and embrace.

"There you have it, folks," Kirk announces. "Lin and Rocha are going to the Grand Prix Final."

GARRETT LIN: We knew Bella and Heath would give us a fight.

KIRK LOCKWOOD: I thought it might be close. But everyone expected Kat and Garrett to win. They were more experienced. They were the reigning world champions.

At the 2005 Grand Prix Final in Tokyo, Japan, Katarina and Garrett sit in the kiss and cry with Sheila, awaiting their free dance scores. In the lead after the original dance, they were the last team to skate. The numbers appear, and Katarina's face falls.

"Incredible!" comes Kirk's voice over the commentary track. "In their first season together, Isabella Lin and Heath Rocha take Grand Prix gold!"

Cut to Bella and Heath backstage, celebrating their win. Bella kisses Heath on the cheek, leaving a smear of pink lipstick. Then back to Katarina and Garrett. Katarina's face has twisted into a furious scowl. Garrett squeezes her knee and smiles, seeming to remind her to be a gracious loser, but it's too late: her reaction has been broadcast for the whole world to see.

ELLIS DEAN: Listen, if you'd just had your ass kicked by your ex-boyfriend and your ex-bestie, you'd be pretty upset too.

Katarina and Garrett leave the kiss and cry. Her expression is more neutral now, but she sweeps past the outstretched media microphones without speaking to anyone.

ELLIS DEAN: If only Heath and Bella had stopped there.

CHAPTER 31

Following our defeat in Tokyo, all I wanted was to fast-forward to Nationals in January, when Garrett and I would have the chance to defend our title and redeem ourselves.

Unfortunately, Sheila had volunteered all the Academy's senior ice dance teams for a charity gala on New Year's Eve. I can't even remember what the cause was—whales or children or something else in perpetual need of saving—but we were to be the night's entertainment, skating an exhibition show on the beachfront ice rink at the Hotel del Coronado.

The hotel was impressive, like a Gilded Age ocean liner run aground on a stretch of pristine island sand right off the coast of San Diego. When we arrived the morning of the event, the place was still decorated for the holidays, with string lights tracing the turrets and, in the two-story lobby, a Christmas tree tall enough to brush the polished ceiling coffers.

Their skating facilities, though, left something to be desired. The rink was a temporary structure, set up every winter for tourists to stumble around in rental skates while sipping spiked hot chocolate. Without any shade from the California sun, the top layers of ice softened until it felt as if you were trudging through slush.

After the preshow practice session, while most of the other skaters seized the opportunity to lounge on the beach or explore the resort, I retreated to my room, exhausted. We'd left LA at daybreak, and my seat on the chartered coach had offered an entirely too clear view of Bella leaning against Heath's shoulder while he listened to the iPod she'd bought him for Christmas. Instead of flying home after the NHK Trophy, the two of them had stayed in Japan for the few weeks leading up to the final, sightseeing and doing who knows what else together.

I didn't want to think about it. But I also couldn't seem to stop.

The elevator in the hotel lobby was an old-fashioned birdcage contraption, operated by a stooped, gray-haired man wearing a uniform complete with little round hat. As he dragged the metal accordion gate closed, he whistled a cheerful rendition of "Auld Lang Syne."

"So you're one of the ice skaters?" he asked.

I nodded. He switched to whistling the Olympic fanfare.

"You going to the Olympics?"

"I hope so," I said.

The polite, humble answer—the one I'd been trained to give in interviews so I didn't come across as an entitled, egotistical bitch. But I knew damn well I was going to the Games.

Despite Bella and Heath's unexpected Grand Prix triumph, Garrett and I were still the top ice dancers in the United States. The U.S. National Championships served as the de facto Olympic trials, but for us, they were a formality. Two American dance teams would compete in Torino, and we would be one of them. My childhood dream coming true at last.

Only it was no longer enough for me.

I'd spent years aching, *yearning* to compete at the Olympic Games. Now that I was well on my way, simply competing didn't feel sufficient. I wanted to go to the Games as reigning U.S. champion. I never wanted to stand on a silver medal step again.

The elevator arrived at my floor. The attendant shuffled over to retract the gate. And there, in the corridor, was Bella, her fist raised to knock on the door to my room.

"Hey," she said. "There you are."

"You were looking for me?"

This was already the longest conversation we'd had since the day I found out she was skating with Heath.

"Yeah. I was wondering if . . ."

She trailed off, twisting her fingers together. I couldn't remember ever seeing her so unsure of herself. I have to admit I enjoyed it.

"Some of the girls were going to get ready together in my suite," she said. "You're welcome to join us. I mean, only if you want."

Like most things with Bella Lin, the invitation might have been an olive branch—or it might have been a trap, ready to bite the second I let my guard down.

I decided to take my chances. I could bite too.

"What time?" I asked.

I heard the noise from halfway down the hall—overlapping voices, girlish giggling, and the grooving bass of a Beyoncé song.

I stopped outside the door, clutching my makeup case against my abdomen. For a moment, I considered fleeing. I didn't know what was behind Bella's sudden friendly overture. But I knew if I backed down now, she'd win. Again.

The door was propped on the swing bar. I arranged my face into a pleasant expression before pushing it open the rest of the way.

"Kat!" Bella broke into what I hoped was a genuine smile. "Come on in."

As Garrett's partner, my days of staying in shabby budget hotel rooms were long gone. Still, I couldn't help comparing my standard room to the Lins' deluxe suite, with its white-shuttered picture windows providing unobstructed views of the sun dipping into the Pacific.

Everyone had gathered in the sitting area. Josie Hayworth was squeezing a cotton candy pink Lancôme Juicy Tube onto her pursed lips. She and Ellis hadn't been invited to perform, but no doubt her senator father was on the guest list, which meant they got to enjoy the free food and open bar with none of the pressure.

The other three—Amber, Chelsea, and Francesca, who went by Frannie—I knew only in passing. I'd made myself scarce around the Academy, dead set on avoiding Bella and Heath or anything else that might distract from my goals. The girls were all young up-and-comers, recently qualified for the senior level. Their entire futures ahead of them—though I knew, after witnessing several years of churn, most of them wouldn't make it to next season.

I perched on an overstuffed ottoman and started applying my makeup, letting their chatter wash over me. They traded tips on the perfect French manicure, talked about the new Harry Potter movie, and harmonized to "Naughty Girl," Frannie hamming it up with a can of glitter hairspray as a microphone.

Was this what normal young women did on a Saturday night? I was only twenty-two, and I felt unspeakably ancient. I had nothing to add to the conversation, no interests outside of skating. It was easier for me to talk to a reporter for a television segment broadcast to millions than to make simple small talk with people my own age.

For the most part, Bella stayed quiet too, concentrating on creating perfect wings of black eyeliner extending all the way to her temples. I assumed she and Heath were performing their free dance program, but she seemed to be going for a more dramatic look than she'd worn for the Grand Prix series.

As I patted on a final layer of setting powder, Bella glanced over. "What are you going to do with your hair?"

"I don't know." So far that season, I'd gone the simple route: half up to keep it out of my face, secured with a hair clip covered in crystals that matched my dress.

"Want me to braid it for you?" she asked.

When I first started skating with Garrett, Bella had done my hair before almost every competition. Those were some of my favorite memories, sitting on the floors of hotel rooms from Spokane to St. Petersburg while Bella twisted and pinned with quick, expert fingers.

"Sure," I said.

She motioned for me to take a seat in front of her, leaning back against the sofa. That put me right in the middle of the group, my knees hitting the metal coffee-table legs. Bella ran her hands through my hair, brushing out the tangles, and a warm tingling sensation spread down my spine. I'd missed this. I'd missed her.

Someone swapped the Beyoncé CD for Madonna's *Confessions on a Dance Floor*, and soon the talk turned to the inevitable: cute boys.

Frannie had a crush on a South Korean pairs skater and was strategizing how to approach him when they were both in the same city for the Four Continents competition.

"Show us a picture," Josie demanded.

Frannie produced her clamshell phone. The others gathered round.

"Oh my god, he's *gorgeous*," Amber squealed.

Chelsea squinted at the screen. "Kind of looks like a younger Garrett Lin."

"He *does*," Frannie sighed.

"First of all, not all Asian people look alike," Bella said. Frannie started to apologize, but Bella cut her off. "And could you *please* refrain from lusting after my brother in my presence?"

"Sorry." Amber shrugged. "But Garrett's a hottie."

I shifted, drawing my knees up under my chin.

"Hold still," Bella told me.

Frannie scooted closer. She'd barely put on any makeup, beyond a few flicks of mascara and tinted moisturizer that emphasized her freckled complexion instead of concealing it. The things you can get away with when you're sixteen. Her mother was the CEO of some global pharmaceutical conglomerate, which made her family even richer than Josie's, but she struck me as a sweetheart rather than a spoiled brat. Maybe *too* sweet to survive this cutthroat sport.

"I've always wondered," Frannie said. "Are you and Garrett, like . . ."

"We're just friends," I said.

She frowned. "Really? But you two are so perfect together."

"He's a great partner."

The sort of answer I would give in an interview—but it was also the truth. The two of us had an easy rapport from the start, and I knew plenty of people assumed we were dating. We denied it, until Sheila told us not to bother. *Let them think what they want* was her advice.

So we let the rumors slide. Sometimes we even played into them, accidentally or on purpose—walking around arm in arm with the natural ease of people who spend hours a day touching, snatching food off each other's plates at post-competition banquets, gushing to reporters about how much we *adored* working together.

Part of me was always waiting for Garrett to make a move. Back in Nagano, Bella had said he liked me—and he did seem to enjoy my company. He'd never dated anyone in the skating world, and we didn't have time to meet many people outside of it.

I could have been disappointed, or even insulted. But it was a relief, in a way. I wasn't sure how I would react if Garrett tried to take things between us to the next level. Better to keep going the way we were, as good friends and colleagues. I knew all too well how wrong a romance between skating partners could go.

Since I'd been such a poor source of gossip, the girls turned their attention to Bella. She was nearly finished with my hair, coiling the plaits and pinning them at my nape.

"What about you, Bella?" Amber said.

"Yeah, what about you?" Chelsea waggled her freshly plucked eyebrows.

Bella stiffened, tugging the braid so tight that my scalp stung.

"Come on, spill," Frannie said. "Cause we all know there's no *way* you and Heath Rocha are 'just friends.'"

CHAPTER 32

"Heath and I are skating partners," Bella said. "That's all."

Her voice had taken on the same smooth, political tone Sheila adopted when asked any question she'd rather not answer. But was Bella uncomfortable because the girls were talking like this in front of me, or because there was some truth to what they said?

"Bullshit," Amber said. "We've all seen the way he looks at you."

Frannie nodded. "And those pictures of you two in Japan! The cutest."

"We were just sightseeing."

"Sure." Chelsea winked, blue glitter eyeshadow flashing. "Sightseeing."

I'd seen the pictures. Everyone had. Heath and Bella posing outside the Sensō-ji Temple, his arm looped around her waist. Smiling and sipping bowls of matcha in the Meiji Jingu Inner Garden. Dancing cheek to cheek under the neon glare of the Harajuku district as street musicians strummed hand-painted guitars.

I refused to believe they were doing anything so mundane as *dating*. No, this was the Lin PR machine hard at work. Bella always insisted she had no time for boyfriends. She'd stayed a virgin until eighteen, when after a ruthlessly analytical comparison of potential candidates, she had a one-night stand with a French skater at the 2003 World Championships. To Bella, sex was a box to check off, another task to put behind her so she could focus on her real priorities.

"Those pictures *were* adorable," Josie said, looking pointedly my way. "Especially the one where Heath was standing behind you and—"

"That's enough," Bella snapped.

Josie's mouth clacked shut. The other girls fell silent too. In the background, Madonna sang *I'm sorry* in several different languages over a throbbing dance beat.

"It's getting late." Bella pushed one last pin into my hair. "We should get dressed."

The others dispersed to their rooms to get into costume. I hung back, pretending to study my elaborate braided hairstyle in the mirror by the door. Bella had extended an olive branch to me, and I felt compelled to do the same for her.

"We need to talk," I said as soon as Bella and I were alone.

"About what?" She'd taken out a compact to touch up her still flawless eyeliner.

"About Heath."

The friendly, flirty demeanor he displayed around Bella—that wasn't at all the way Heath would've acted if he actually had feelings for her. It was a show, and I was the audience.

"Look," I said, "I don't know what's going on between you two—and I don't want to know." I took a deep breath. "But wherever Heath was for all those years, whatever he was doing, he wouldn't have come back solely to skate. Once he's gotten what he wants . . ."

"And what is that, exactly?" Bella said. "You?"

"No, that's not wh—"

"Not everything is about you, Kat." She snapped the compact shut. "And it's not like you give a damn about Heath anyway."

"Excuse me?"

"You didn't want him. You tossed him aside for my brother."

"Because *you* told me to!"

"As if anyone could ever make *Katarina Shaw* do something she didn't want to do."

It sounded like something Heath would say. It was probably something he *had* said to her, in a moment alone after practice. Or huddled close on a long-haul flight.

Or in bed in a Tokyo hotel room, whispering together in the dark.

"Our friendship never meant anything to you, did it?" I asked, though I wasn't expecting an answer. "All you care about is winning."

"That's all we both care about." Bella turned away, busying herself with stowing brushes and palettes back in her custom monogrammed makeup case. "That's *why* we're friends."

I wrenched open the door. "Not anymore."

When I made my way to the rink after dark, I was still seething. If only the event that night had been a competition. Then I could have focused my fury on beating Heath and Bella.

But this was some frivolous party, a bunch of SoCal businessmen getting soused on overpriced champagne while their trophy wives hung off the arms of their designer jackets. There would be no winning, no medals. No satisfaction at all.

Garrett waited for me beside the rink, the glow of the firepit next to him glinting off the crystals that decorated his shoulders like fresh snowfall. The flames danced over faux stone pellets, so there was no comforting scent of woodsmoke, only the chemical tang of propane.

He took one look at me and asked, "You okay?"

My head burned from the braids—which I was starting to suspect Bella had made too tight on purpose. My makeup was already melting in the balmy evening air. The crystals on my bodice scoured my bare arms like steel wool. My former best friend was probably sleeping with the only man I'd ever loved, and I wanted to open my mouth and scream until every rich asshole on Coronado Island turned to gape at me in horror.

"I'm great," I said. "When do we start?"

"Any minute now. We're skating second."

"Second? Who's skating first?"

Garrett shrugged. In a competition setting, the later you skated, the higher your rank. But at an event like this, where the crowd would grow more distracted (and drunk) as the evening wore on, opening the show was the plum spot. All I wanted was to get our performance over with, so I could focus one hundred percent of my attention on Nationals.

The lights shifted, projections of snowflakes swirling across the ice. *"Ladies and gentlemen,"* came a male voice over the sound system. *"Please gather round for a special performance from the Lin Ice Academy!"*

A spotlight hit the other side of the rink, and music started to play. A trumpet fanfare.

I knew that music. But not because I'd heard it during a practice session.

Heath stepped on the ice, dressed all in black, arms bare except for a band of leather across his left bicep. He held out his hand. The spotlight hit his partner, and there was a blinding blaze of gold. The crowd gasped with delight.

I didn't gasp. I could hardly breathe. Because there was Bella, in her mother's Cleopatra dress, smiling the same way Sheila had at the Calgary Olympics.

Like she'd already won.

INEZ ACTON: Even if you don't know a damn thing about ice dance, you know Lin and Lockwood's Antony and Cleopatra program.

Sheila Lin and Kirk Lockwood take the ice for the free dance at the 1988 Winter Olympics in Calgary, dressed as the tragic lovers Queen Cleopatra and Mark Antony. Kirk's costume has the look of leather armor molded to his chest. Sheila's dress is pure gold, as is her headpiece, which is shaped like a serpent with red gemstone eyes.

FRANCESCA GASKELL: I wasn't even born until 1989, but of course I know that program!

INEZ ACTON: Their performance from the '88 Games has millions of views on YouTube. It's iconic.

JANE CURRER: Breathtaking.

ELLIS DEAN: Motherfucking *legendary*.

KIRK LOCKWOOD: The gold standard, you might say. *(He laughs.)*

Sheila and Kirk perform a fast-paced footwork sequence to the sounds of crashing cymbals and syncopated war drums from the score of the 1963 Elizabeth Taylor film Cleopatra. *The music transitions into the movie's haunting love theme, and they move into a close dance hold.*

KIRK LOCKWOOD: Interestingly enough, our Russian rivals chose a royalty-themed program for the 1987–1988 season as well.

At the 1988 Winter Games, Veronika Volkova and Mikhail Zolotov skate a free dance inspired by the marriage of Catherine the Great and Emperor Peter III. Veronika wears a red velvet dress with glittering gold embellishments. Mikhail is also dressed in red, with a military-style sash.

VERONIKA VOLKOVA: For us, this was not some cheap cinematic gimmick. My costume was inspired by the Imperial Crown Catherine wore in her coronation portrait. Our music was by Catherine's favorite court composer, lost to history until the Russian National Orchestra recorded it especially for us. We worked with principal dancers at the Bolshoi on our choreography. We were honoring our heritage. Honoring Russia.

JANE CURRER: In the lead-up to Calgary, the rematch of Lin versus Volkova was all anyone could talk about. The media dubbed it "The Battle of the Ice Queens."

ELLIS DEAN: I was like six at the time—but yeah, I remember it. Every two minutes on Channel 6, "Don't miss The Battle of the Ice Queens, broadcast live this Tuesday!"

VERONIKA VOLKOVA: Catherine was not a queen. She was an empress.

KIRK LOCKWOOD: The whole "Battle" thing was pretty over the top. In my opinion, there was no comparison. Veronika Volkova was pretending to be a queen, but Sheila?

Later in the Antony and Cleopatra program, Kirk takes Sheila's face in his hands as if he's drawing her in for a passionate kiss. Before their lips meet, Sheila twists away, taking the lead.

KIRK LOCKWOOD: Sheila *was* a queen. And she wasn't leaving without her crown.

INEZ ACTON: The absolute lady balls it takes to wear a gold dress to the Olympic final when everyone watching thinks you're past your prime and couldn't possibly win.

At the end of the program, Sheila and Kirk collapse dramatically on the ice, pretending to die in each other's arms. The music fades, and there's a moment of total silence. Then the audience explodes into a standing ovation.

INEZ ACTON: Like I said: iconic. No wonder Katarina Shaw idolized Sheila so much.

Sheila and Kirk take their bows, waving to the crowd. The camera zooms in on little Bella and Garrett Lin, sitting with their nannies in the front row.

The twins' ears are ensconced in toddler-sized noise-canceling headphones. Garrett glances around, bewildered by the commotion. Bella never takes her eyes off their mother.

GARRETT LIN: My sister and I were there that day. We don't remember anything, of course. We were only three years old.

In the kiss and cry, Garrett sits on Kirk's lap, Bella sits on Sheila's. The gold medal–winning marks appear, and the arena explodes with applause again. Garrett screws up his face and starts to cry, trying to squirm away from Kirk and all the cameras, but Bella claps her tiny hands and smiles wide. Sheila kisses her daughter on the cheek.

GARRETT LIN: It was a lot to live up to. Bella and I had no choice. We were always going to be stuck in the shadow of our mother's greatness. But Kat ... she wanted it. She actually *wanted* to spend her life trying to live up to the great Sheila Lin.

CHAPTER 33

So many times, I'd imagined myself skating that program, in that dress. In Heath's arms.

I knew every step, every gesture, every note. I would be able to tell, in an instant, if they faltered, even if they covered it well for the crowd.

They were absolutely perfect.

Bella's hips marking every beat of the drums. Heath's hand on the curve of her back. The magnetic desire pulsing between them as they came near enough to kiss, then spiraled away, then drew close again. Lips parted, breathing each other in.

I hated them. I wanted to be them. I couldn't take my eyes off them.

Every expression, every edge, exactly like Lin and Lockwood seventeen years earlier.

Until the end of the program.

They flung themselves down on the ice, just as Sheila and Kirk had, snow sparkling in the pleats of Bella's golden skirt as she and Heath clutched each other, feigning death throes in time with the final crescendo of the music.

I knew what was supposed to happen next. He would die first, and then she would succumb, still wrapped in his arms.

But Heath didn't slump over. He didn't go still. He cradled Bella's face in his hands, smoothing her hair back.

Then he pressed his lips to hers.

GARRETT LIN: There was nothing going on between my sister and Heath Rocha.

FRANCESCA GASKELL: We all knew there was *something* between those two.

A clip from the conclusion of Bella Lin and Heath Rocha's Antony and Cleopatra performance. As he kisses her, the camera zooms in on their faces.

ELLIS DEAN: Why do I think Heath kissed her? Oh, come on. You know why.

Heath and Bella take their bows. Her cheeks are flushed. They keep looking at each other rather than out at the audience.

GARRETT LIN: We were all so focused on the Olympics. Even if Bella had a crush, or . . . she wouldn't have risked it. No way. That was all for show.

Now the video focuses on Katarina Shaw, standing in the front row. She's the only one not applauding. As Bella takes her final solo bow, Katarina and Heath's eyes meet. Heath is still smiling. Katarina's expression is murderous.

INEZ ACTON: I won't even pretend to know what was going on between Heath and Bella back then. But it was messy and manipulative. Real fuckboy shit.

ELLIS DEAN: There's a reason so many skating partners end up banging. It's like movie stars on set—all that time working together, touching each other, pretending to be in love. You're bound to catch *some* feelings, whether it's love or hate.

VERONIKA VOLKOVA: It is a special talent some men have: they stare into your eyes, and you feel like the most beautiful woman in the world. These men must never be trusted. Because if they can make you feel that way, they can make any woman feel that way.

ELLIS DEAN: It was a game—not only for Heath, for all of them. They knew exactly what they were doing to one another. And they weren't gonna stop until somebody won.

CHAPTER 34

Heath kissed her to hurt me. To twist the knife. That was the only explanation.

Not everything is about you, Kat, Bella's voice echoed in my head.

They wanted to force me to fall apart. I couldn't let them.

Heath and Bella exited the rink. Garrett and I were next. The emcee announced our names. The audience applauded. They were waiting.

Something brushed my hand. I assumed it was Garrett, trying to lead me out onto the ice.

I blinked. Garrett was already past the boards, taking off his blade guards. Heath stood beside me. Heath was the one who'd touched me. He looked at me like a cat observing his squirming, wounded prey.

A few feet away, Ellis Dean eyed us over his plate of hors d'oeuvres, popping a miniature puff pastry into his mouth as if it were popcorn.

I shouldered past Heath and joined Garrett without a backward glance. Showtime.

Opening position: facing in opposite directions, the only point of contact Garrett's hand reaching back to rest on my hip. Cue the music: the groovy, looping bassline of Sade's "Turn My Back on You." Garrett spun me around with a quick flick of the wrist that sent my filmy white skirt fluttering like a spiderweb in a storm, and we were off.

I told myself not to think about Heath. I told myself to be in the moment, to be in my body. Feel the fabric slipping over my thighs, the cool breeze off the ocean, the heat of Garrett's shoulder under my palm. The contrast between the smooth velvet and the scrape of rhine-stones.

But I couldn't get it out of my mind. The kiss. The brush of Heath's knuckles over mine. The smug, triumphant look on his face.

Despite my distraction, I kept up with Garrett. The first part of the program—with its hip hop–inflected muscle isolations, dynamic foot-work, and flirtatious interplay—was easy for both of us, even with the constraints of the compact rink.

Our problems always came in the latter half, when we shifted into the yearning classical guitar and soft piano of "Haunt Me." No matter how many times we practiced, it felt counterintuitive—all that kinetic energy building, only for us to slam on the brakes for a smooth, re-strained midline step sequence to match the slower music.

We came to the transition point. A pause at the center of the rink, a breath with Garrett's arms around me and my head on his shoulder. Usually I closed my eyes for that moment, centering myself. But that night, I kept them open.

And there was Heath, standing in the front row of the crowd. Our eyes met. My hands clawed, digging into the back of Garrett's head. He gave a little gasp and flinched.

Heath smiled.

All the months we'd been working on the program, drilling it over and over and over again, I'd had it all wrong. Shoring up all that energy wasn't counterintuitive. It was the whole damn point. "Turn My Back on You" was a seduction—a push-pull of warring lusts, seeming to give in to Garrett one moment, forcing him to follow me like a lovesick puppy the next.

So once we reached "Haunt Me," the tension was almost tantric. My mistake before had been trying to tamp down the fire, instead of hold-ing it inside me for as long as possible. Everything I was feeling that night—the rage, the jealousy, the frustration, the desire—all of it was more fuel for the inferno.

Garrett met my sudden intensity spark for spark. Our combination spin had always felt a bit stilted and mechanical; now our bodies curled together like plumes of smoke. He touched my face, and I could feel his longing extending from every fingertip. When we reached the climactic lift, timed to the song's sultry tenor saxophone solo, I threw myself into his arms. No hesitation, no holding back. We whirled across the ice, my spine arched, hand reaching back to grab my blade, only the strength of Garrett's interlaced fingers keeping me aloft.

It felt like flying. It felt like victory.

When we finished, the applause seemed to last forever. I didn't look for Heath in the crowd again. Instead, my eyes sought out Sheila. She stood next to a firepit, wearing a cocktail dress covered in iridescent sequins that caught the reflection of the flames, making her look like a goddess emerging from a pyre.

She wasn't applauding. Instead, she smiled at us and lowered her chin in a subtle nod of approval. Garrett and I exchanged glances. We both knew what that meant.

We were ready.

CHAPTER 35

As I changed out of my costume into party clothes—a long velvet dress with a low V in both the front and the back, snakeskin stilettos gifted to me by a designer following a magazine shoot—I was still vibrating with adrenaline.

Garrett and I were peaking at exactly the right time. Finally, our free dance felt like a cohesive program instead of a series of elements strung together. All we had to do was skate at Nationals the way we'd skated that night, and they'd have no choice but to hand us the title—and our ticket to Torino.

So what if Bella had worn her mother's old costume and put on a nostalgic show to impress a bunch of people who didn't know a twizzle from a one-foot turn. It must have taken her and Heath weeks to learn that choreography—time they could have spent perfecting their competition programs. Sheila should have known better. In fact, I was sure she did. She might have put Bella and Heath in the spotlight, but Garrett and I were still the ones to beat.

The elevator car was empty when it arrived; the whistling operator must have taken off for the evening. I stepped inside and started examining the control panel, which had directional arrow buttons in addition to the options for each level.

Then I felt the floor shift as another passenger boarded.

"Going down?" Heath asked.

He'd changed out of his costume too, into a slim-cut black suit and leather brogues. Interesting how content he seemed to let Bella dress him up like a doll, considering how stubbornly he'd held on to his scuffed sneakers and ripped jeans when he was with me.

I mashed a combination of buttons. The elevator didn't move. Heath stepped closer.

"Here, you just—"

"I've got it." I bumped him out of the way with my hip, trying another sequence.

The elevator started to descend. I yanked the gate closed.

Heath was right behind me. The heat of him radiated across my spine. We stood still like we were waiting for music to start, but the only sound was the whir of the elevator gears.

I spun to face him. Stepped back. My shoulders hit the side of the car, the cool metal bars sending a shiver through me.

There was nowhere to go. And worse, I didn't *want* to go anywhere. Heath moved toward me, hands gripping the bars, hips flush against mine, breath on my mouth, and it felt more natural than anything I'd ever done with Garrett Lin.

My body remembered everything I'd tried so hard to forget.

The elevator stopped. We didn't move. There was no one waiting. No one to see us pressed together through the lattice of the gate.

Our breathing started to sync, his inhales quickening to catch up with mine the way they used to before we took the ice together. His fingertips brushed the shell of my ear, not taming wayward strands into place, but winding my hair around his knuckle, turning it wilder.

I could have reached for the control panel, pressed the number for my floor again. I could have taken him into my room, into my bed, and pretended, for a few hours at least, that the past three and a half years were nothing but a bad dream.

That was what he wanted. For me to forget myself. For me to forget everything I'd worked for.

So I pushed him away. I grappled with the gate, snapping a nail in my rush to get it open.

Heath said my name. Like a prayer, like a promise. Like he used to say it.

Like he still loved me after all.

I gripped the gate so tight the metal rattled. No. I would *not* turn around. This was another act. A part of the show. And I refused to stay for an encore.

I stumbled out of the elevator, running toward the lobby doors and out into the night air. At the party, I paused only long enough to seize a bottle of champagne from the maw of a half-melted ice sculpture shaped like some kind of sea creature. Then I kept running until my heels sunk into sand.

The hotel was on the west side of the island, facing open ocean rather than the shining lights of downtown San Diego. In the daylight, it had been beautiful, a never-ending sweep of cobalt reflecting the clear winter sky.

Now all I could see was darkness. The moon was barely a sliver in the sky, giving off only enough light to make out the jagged crest of the breakwater at the end of the beach. I left my shoes next to an Adirondack chair and wandered toward the sound of the waves, clutching the champagne bottle by the neck. When cold water surged over my feet, soaking the hem of my dress, I closed my eyes and tried to pretend I was back home by the lake.

It didn't work. The sand was too smooth, the wind too warm. The spray tasted of salt.

I opened my eyes. My vision had adjusted now, well enough to see the waves crashing against the breakwater.

Well enough too that I could no longer miss the two figures intertwined in the cove.

Garrett. And Ellis Dean.

KIRK LOCKWOOD: Figure skating has this reputation as a super gay sport.

ELLIS DEAN: So many sports are gayer than figure skating.

KIRK LOCKWOOD: The truth is, it's heteronormative as hell.

ELLIS DEAN: Two-man luge, American football, beach volleyball. Fucking *wrestling*, hello?

KIRK LOCKWOOD: Back in my day, there was pressure to stay closeted— officially, at least. It was a very *do what you want in private as long as you don't talk about it in public* atmosphere. Fortunately, the sport has become much more open and accepting.

ELLIS DEAN: Even now, plenty of male skaters—more than you might think, I could name names if I weren't such a *gentleman*—get away with hiding in the closet. That wasn't an option for me. I might as well have been wearing a big-ass neon rainbow sign.

GARRETT LIN: My mother never told me to hide my sexuality. She never mentioned it at all. I'm not even sure whether or not she knew I was gay.

KIRK LOCKWOOD: Sheila knew about Garrett, of course. A mother always knows.

GARRETT LIN: I always got this . . . sense. That I had to carry myself a certain way. Be a certain type of man, on the ice and off. I wanted to be perfect.

ELLIS DEAN: The *shit* I had to put up with, being out and proud back then. I don't want to say Garrett Lin was a coward. But yeah, if he'd come out—with his status in the sport, and all that straight-passing hot guy privilege? It would've made things a hell of a lot easier.

GARRETT LIN: If I could go back, I'd do things differently. But I wasn't being truthful with myself at that age, so how could I tell other people the truth?

ELLIS DEAN: I'm glad the sport is catching up with the times. Then again, I wouldn't be where I am today without the pathetic self-loathing of my elders. It's like I always say: suck a man's dick, and he'll be satisfied for a night. Let him suck *your* dick in a hotel suite at the World Championships of Figure Skating? Then you'll have blackmail material to last a lifetime.

GARRETT LIN: I think a part of me wanted to be found out, forced to face who I really was. Honestly, I'm surprised it took so long.

CHAPTER 36

Ellis spotted me first. Garrett was too occupied with kissing the bare skin below Ellis's undone collar.

I stumbled backward, feet slipping in the wet sand. "Sorry, excuse me, I'll—"

Garrett turned too.

"Shit," he said. The first time I'd ever heard him swear.

"I'll go," I said.

"No." Ellis pulled away, tucking in the tails of his shirt. "I'll go. You two need to talk." He shot Garrett a look. "Clearly."

He strode back toward the hotel, leaving Garrett and me alone on the beach.

I had no idea what to say. Realizing Garrett was into guys wasn't such a shock. It explained a lot, actually. Realizing what a good liar he was, though? That threw me.

"So." I glanced after Ellis, now nothing but a gangly shadow against the distant glow of the party lights. "You and Ellis Dean."

"Listen, Kat." Garrett swallowed. "It's not what it—"

"I'm not going to tell anyone. If that's what you're worried about."

He sighed, shoulders slumping. "Thank you."

"I *am* curious why you never told me, though. This whole time I thought I just wasn't your type."

I smiled, trying to make a joke of it. But Garrett took my hand and gazed into my eyes, deadly sincere.

"I wish you were my type, Kat. I can't tell you how much."

"It doesn't make any difference to me," I told him. "I hope you know that."

In some ways, it made things a hell of a lot easier. If only I'd known back when Heath and I were together; all of that jealousy over Garrett's intentions toward me, when in reality there was nothing to worry about.

"Who else knows?" I asked.

"No one."

"Not even—"

"No."

"Why not?"

Bella wouldn't have cared. Sheila, I wasn't so sure about. She wasn't homophobic. She and Kirk had remained close since their retirement, and she'd done plenty of fundraising for AIDS patients in the '80s and '90s. But she'd spent decades building the Lin family brand, packaging Garrett as a handsome prince for all the young female fans to fantasize over. Being gay wasn't part of the business plan.

"At first I was scared," he said. "I felt like I needed to figure it out on my own, before I shared it with anyone. But now . . ." He scrubbed a hand over his neck. "Maybe I like having a part of myself that's not public."

"Well, your secret's safe with me. And if you want to let people think I'm your girlfriend, that's fine."

He smiled. "Are you seriously volunteering to be my beard?"

"I mean, I kind of am already?"

"The way we skated tonight isn't going to hurt those rumors, is it?"

"Not at all."

Garrett gestured to the champagne bottle in my hand. "Shall we toast to that?"

"I don't know how to open it," I admitted.

"Allow me."

Garrett popped the cork with a practiced twist, and foam spilled into the surf. He took a sip before handing me the bottle. The champagne was lukewarm, and despite how much I'm sure the stuff cost, my face screwed up in disgust at the tart taste. I made myself swallow, then took another gulp for good measure.

We sat on one of the flatter rocks in the breakwater, facing the hotel.

Though the performances were over, the party was still going strong, with a DJ spinning remixes of pop songs. Over the breeze, I could make out the soaring chorus of "Somewhere Only We Know."

Garrett draped his suit jacket over my shoulders, and we spent a few minutes passing our stolen Dom Pérignon back and forth.

"You want to go back to the party?" he asked.

"So some dude old enough to be my grandfather can try to grab my ass when his third wife isn't looking? No thanks." I took another swig of champagne. "Besides, I'd rather steer clear of—"

"Heath?"

I almost told Garrett about the moment in the elevator. How close I'd come to ruining everything.

"It's got to be hard for him," Garrett said. "Seeing you with another guy."

Classic Garrett Lin: always able to put himself in someone else's shoes, to empathize even when the other party didn't deserve it.

"He used to hate all this," I said. "The parties, the schmoozing with fancy people. Now he's better at it than I am. I swear, they take one look at me, and they can sense it."

"Sense what?"

"That I'm small-town Midwestern trash."

After learning Garrett's big secret, my own seemed trivial in comparison.

He wrinkled his brow. "I thought you were from Chicago."

"North of Chicago—this tiny suburb called 'The Heights.' *Very* different."

I'd spent most of my waking hours with Garrett over the past few years, but we rarely spoke about anything besides skating. That night on the beach, it felt like we were meeting each other for the first time.

"Trust me," he said, "they're all as self-conscious as you are. Everyone's way too busy worrying how *they* look to look twice at anyone else."

"Easy for you to say. You're rich."

"My mother's rich."

"Same thing. You grew up in this world."

"That's true. But she didn't."

I looked at him. "What?"

"She grew up in Sugar Land, Texas. Her family owned an office supply store."

"*What?*"

"They lived in an apartment above the storefront. *Sheila's* not even her real name."

"What's her real name?"

"Lin Li-Mei. She changed it when she left home, I guess. Her parents both died in the '90s, but that's what it said in their obituaries. 'Survived by a daughter, Lin Li-Mei.'"

Garrett tipped the bottle back again, then passed it to me; there were only a few swallows left. My head was swimming, but I couldn't tell how much was from the alcohol and how much from what he'd told me.

"Bella never mentioned any of this," I said.

"She doesn't know. At least, I don't think she does."

More secrets between the twins. I'd truly believed they told each other everything.

"I always knew she was hiding something about her past," Garrett said. "I thought it would be . . . I don't know, scandalous or shocking. But her parents sounded totally normal."

That was exactly why she'd hidden them. Their mundanity didn't fit into the narrative she wanted to create. The legend of Sheila Lin.

Bella told me once about how, when she and Garrett were kids, they'd spend hours combing through newspaper clippings about the male gold medalists from the Sarajevo Games, searching for any family resemblance. *Why only the gold medalists?* I'd asked her.

Because, she said, *whoever our father was, he must have been exceptional. Otherwise she wouldn't have decided to keep us.*

Now I know Garrett better, and I understand what he was trying to tell me: the Sheila Lin I idolized wasn't real. She was a carefully constructed character, a beautiful mask not even her own children could glimpse behind. But that night, fizzing with expensive champagne and Olympic dreams, that isn't at all what I heard.

Learning Sheila had come from nothing and nowhere didn't disillusion me. It gave me hope—that I could transform myself as completely as she had.

The champagne bottle was empty. I stood up, swaying a bit—the hazards of being an infrequent drinker with an elite athlete body-fat percentage. Garrett stood too, and had to grab the edge of the rock to steady himself.

"We should eat something," he said. "Maybe there's still food left at the party?"

"Or we could be antisocial and order room service."

The party guests were probably too wasted themselves to notice the state we were in, but I didn't want to take any chances.

Garrett tucked my arm through his, and we staggered up the beach together to collect my shoes. As I reached down to retrieve them, his suit jacket slipped off my shoulder, dragging in the sand. He pulled it back into place and wrapped it tighter around my shoulders. I felt warm and cared for, closer to him than ever. If I hadn't seen him with Ellis earlier, I would have given serious thought to kissing Garrett at midnight.

"What sort of food should we order?" he asked as we continued toward the hotel.

"Something with *cheese.*"

Garrett laughed, knocking into my side. He slipped his arm under the jacket to hold my waist. "You can take the girl out of the Midwest, but you can't take the Midwest out of th—"

He stopped. Someone stood ahead of us, blocking the path.

Heath.

CHAPTER 37

"Rocha." Garrett dropped his hold on my waist. "We were just—"

"Down on the beach together," Heath said. "You've always loved the beach, haven't you, Katarina? Couldn't get enough of it when we were younger. All those long nights by the lake."

I glared at him. "Are you finished?"

"I suppose I am." Heath stepped out of our way with an exaggerated sweep of his hand. "She's all yours."

Garrett shook his head. "No, no. It's not like that."

I could see the warring emotions on his face, the weighing of options. I knew what he was about to do—and I couldn't let him. Not for my sake.

So once again, I chose Garrett. I stood beside him, I took his hand. I turned on Heath and spat, "What right do you have to be jealous? You're nothing to me."

"Kat," Garrett said, tugging on my hand. "Let's go."

But I couldn't stop. The champagne gave me the courage I hadn't had earlier in the evening. How dare Heath try to shame me. How dare he imply that I'd belonged to him, that he was somehow ceding his claim to Garrett. I didn't belong to anyone.

"Did you really think," I said through gritted teeth, "you could spend three *years* God knows where, doing God knows what, and then we'd go back to the way things were before?"

"We can never go back to the way things were." Heath's voice was low and dangerous, his eyes frozen over with fury. "You made sure of that, didn't you?"

"You disappeared!" I was shouting now, voice echoing off the hotel's elegant facade. "You could've been dead, for all I knew. Where *were* you?"

"There you three are."

Bella. She'd come from the party, wearing a shimmery gold bandage dress that looked like a sexier version of the Cleopatra costume.

"They want all the skaters by the rink," she said, "for the champagne toast at midnight."

We didn't move. Unspent tension crackled in the air. Bella planted her hands on her hips.

"Okay, what the hell is going on?" She rolled her eyes. "If this is about the kiss, I—"

"Not everything is about *you*, Bella."

She flinched at my words, looking genuinely wounded, even though I was only repeating what she'd said to me mere hours before.

"Don't talk to her like that," Heath said.

"You used to say a lot worse about her." I looked at Bella. "He always hated you, do you know that? And I always defended you."

"I never hated Bella," Heath said. "I hated who you became around her."

The countdown had begun. The party guests raised their champagne flutes and chanted.

Ten, nine, eight—

I dropped Garrett's hand and stepped toward Heath. Close, my lips at his ear.

Seven, six, five—

"You hated that I was better than you," I whispered. "You hated that I didn't need you."

Heath's nostrils flared and his fists clenched.

Four, three, two—

"You hated yourself, because you knew you weren't enough for me. You still aren't."

I pulled back. Heath's eyes locked on mine. Bella and Garrett were there too, flanking us like seconds in a duel, but they might as well have been ghosts.

All Heath and I could see was each other.

One.

Happy New Year!

Fireworks strafed the sky. People cheered and clinked and kissed as confetti rained down. The string quartet struck up "Auld Lang Syne."

Two thousand and six, the year of the Torino Olympics. The year all my dreams would come true.

The year I would make Heath Rocha regret everything.

GARRETT LIN: Everything changed after New Year's Eve.

During a practice session a few days before the 2006 U.S. National Championships in St. Louis, Missouri, young ice dancer Frannie Gaskell and her partner, Evan Kovalenko, are working on their Ravensburger Waltz when Katarina Shaw and Garrett Lin cross paths with them.

FRANCESCA GASKELL: That year was my first time competing at senior Nationals. I didn't expect to medal, I was just excited to share the ice with all those skaters I admired. Like Kat.

Katarina doesn't slow down. Frannie and Evan have to flatten themselves against the wall to avoid a collision. Garrett looks back at them with an apologetic wince. Katarina keeps going.

ELLIS DEAN: Kat had always been intense, but this was a whole new level. She was a shark moving across the ice. (*He jokingly hums the Jaws theme.*) Get in her way, and you were chum.

JANE CURRER: Olympic team slots are allocated based on each nation's performance at the previous Worlds. Although Ms. Shaw and Mr. Lin won the world title, since no other American team ranked highly, the United States could only send two ice dance teams to the Games that year.

ELLIS DEAN: No official decisions about the Olympic team are made until after the National Championships. But we all knew, barring some bizarre act of God, one of those Olympic spots was going to Shaw and Lin, and the other to Lin and Rocha.

KIRK LOCKWOOD: The first two events were held on the same day. Shaw and Lin won the compulsory, and it looked like they would increase their lead in the original. Until the final moments of their program.

Katarina and Garrett skate their original dance—a fast-paced Latin combination program to the music of Shakira—at 2006 Nationals. Partway through an intricate step sequence to the song "Ojos Así," Katarina mixes up a few steps, getting out of sync with Garrett.

GARRETT LIN: Ideally, before a major competition, you want to taper off your training, so you have enough left in the tank to skate your absolute best on the day.

ELLIS DEAN: Kat kept pushing. It was bound to bite her in the ass eventually.

Bella Lin and Heath Rocha skate their Latin combination original dance at Nationals: a slower, more sensual number to a trip hop–inflected version of "Bésame Mucho."

GARRETT LIN: We did well. But Bella and Heath, they did better.

KIRK LOCKWOOD: Lin and Rocha pulled ahead by a point.

Katarina and Garrett do a rink-side interview immediately following the original dance. They're both in their Latin dance costumes, faces shining with sweat.

"I'm happy for my sister," Garrett says. "And for Heath. They've been working hard, and they were fantastic out there today."

"Is it difficult, facing off against your former skating partners? Especially considering th—"

Garrett cuts the reporter off with a good-natured grin. "Oh, Bella and I have been competing since the womb. Our mother wouldn't have it any other way."

Laughter from the crowd. Garrett slips his arm around Katarina. She keeps staring straight ahead, posture stiff and face expressionless.

The reporter turns to her, sticking the microphone in her face. "So Kat, tell me: what's your plan going into the free dance tomorrow?"

Katarina gives him a blank look. "My 'plan'?"

Garrett shifts nervously, tightening his hold on her shoulders.

"My plan," she says, "is to win."

CHAPTER 38

The worst thing about figure skating competitions isn't the pressure.

It's how much time you have to sit around and wait.

The 2006 U.S. National Championships was worse than most in that regard. After busting our asses doing back-to-back programs on our first day of competition, we had two full days off before the ice dance final. Some skaters attended other events. Some took advantage of the unseasonable warmth in St. Louis and went sightseeing, riding to the top of the Gateway Arch or touring the Anheuser-Busch stables. In the evening, anyone old enough to drink (and even a few who weren't) descended on the bar at the official headquarters hotel to gossip the night away.

Not me. Sheila had booked us accommodations at the Chase Park Plaza, a luxury hotel a few miles from the whirlwind of the competition venue, and aside from scheduled practice sessions, I didn't leave my room.

I stretched to keep my muscles limber. I ordered room service meals full of balanced proteins. And most of all, I visualized: not only the details of our free dance program, but everything that would come after our victory. I lay starfished on the king-sized bed with my eyes closed and repeated it over and over, a movie in my mind.

By the time I arrived at the Savvis Center for the free dance, my fantasies felt so real, it was if they'd already transpired. In the dressing room, the other girls steered clear, like I had a force field surrounding my body. Nothing could rattle me.

Not even Heath and Bella. When I emerged in full costume and makeup, they were still in their warm-up clothes, getting a pep talk from Sheila.

I didn't need a pep talk. I didn't need anything, except to get out there and win. The technical base value of our free dance was higher than theirs; when we performed it perfectly, the way I'd been picturing for days, we would triumph.

Finally, it was time for the last group, the top five couples in the competition. Gaskell and Kovalenko. Hayworth and Dean. Fischer and Chan, a solid but unremarkable pair who trained near Detroit. Garrett and me. Heath and Bella.

So what if they got to skate in the coveted final spot? That just meant all eyes would be on them when they got their scores in the kiss and cry and realized they'd lost.

The clock started for the group warm-up, and I took off so fast, Garrett had to scurry to catch up.

"You good?" he asked once he got ahold of my hand.

"Why wouldn't I be?"

I didn't even look at him. We had our warm-up routine down to a science: stroking two full laps of the rink side by side, forward and backward progressives switching between several different dance holds, then running through a few of our trickier program elements to make sure we were completely in sync.

"You seem . . ." Garrett leaned down. "Distracted."

Distracted? Ridiculous. I'd never been more focused in my life. Distracted was what I'd been before, when I was still letting Heath's machinations get to me, but I was finished with that. I had wanted to go to the Olympics since before I even knew Heath Rocha *existed.*

Out of the corner of my eye, a swirl of emerald silk—Bella and Heath whizzing past, close enough for the flare of her skirt to brush my leg.

Garrett tugged me closer, keeping me clear of their path. My temper flared. They should be the ones getting out of *our* way.

Two minutes left in the warm-up. We ran through our midline step sequence and moved on to the twizzles. I cued up my mental movie again, zipping through it on fast-forward.

First, every step of our free dance, flawless, even better than we'd done it in San Diego.

Garrett and I standing on top of the podium, the national anthem heralding our fourth consecutive U.S. title. Heath and Bella an inconsequential blur on the silver medal step.

Then the Olympic team announcement. The flight to Italy. Our arrival in Torino. Walking in the opening ceremony in our Team USA uniforms. Everything up to the moment when we had those golds around our necks. Shaw and Lin, the first Americans to win Olympic medals in ice dance since Lin and Lockwood in 1988.

As I entered the final turn of the twizzle sequence, I was smiling. I was so close. Soon it would all be mine. The gold, the fame, the security. Everything I'd longed for since I was four years old, and more.

I reached for Garrett. He reached back. Behind him, a flash of green and black.

And then blinding white, rushing toward me.

GARRETT LIN: Of course it was an accident.

ELLIS DEAN: That bitch did it on purpose.

Katarina Shaw and Bella Lin collide during the warm-up at the 2006 U.S. Nationals free dance. Katarina attempts to brace with her hands but reacts too slowly. Her head smacks into the ice.

JANE CURRER: Ms. Shaw should have paid more attention to where she was going. Sometimes she seemed to forget she wasn't the only skater on the rink.

Garrett crouches down to check on his partner. Katarina gets back up on her own. Her balance wavers, and Garrett catches her by the arm to steady her. There's no audio, but Bella skates closer, seeming to ask if Katarina is all right. Heath stands slightly apart from the others, watching the whole interaction. His face is difficult to read.

VERONIKA VOLKOVA: I would not care to speculate. I have never paid much attention to what happens at the Americans' little championship.

Katarina brushes past Bella with a blatant shoulder check on the way to the boards. Garrett follows Katarina off the ice. Heath stares after them, until Bella grabs his hand.

ELLIS DEAN: I'm telling you. Watch the video.

A slow-motion replay of the collision shows the moment Bella and Heath skate toward Katarina and Garrett. It looks as if the two couples have enough room to maneuver past, but at the last second, Bella and Katarina crash into each other.

ELLIS DEAN: The way Bella glances over her shoulder, then shifts her heel? It's *so* obvious.

The slo-mo replay again, this time zoomed in on Bella's face. At the moment of impact, she's looking right at Katarina with a resolute expression.

GARRETT LIN: She and Heath had the lead. And she could have been injured too, you know.

Medical staff intercepts Katarina to examine her, though she tries to wave them off. The camera follows until a medic leads her into a private room and shuts the door behind them.

GARRETT LIN: We all wanted to win. But not like that.

Sheila Lin goes into the private room where the medic took Katarina. Garrett stays outside, pacing back and forth. The warm-up session now concluded, Bella and Heath come backstage too, standing off to the side. Heath keeps glancing over at the closed door.

VERONIKA VOLKOVA: All I will say is this: it certainly seemed like something Sheila Lin would have done.

CHAPTER 39

"Ms. Shaw, can you tell me where we are right now?"

I blinked into the flashlight beam as the medic checked my pupil dilation. Behind him, Sheila stood, arms folded across her white leather moto jacket.

"St. Louis, Missouri," I answered. "The Savvis Center."

The most important competition of my career. But by all means, take your time.

Frannie and Evan had finished their skate to the *Lord of the Rings* score, and the first notes of Lou Bega's "Mambo No. 5" blared through the arena, which meant Josie and Ellis were on the ice. I'd already given a detailed report of my symptoms (dull pain, no nausea, no blurred vision) and listed the months of the year in reverse order to prove I was lucid. But this guy kept asking me inane questions and shining that damn light in my eyes.

"And what's today's date, please?"

I sighed. "Friday, January thirteenth, two thousand six."

I'd heard some of the other skaters joking about the date, what bad luck it was to have the final on Friday the 13th. Figure skaters are a superstitious bunch at the best of times—tying their boot laces a certain way before every skate, carrying lucky charms at competitions, repeating prayers and affirmations under their breath as they take the ice.

I thought it was all absurd. I didn't need luck, I had skill and determination and an unwavering desire to win.

The medic sat back on his heels and clicked off the light.

"Well?" Sheila said.

"She may have a mild concussion."

"So I can skate," I said. "Right?" My skull still throbbed, but I was prepared to chalk that up to Josie and Ellis's earworm music.

The medic hesitated. "You should be examined at a medical facility. They can run scans. Give you a more conclusive diagnosis."

"I can do that after the competition."

I stood up. My head swam a bit, but quickly leveled off.

Four minutes. That was all the time I needed, and then they could scan me with every piece of equipment in the hospital.

Garrett waited right outside the door. I might not have been experiencing nausea, but he sure looked like he was. He rushed toward me, arms outstretched, then pulled back as if he was afraid I might break.

"Are you okay? Your head, is it—"

"I'm fine."

On the monitors, Josie and Ellis took their seats in the kiss and cry. Tanya Fischer and Danny Chan stepped onto the ice for their two-minute warm-up. Garrett and I were next.

"You're sure?" he said. "It looked like you smacked it pretty hard."

I shrugged. "Maybe a mild concussion, but nothing I can't—"

"A concussion? That sounds serious, Kat."

He looked to his mother. She said nothing.

Bella, though, couldn't help inserting herself into the conversation.

"If you have a concussion," she told me, "you shouldn't skate."

I whirled on her. "Oh, you'd love that, wouldn't you? Was that your plan all along?"

When we'd collided during the practice session at our first Nationals in Cleveland, it had been an accident, pure and simple. This time, I wasn't so sure. Bella certainly didn't look sorry.

"That's enough." The slender blade of Sheila's voice slipped between us. "I'm sure I don't need to remind you where we are."

Backstage at a major competition, which meant skaters and coaches and officials and reporters watched our every move. The cameramen were keeping a respectful distance, but no doubt they had their zoom lenses trained on us.

Heath kept his distance too, leaning against the wall a few feet away. But he hadn't taken his eyes off me for a second.

"Let's go." I took Garrett's hand. "It's almost time."

I started toward the curtained-off tunnel between the backstage area and the rink, where we'd wait for our names to be announced.

Heath blocked my path. "What the hell do you think you're doing?"

I glared at him. "Get out of my way."

The final movement of Fischer and Chan's Chopin sonata had begun. Garrett and I should already be in position.

Heath turned to Garrett. "You're just going to stand there and let her—"

"He's not *letting* me do anything," I said. "It's my decision."

"It's her decision," Garrett repeated in a numb monotone.

"You've won this thing three times in a row," Heath said. "Even if you withdraw, they'll send you to Torino. You can submit one of those, what do they call it . . ."

"Appeals," Bella supplied. "Heath's right, you can petition to be on the team no matter what happens today."

Garrett turned back to Sheila. "Do you think they'd still name us to the team?"

Sheila lifted her shoulders. "They might, they might not. There's no way to be sure."

I thought about asking Sheila what she would do in my situation, but I already knew the answer. Sheila Lin wouldn't withdraw from a competition unless she was stone-cold dead.

Yes, my head hurt, but it was nothing in comparison to the agony I'd gone through to get to that moment. Not only the physical pain of pushing my body to the limit, but all the grief, the struggle. The heartbreak.

I couldn't stop. Not when I was so close. I could see it all—the rest of my career unrolling in front of me like a red carpet. Garrett and I were going to win our fourth U.S. title, and we were going to be Olympic champions.

"I can do it," I said. I'd never felt more certain of anything in my life.

Sheila nodded. "All right."

Bella pursed her lips and turned away. Garrett stared down at his skates, taking slow, deep breaths.

Heath gripped my shoulders like he wanted to shake sense into me. "Katarina, you're *hurt*. You can't seriously—"

"Don't touch me."

I tried to writhe free, but he held fast. My vision blurred, pain spiking between my eyes.

"Please." Heath's voice was a whisper, meant for no one but me. "Don't do this. If anything were to happen to you . . ."

I was so relieved he didn't finish the sentence. That way, I could go on telling myself that this plea was merely another manipulation, the latest phase of his revenge plot. He didn't mean it. He didn't care what happened to me.

As I headed for the ice, hand in hand with Garrett, I felt Heath's eyes hot on my back. Same as when we were kids, when he sat in the stands watching me spin and jump for hours.

Watch me now, I thought. *Watch me win.*

Without you.

Shaw and Lin take the ice at the 2006 U.S. National Championships to supportive cheers from the crowd, showing solidarity after Katarina's fall in the warm-up.

Garrett smiles and waves up at the stands. Katarina is all business.

INEZ ACTON: I remember seeing Kat looking fierce and thinking: wow, what a badass.

ELLIS DEAN: Josie and I were in silver medal position, behind Fischer and Chan, but we knew once the top teams skated we'd be bumped down to fourth. At least we were ahead of those little pipsqueaks Gaskell and Kovalenko.

Katarina and Garrett take their opening position. The applause fades. Their music begins.

FRANCESCA GASKELL: I wasn't even thinking about scores or medals. We were all worried about Kat. That was a nasty bump to the head. She seemed fine, though—at first.

As they start their first choreographic sequence, Katarina attacks every step. Garrett is more tentative and ends up lagging behind her.

KIRK LOCKWOOD: Garrett was trying to play it safe—the kiss of death, especially in a final.

GARRETT LIN: I was scared. I didn't want to hurt her.

INEZ ACTON: The more Garrett held back, the harder Kat pushed.

GARRETT LIN: It wasn't our best skate, that's for sure. But we were getting through it, and there was a big gap between our scores and Fischer and Chan's. I thought, okay, we'll get silver. Kat will be upset we didn't win, but we'll still go to Torino.

They transition into the slower part of the program. Garrett seems more comfortable with the languid tempo of "Haunt Me." Katarina continues to skate with intensity. Coming out of their combination spin, she loses her balance for a second, but quickly recovers.

KIRK LOCKWOOD: When they got into the lift, I could tell right away.

Katarina and Garrett begin their rotational lift. She arches her back and grabs her skate blade.

GARRETT LIN: The entry was a little shakier than usual, but I thought I had her.

They spin faster and faster. Garrett's arms are shaking. Katarina's body tenses.

KIRK LOCKWOOD: He didn't have her.

ELLIS DEAN: They fought for it, I'll give 'em that.

KIRK LOCKWOOD: It's a miracle she got up there. Maybe better if she hadn't, though.

Katarina jerks, letting go of her blade. Garrett stumbles, momentum slowing. Katarina grasps for the blade again. It slashes across her palm, spraying blood.

GARRETT LIN: I thought I could save it. I thought I could save her.

He loses his grip. They're still rotating. Katarina is thrown onto the ice, the back of her skull hitting with a sickening crack audible even over their music.

KIRK LOCKWOOD: There was so much blood. You couldn't tell where it was coming from.

ELLIS DEAN: Everyone was freaking out. And that sexy slow jam's still playing. It would've been funny if it wasn't so *insane*.

FRANCESCA GASKELL: The whole thing was terrifying! Every skater's worst nightmare.

KIRK LOCKWOOD: They finally turned off the music. And the place went *silent*. Kat must have been in a lot of pain, but she didn't cry out, didn't scream. Maybe she was too stunned.

GARRETT LIN: I was on my knees on the ice, and she seemed so far away. She wasn't moving. For a second, I thought she was dead. I thought I'd killed her.

The crowd stands in shocked silence, staring like rubberneckers at a car crash. Then the camera zooms in close on Katarina, focusing on the blood staining her white dress.

"Falls like this are always awful to witness," Kirk says from the commentary booth. "But medical personnel are on their way, and—wait, who is that?"

The shot zooms out again. The medics rush toward the rink carrying a stretcher, but before they can get to Katarina, someone else vaults over the boards and runs onto the ice.

GARRETT LIN: And then . . . there he was.

CHAPTER 40

The first thing I felt when I woke up was Heath's hand in mine.

Then the IV stuck in my skin, the heart monitor clamped on my finger. The pain so urgent and diffuse I thought my whole body must be an open wound.

Heath's head was bowed, like he was praying. His heel tapped nervously, the way it used to before we took the ice at novice competitions.

I laced my fingers through his. He went still, then lifted his head to look at me.

He looked at me like he'd been wandering in the dark for years, and I was the sunrise.

"What happened?" I asked.

"It's okay," he said. "You're at Saint Louis University Hospital."

He was still in his free dance costume. Red stains smeared the front of his tuxedo shirt.

My white dress was draped over a chair by the window. Even in the dim light, I could see it was ruined, the delicate fabric stiff with dried blood. My blood.

I remembered Heath telling me not to skate. I remembered taking the ice anyway. After that, only a blur. A stomach-lurching sensation, like dropping from a height.

"What happened at Nationals?" I asked.

"You fell. You hurt yourself."

"No, I meant . . ." I tried to sit up. Heath was on his feet in an instant, ready to stop me—but I thought better of it on my own, sinking

back down into the pillows. "What happened after that? Did they announce the Olympic team?"

"I don't know," Heath said. "I don't care."

More fractured memories: glaring lights in my eyes. Satin against my
cheek. Lifting off the ice—up, up, up, like I was floating into the rafters.

Bella's voice, right beside me. Only it didn't sound like Bella, because she was so weak and pleading. Desperate.

You can't. Please, Heath, don't do this, we have to—

"Heath," I said. "What did you do?"

"It doesn't matter." He sat on the edge of the bed and squeezed my
hand. "All that matters is you're all right, Katarina."

ELLIS DEAN: It all happened so fast.

GARRETT LIN: It was like time stopped.

Katarina lies motionless on the ice. Heath kneels beside her. As Garrett struggles to his feet, looking dazed, Heath scoops Katarina up in his arms.

GARRETT LIN: I'd never dropped my partner. Not since Bella and I were little kids, practicing off-ice on pads. And then I cried way harder than she did.

Heath carries Katarina off the ice. She's barely lucid, her head lolling against his shoulder, but she clings to his jacket lapel.

GARRETT LIN: I let her down. I had her, and then I didn't.

Garrett watches helplessly as Heath and Katarina exit the rink. Bella runs over to Heath, grabbing at his sleeve. He shakes her off and keeps going.

KIRK LOCKWOOD: I've seen some shocking upsets in my time, but that was something else.

ELLIS DEAN: I thought Josie and I were going to leave with the pewter medal at best. All of a sudden, we're going to the goddamn *Olympics*?

On the final day of the 2006 U.S. National Championships, the Olympic figure skating team for the Torino Games is announced. Fischer and Chan and Hayworth and Dean are selected to represent the United States in the ice dance competition, while Gaskell and Kovalenko are named as alternates.

FRANCESCA GASKELL: Of course, I was excited to be on the Olympic team.

The skaters all look a bit shellshocked and uncomfortable—except for Frannie, who waves enthusiastically and grins at the spectators.

FRANCESCA GASKELL: But I couldn't really celebrate, you know? The *reason* I was on the team was too awful.

JANE CURRER: Sheila did enter a petition for Isabella and Heath to be named to the team. However, because of Mr. Rocha's lack of international competition experience—not to mention the fact that he'd abandoned his partner in the midst of the National Championships final—the committee was unmoved.

As the Lins climb into a car outside the Chase Park Plaza in St. Louis, reporters jostle around them, shouting questions. The vehicle's windows are tinted, but one photographer still manages to get a close-up of Bella's tear-swollen face through the darkened glass before they drive away.

GARRETT LIN: All that anticipation, all that work. And then it was just . . . over.

CHAPTER 41

We waited all night for the hospital to release me. Heath climbed into the narrow bed, and it felt like we were sixteen again, holding each other in my childhood room.

The doctors told me not to go to sleep, but I couldn't have anyway. Everything hurt too much. I had a concussion—from the first fall or the second, they couldn't be sure. The gash on my palm took ten stitches to close, the wound on my leg even more. I would have scars.

Finally, sometime around daybreak, they told me I could go.

I had to leave in a wheelchair. As Heath pushed me through the lobby, there was a flash like lightning. Then another. Then a whole storm.

Reporters, gathered outside the hospital entrance. Pressed up against the glass like tourists at the zoo. It took me a second to realize they were there for us.

Heath swore under his breath and steered back the way we'd come. "There has to be another exit we can use," he said. "I'll be right back."

He left me sitting by the elevator bank, staring at my distorted re-flection in the dented stainless-steel doors. My hair was a wreck, a nest of curls standing out on one side of my skull, the other side flattened from being pillowed against Heath's chest for hours. My eyeshadow and mascara had blurred into a gray murk around my eyes. My posture was slumped and careless, shoulders bowed under my wrinkled warm-up jacket.

I looked like a mess. But I also looked like myself, for the first time in a long time—raw and wild instead of pretty and refined. I looked like the fearless girl who used to ramble all over the lakefront with Heath, skinned knees and windblown hair and dirt under my nails.

I'd tried so hard to become the perfect skater, the perfect partner for Garrett. The next Sheila Lin. And where were the Lins now? As far as I knew, they hadn't come to the hospital to check on me. Hadn't even sent flowers. They weren't there for me when I truly needed them. They weren't my family.

Heath was.

He came hurrying back, like he'd promised. "They're going to let us leave through the ambulance bay in the back," he told me. "A taxi can meet us over there."

"I want to go home," I said.

"Of course." He pivoted the wheelchair toward our escape route. "When we stop off at the hotel to get our luggage, I'll call the airline, and—"

"No." I twisted to look up at him. "*Home.*"

CHAPTER 42

A soft haze of rain fell as Heath drove us out of St. Louis, turning to shards of sleet the farther north we traveled.

I still don't know how he got the car—a gray Kia with a dented fender and crumbs left on the seat cushions by the last occupants. We were old enough to represent our country at the Olympic Games, but too young to legally rent a vehicle.

We didn't play music. We barely spoke. But we held hands over the gearshift, like we'd done on that trip to Cleveland when we were teenagers. Heath kept squeezing my fingers to make sure I didn't drift off in the passenger seat.

Only during the final hour of our approach did it occur to my concussion-addled brain that returning to my childhood home meant dealing with my brother. The house was as much mine as his, though. I had every right to be there.

When we pulled up, the place looked unoccupied: windows dark, gutters choked with dead leaves. Lee's truck wasn't parked in its usual spot, and ours were the first tire tracks through the dusting of snow on the driveway.

"Wait here." Heath got out of the car, leaving the motor running and the heat full blast.

After living in the Lins' mansion, my childhood home seemed small and lonely, a stray animal cowering on the craggy shoreline. Still, as much as I dreaded seeing him, I was grateful Lee had refused to sell the property. Even sitting outside, I felt something unfurl in me that had been clenched tight for far too long.

The doctors had assured me that, with rest and time, I would recover. But I wouldn't be able to step on the ice for months. It might be a year or more before I could skate full-out again—if I ever could. All because of one stupid mistake. That's all it takes in our sport, to change the entire course of your life.

I'm not sure how much time passed before Heath returned. The painkillers they'd given me before we left the hospital had worn off, and my head felt as foggy as the air.

"Lee's not here," he said. "I don't think he's been here in a while."

I was so relieved I wouldn't have to face my brother, I didn't think about where he might have gone, or when—or even *if*—he might return.

"The power's off, and it's pretty cold in there," Heath said. "We should find a hotel."

I shook my head. Pain throbbed from my skull to the base of my spine.

"At least for tonight," Heath insisted.

"It can't be worse than the stable. I want to stay."

He helped me out of the car. As I limped toward the front door, leaning against Heath, tendrils of lake breeze caressed my cheek. Welcoming me home.

Inside, it was somehow even colder, as if the building had been holding its breath, waiting for our arrival. Dust draped every surface like a shroud.

It finally occurred to me that Lee could be dead, his corpse rotting in his bed or broken at the bottom of the cellar stairs or bloated in the lake.

"I checked every room," Heath said, as if he'd read my thoughts. "And the stable, and the beach. We're the only ones here, I promise."

He took me into the parlor, draping his coat around my shoulders and pressing another dose of painkillers into my palm before getting to work building a fire. Soon the room was so warm I didn't need the coat—or my jacket. I doffed them both, stripping down to a thin tank.

"Come here," I said.

Heath stretched out on the sofa beside me—slowly, gingerly, so I wouldn't be jostled. I'd been furious with him for so long. And yet, in that moment, I couldn't remember why.

We leaned back against the cushions, my head resting on his chest. The day before, we'd both woken up in a luxury hotel, ready to battle it out for the national title and berths on the Olympic team. Now we were back in our childhood home. Together.

"How are you feeling?" Heath cupped my chin and looked into my eyes. He was only checking the dilation of my pupils, as the doctor had instructed, but my breath caught in my throat all the same.

"Better," I said. The meds were kicking in, covering my agony in a plush layer of calm.

I touched his face, tracing the scar under his eye. I still didn't know how he'd gotten it. There was so much I didn't know.

"Katarina," he said.

I had no idea what he was going to say next, but I felt sure it would ruin the moment. There would be plenty of time later for dissecting all the ways we'd hurt each other. For figuring out what the hell we were going to do next.

I laid my head back down and closed my eyes. Heath draped his arm across my stomach. Cold wind howled outside, but we were both so warm from the fire and the heat of each other's skin, it was difficult to tell where he ended and I began.

"You shouldn't fall asleep yet," he whispered. "The doctor said—"

I tipped his chin down until his mouth met mine, and that felt like coming home too.

"Then keep me awake," I said.

GARRETT LIN: I would never have admitted it back then. Certainly not to Bella or my mother. But I can say it now: I was relieved to miss the Olympics.

VERONIKA VOLKOVA: All this salivation over Sheila Lin and her elite skating academy and her superstar children with their gold medal–winning pedigree, and then their Olympic hopes are shattered in an instant. By two no-name orphans from the middle of nowhere.

GARRETT LIN: All that guilt eating me alive every minute of the day, and it still felt like a welcome reprieve from the pressure I'd been under. How messed up is that?

VERONIKA VOLKOVA: I might find it amusing, were I not such a professional.

GARRETT LIN: But I'd never seen my sister so upset. Bella wouldn't come out of her room for at least a week, and she wouldn't let anyone in. Not even me.

ELLIS DEAN: Karma's a bitch, and so is Isabella Lin. She thought she was going to take out her competition, and instead she fucked herself out of the Olympic Games *and* out of a partner.

GARRETT LIN: I thought our mother might . . . I don't know. But she left us alone for the most part. I think she could tell we were punishing ourselves more effectively than she ever could.

ELLIS DEAN: Josie and I were the ones actually *on* the Olympic team, but no one gave a damn about us. All they wanted to talk about was Shaw and Rocha.

GARRETT LIN: I couldn't understand why people were so interested in Kat and Heath. But the story was everywhere. All those awful pictures too.

A montage of tabloid articles and gossip blog posts covers the saga so far, with images of Katarina prone on the bloodstained ice, then leaving the hospital in St. Louis.

GARRETT LIN: I was just glad the focus wasn't on me. All I wanted was to be left alone.

ELLIS DEAN: The Olympics are so overblown anyway.

FRANCESCA GASKELL: Oh, alternates don't actually get to go to the Games—I wish! That's a common misconception. But it's still a *total* honor.

ELLIS DEAN: Like this one competition every four fucking years is supposed to define who you are? It's ridiculous.

At the 2006 Winter Olympics in Torino, Italy, Josie Hayworth and Ellis Dean perform their free dance to Lou Bega's "Mambo No. 5." They're out of sync, behind the music, stumbling over the ice. As they hit their final pose, they lose their balance, ending the program in a heap.

ELLIS DEAN: Not to mention the corruption behind the scenes, the expense and damage inflicted on the host cities. You have to wonder why we keep this antiquated tradition going.

In the kiss and cry, Josie and Ellis can't even meet each other's eyes. Their scores appear, putting them in last place out of 24 teams.

ELLIS DEAN: Anyway, after Torino, I decided it was time to move on to new opportunities. My competitive career might have been over, but I knew I still had plenty to offer the sport. Whether they liked it or not.

CHAPTER 43

In the Midwest, we call the first warm spell of the year "Fool's Spring," because we know from bitter experience the lovely weather can't last. Another cold snap lurks right around the corner, ready to lunge as soon as we shed our winter coats.

That doesn't mean we don't enjoy every minute of it, though.

In late March, it hit 60 degrees, and I made it to the ten-week mark in my recovery—which meant I was finally allowed to do a real workout again. Heath and I jogged through the woods to the stable, then sprinted back to the house.

We still had the place all to ourselves. The flood of invoices from a Lake County law firm helped us figure out where my brother had disappeared to. He was in prison, serving a sentence for drug possession with intent to sell—his second time behind bars, apparently, following a misdemeanor DUI a few years prior. Lee being in prison wasn't a shock, but the fact that he'd attempted a business venture, however illegal and ill-advised, did surprise me.

Heath kept pace with me as we ran, weaving between maple trees spotted with spiky crimson buds. Red-winged blackbirds, just returned from their southern migration, trilled overhead as if they were cheering us on. I lengthened my stride, overtaking him.

It felt so good to push my body, to feel my muscles responding, the satisfying burn spreading through my legs. As an athlete, you come to appreciate all the different flavors of pain. Some are unbearable, others a kind of delicious, aching pleasure.

The house came into view, specks of mica in the gray stone facade glittering in the sun. Heath had caught up, running right at my shoulder again. But I had something to prove.

I stretched forward with all the strength I had left, seizing a photo finish victory across the tree line. We both flopped down on the winter-browned lawn, breathing hard.

"You better not have let me win," I said.

Heath grinned. "Never."

I felt charged, vital, adrenaline arcing through me. My injuries were a distant nightmare—though I had shiny pink scars across my palm and shin to spark my memory. The first few weeks after Nationals had been the worst: headaches, brain fog, the slow torture of my skin knitting itself back together.

But since then, I'd gotten better, progressing from limping around the house to gentle walks along the lakeshore to today's flat-out run. Heath and I had progressed too, from cautious lovemaking to the sort of athletic, passionate sex we'd always had to hold ourselves back from during our forbidden liaisons in the Academy dorms, or our rushed, exhausted hotel room encounters between flights and full days of competition.

Heath didn't touch me carefully anymore. He knew what I could take.

Every time I brought up returning to the ice, though, he hesitated. *The next season doesn't start for months,* he'd say. *We don't need to decide right away.* If I made any reference to our time apart, he'd change the subject entirely.

Or he would distract me, and I would let him.

He pushed me back onto the ground and leaned in for a kiss, hair tumbling across his forehead. His curls had grown out now, even wilder than they used to be. Just before our lips met, I stopped, staring toward the house.

Two people stood on the porch. At that distance, all I could make out was their stature—one tall, one short.

Heath stood, brushing grass off his clothes. "This is private property," he called out.

Our uninvited guests turned around—in such perfect, graceful sync, I recognized them before getting a glimpse of their faces.

Bella and Garrett Lin.

CHAPTER 44

"Your hair." That was the first thing Bella said when she saw me. A few weeks before, I'd tried to hack off the remaining blond with a pair of dull kitchen shears. I made such a mess of it, Heath insisted on taking me into town for a proper haircut—the only time I'd left the property during our time in seclusion, aside from doctor's appointments. The hairdresser had tamed it into a pixie cut, the shortest style I'd ever had.

"It suits you," Bella added. It could have been a compliment or an insult.

"What are you doing here?" I asked.

"We tried to call," she said. Garrett stayed silent, shifting his weight back and forth, weatherworn planks creaking under his polished shoes. "We were worried about you."

Heath had gotten the house's phone service restored along with the other utilities, but after a week of nonstop phone calls from the press, we'd ripped the cable from the wall. My cellphone was in a drawer somewhere, drained of power, and Heath still didn't own one.

"We're fine," Heath said. He had his arm lashed across me. Protective.

I pushed past him, approaching the twins. "Really, you were worried? So worried, you didn't bother coming to see me in the hospital?"

Garrett finally spoke up. "We did come to see you." His voice sounded hoarse, like he hadn't used it in days.

"What?" I looked at Heath. His jaw was set in a hard line.

"We both came," Bella said. "We brought you flowers and everything." She nodded in Heath's direction. "*He* said you didn't want to see us."

"He was right. I didn't."

Heath should have given me the choice, though, instead of making it for me. At the very least, he should have let me know later on about their visit.

I wondered how I would have reacted if I'd seen Bella that night. Maybe I would have screamed in her face and thrown the flowers in the trash. Maybe I would have forgiven her.

I couldn't know for certain whether she'd collided with me on purpose, but my gut told me she hadn't. Bella Lin rarely *intended* to hurt anyone. She just didn't care if she did.

"Can we talk?" Bella asked.

"We're talking right now."

She shot a sharp look at Heath. "Alone?"

I suggested taking a walk. Heath and Garrett stayed behind on the porch. "Be nice," I whispered in Heath's ear before heading toward the lake. He made a grunting sound that wasn't exactly agreement, but wasn't refusal either.

Bella struggled to keep up with my stride across the uneven ground, heels sinking into the soft earth. Her shoes would be ruined. I hoped so anyway.

At the end of the lawn, I clambered onto one of the limestone slabs overlooking the shoreline. Bella gingerly took a seat beside me, on the edge of the rock, tilting her weight onto one hip so the smallest possible part of her made contact.

We both stared out at the horizon. Stratus clouds had blown in to cover the sun, and a hint of winter sharpened the edges of the air again. The water was a silvered mirror.

"I'm really sorry, Kat," Bella said.

I turned to face her. "So you *did* do it on purpose."

"That's not what I said." She swiveled toward me too. The stone left a smear of dirt on her designer coat. "I'm sorry this happened. I'm sorry you got hurt."

"And you're sorry you didn't get to go to the Games."

"Did you watch?" she asked.

I shook my head. Heath and I hadn't so much as spoken about it. I didn't even know who had won the gold.

Bella tugged the coat tighter. "Mom made us."

Rubbing her children's faces in their failure, like puppies who'd soiled the carpet. Sounded like Sheila Lin.

"How did Ellis and Josie do?" I asked.

"You don't want to know."

I winced. "And the Russians?"

"Gold for Yakovlevna and Yakovlev," she said. "They won the world title last week too, even though Polina's twizzles were a total mess."

Garrett and I had competed against the second-tier Russian couple plenty of times, and they'd never beaten us. They only won those medals because we weren't there.

But it didn't matter. They were in the record books, and we were a cautionary tale.

The wind blew harder, colder, heaving water at the base of the rocks. When Bella spoke again, her voice was barely audible above the waves.

"Your friendship means so much to me, Kat."

"More than winning?" I asked.

I just wanted to see if she would lie.

Bella met my eyes without hesitation. "Of course not. You want to know why I'm here? Because it's about damn time you stopped playing house and feeling sorry for yourself."

There she was—my cutthroat, ambitious best friend.

"When are you coming back?" she asked.

"Who says I'm coming back?"

She rolled her eyes. "Let me guess. Heath doesn't want to."

He hadn't gone that far. Not yet. But he was content in our little stone house by the lake, more at ease than I'd ever seen him.

Some days, I was content too. Other days, I felt trapped in a purgatory of my own making. Every day the same as the next, not working toward anything, not improving, not striving. Simply existing. Heath might be able to live like that, but I couldn't.

"We haven't discussed it," I said.

"Seriously? What the hell have you been doing out here in the middle of nowhere for all this time, then?"

I raised a suggestive eyebrow.

Bella scowled. "Don't answer that. And if you're worried about me getting between you two again, don't. You were right about him." She laughed, but it did nothing to douse the spark of fury in her eyes. "Guess it was all about you after all, huh?"

I didn't know what to say to that. Bella had every right to be angry. Heath had wasted her time, toyed with her emotions—and worst of all, derailed her career when it mattered the most.

"Anyway," she said with an imperious sniff. "He's all yours. At least you'll have no trouble getting sponsors now."

"What do you mean?"

"You know, because everyone's so obsessed with you." Bella fluttered her lashes. "Shaw and Rocha, the star-crossed childhood sweethearts of U.S. Figure Skating."

I stared at her, confused. Her eyes widened.

"I thought you knew. You really haven't seen it?"

"Seen *what*, Bella?"

She bit her lip. "Let's go inside. Heath should know too."

ELLIS DEAN: Everyone lost their minds over that damn picture.

The picture in question: a close-up of Katarina Shaw and Heath Rocha as he carried her off the ice at the 2006 U.S. National Championships.

INEZ ACTON: They looked like fucked-up Gothic wedding cake toppers. Him in a tux, her in that gauzy white dress with blood all over it.

JANE CURRER: It was rather grotesque.

FRANCESCA GASKELL: I mean, at the time, the situation was really scary. But that picture? (*She sighs.*) It was *so* romantic!

INEZ ACTON: It was romantic, but also raw. All that blood, and the intense look on his face, like he's carrying a fellow soldier off the battlefield.

GARRETT LIN: The last thing I wanted was to be reminded of that day, but when I saw the picture ... well, I couldn't look away. It made me think: of course. Of course it was always going to be the two of them together, in the end.

ELLIS DEAN: Their disappearing act following Nationals made everyone even more frantic for information. So I figured, why not give the people what they want?

KIRK LOCKWOOD: In early March 2006, after announcing his retirement from competitive ice dance, Ellis Dean launched a figure skating gossip blog called Kiss & Cry.

ELLIS DEAN: It was a shitty-ass WordPress site at first. But it was a big hit—and not only with hardcore skating fans. Anytime I posted about Kat and Heath, the link would get shared around, and traffic would go nuts.

Screenshots of early Kiss & Cry stories about Katarina Shaw and Heath Rocha: "Wild Children—All About Kat and Heath's Hardscrabble Early Years,"

"'They Couldn't Keep Their Hands Off Each Other': Shaw and Rocha's Training Mates Tell All," "Every Cold Hard Fact We Know About Skating's Hottest Couple."

JANE CURRER: That site is not at all representative of our sport. The focus should be on our athletes' performances on the ice, *not* salacious details of their personal lives.

ELLIS DEAN: The Powers That Be got their granny panties in a bunch about it.

FRANCESCA GASKELL: Sure, I read it. Everyone did—whether they admitted it or not.

ELLIS DEAN: I was pulling back the curtain and showing people what the skating world was really like—not the pretty image they try to project.

GARRETT LIN: Ellis and I weren't in touch then.

ELLIS DEAN: I dumped his closeted ass.

GARRETT LIN: He could have outed me on his site, and he didn't. I'm grateful for that.

INEZ ACTON: Calling Kiss & Cry "just" a gossip blog is so reductive. Gossip is a powerful tool the marginalized can wield against the establishment. Sometimes the only tool we have.

ELLIS DEAN: It's not like I was just spilling the tea on which skaters were fucking and/or fighting at any given time. I reported on serious issues— harmful coaching practices, biased judging, disordered eating, sexual misconduct.

Screenshots of some of the Kiss & Cry stories Ellis mentions: "10 Signs Your Coach Doesn't Deserve You," "Shocking News: Figure Skating Still Terrified of Real Women's Bodies," "Olympic Pairs Skater Breaks Silence About Abusive Partner—and the High-Level Officials Who Enabled Him for Years."

ELLIS DEAN: But yeah, in those early days, the Shaw and Rocha Saga made the best clickbait. That picture turned them into the Brad and Angelina of skating, and there was no going back.

A clip from a television interview with Katarina's brother, Lee Shaw. He's in his late twenties, but he looks at least a decade older. The wall behind him is gray, nondescript.

"Yeah, I saw the picture," he says. "It was the first time I'd laid eyes on my little sister in years. Ever since she ran away from home."

CHAPTER 45

When Bella showed me the photo, I almost didn't recognize myself.

I looked delicate. Fragile. All that blood marring my white skates and my white dress somehow made me seem even more virginal and feminine.

And Heath looked like he would kill anyone who tried to tear us apart.

After the twins left—for a fancy dinner party with some sponsor in Chicago, which they'd used as an excuse to fly to the Midwest unsupervised—I fell down the rabbit hole. I read every news story, every post about us on Ellis's obnoxious new blog.

I was shocked by the frenzy. Usually the American public cares about figure skating for two weeks every four years during the Winter Olympics. Even then, it's the singles and the pairs who capture their attention; we ice dancers are an afterthought. But everyone loves a love story, and that's what they thought this was.

When I was strong and self-assured, people recoiled from me. They told me I was too competitive, too ambitious, too much. But when I was brought low, bruised and bleeding, a princess in need of rescue instead of a conquering queen, they loved me.

I finally came to bed after midnight, eyes bleary from staring at the computer screen. Heath was still awake. He took off his headphones—I caught a few notes of Sigur Rós before he pressed *stop* on the click wheel—and pulled back the covers.

Since Nationals, Heath had made me feel so safe and comfortable. It would have been easy to stay, to choose a quiet life with him over the pain and punishment of skating. Easy as falling asleep in a snowdrift, the warm feeling that lulls you to sleep before you freeze to death.

I reached toward him. He closed his eyes, anticipating my touch. My fingers kept stretching, until they brushed over the carving on the headboard.

"Remember this?" I asked.

Shaw & Rocha. I traced the letters. We'd written them only six years before, but it felt like a lifetime.

Heath nodded, something guarded in his expression. "You want to go back," he said. "Don't you?"

"I miss it," I admitted, though that word was far too small to encompass the bone-deep longing I felt to get back on the ice. "I miss—"

"Him." Heath set his iPod on the nightstand and crossed his arms.

"No, that's not . . . I mean, I have missed Garrett, and Bella, but—"

"I won't lose you again, Katarina. Not to him, not to—"

"I don't want to go back to him." I sighed and stood up on my knees, taking Heath's face in my hands. "I want to go back with *you.*"

Heath's lips ticked upward, but his eyes stayed wary. "You're sure?"

My thumb found the smooth edge of the mark under his eye. I'd relearned the topography of his body, turned all his scars into familiar terrain. We still hadn't talked about them, though, or spoken at all about his three years away. I'd started to believe it was for the best. The past was the past. We couldn't change it.

But the future—the future could be anything we wanted.

"I love you," I told him. "And I don't want to skate with anyone but you, ever again."

Heath's smile blazed like a torch in the shadows. "I love you too, Katarina."

Shaw & Rocha, Olympic champions. We could still make it true, it wasn't too late. We had four years until Vancouver.

He kissed me and pulled me down beside him, and as we tangled the sheets around us, I told myself that this time everything would be different.

Katarina Shaw and Heath Rocha arrive at LAX airport in April 2006. They're immediately mobbed by paparazzi snapping photos and shouting questions.

ELLIS DEAN: From the second they set foot in LA, it was a circus.

Both Katarina and Heath seem knocked off balance by the sheer number of people waiting to see them. There are fans too, holding handmade signs covered in glitter hearts.

"Katarina, how are you feeling?" a reporter asks.

"Much better," she replies. "Ready to get back to work."

"Where have you two been all this time?"

Heath puts his arm around Katarina. "Home," he says, steering toward the exit.

GARRETT LIN: My mother and Kirk dealt with their fair share of media attention back in the day, and Bella and I had some run-ins with the paps too. But this was on another level.

A montage of paparazzi photos from Shaw and Rocha's first summer back in Los Angeles: Katarina and Heath leaving their apartment complex, Heath carrying both of their skate bags. Skating together at the Academy, blurry shots taken through the windows. Katarina falls, Heath helps her up. She buries her face in her hands, and Heath embraces her at the edge of the ice.

FRANCESCA GASKELL: I know it's not like they *asked* for all that hoopla. But yeah, it was pretty disruptive for the rest of us at the Academy.

INEZ ACTON: They couldn't have picked a worse time to become famous. It was like the Wild West in those days. The internet made the public feel entitled to intimate access to all their favorite stars—but social media hadn't taken off yet, so celebrities couldn't take charge of the narrative the way they do now.

Katarina and Heath return home after a practice session. They've moved to a different building, with a burly doorman who sternly shoos the crowd away, but the photographers still get what they came for: Katarina looking wrung out with exhaustion, Heath with a protective arm around her as though he's her bodyguard rather than her boyfriend.

ELLIS DEAN: The general public had never been so interested in ice dance, that's for sure. Hell, before Kat and Heath went viral, most people had never even *heard* of ice dance.

JANE CURRER: We wanted to attract more attention to the sport. But not *that* sort of attention.

ELLIS DEAN: The figure skating association should've sent me a fucking fruit basket. Instead they tried to have my site shut down—emphasis on *tried*.

Screenshot of a Kiss & Cry headline: "Ever Heard of Free Speech, Bitches? (And By 'Bitches' I Mean the U.S. Figure Skating Association)." The website has been updated from the basic WordPress template to a more professional design, with a sparkling animated logo.

ELLIS DEAN: Maybe I should've sent *them* a fruit basket for all that free publicity. Ad revenue shot up so fast I had to hire an assistant.

GARRETT LIN: Once Kat decided to partner with Heath, I thought about retiring. Possibly going to college. But Bella kept talking about 2010, the next Olympics in Vancouver. She didn't ask if we could skate together again. She just assumed we would.

Video of the Lins learning choreography for their 2006–2007 original dance. They perform a one-foot turn sequence, but they're out of sync. Garrett finishes a few notes ahead of Bella, and she has to scramble to catch up.

GARRETT LIN: I thought it would be easy, skating with my sister again. But after four seasons with Kat, it was a tough adjustment. We were faring better than her and Heath, though.

Kirk Lockwood reports from Skate America 2006 in Hartford, Connecticut. "We were expecting a showdown this weekend between the new—or should

I say old?—ice dance teams of Shaw/Rocha and Lin/Lin, but unfortunately Shaw and Rocha decided to withdraw after a rough practice session this morning."

ELLIS DEAN: All this furor over them, and they hadn't even taken competition ice together yet.

FRANCESCA GASKELL: She was fine, physically, as far as anyone could tell. But injuries like that, they can really mess with your mind.

GARRETT LIN: Kat and Heath stayed in Hartford and cheered us on. That meant a lot.

Katarina and Heath sit in the front row of the Hartford Civic Center, while Bella and Garrett skate the Westminster Waltz for the compulsory dance portion of the event.

When the Lins finish, Katarina and Heath stand and applaud for them, both smiling—except for a split second where Katarina looks down and brushes something off the sleeve of her jacket.

Cut to a screenshot of a post on the Kiss & Cry homepage, featuring the image of that unsmiling moment. "With Frenemies Like These . . . Bella Lin Better Watch Her Back" reads the headline.

ELLIS DEAN: Look, women supporting women doesn't get clicks. I didn't invent misogyny, I just shamelessly profited from it.

Back to Kirk in the commentator booth: "Skate America is the second event the reunited team of Shaw and Rocha has withdrawn from this season; they were also slated to compete at the Nebelhorn Trophy in September, but decided against it before making the trip to Germany. We'll see if they show up in Paris next month for their second Grand Prix assignment.

"Until then, we're wishing Katarina Shaw continued success with her recovery. And don't miss my exclusive interview with her brother, Lee Shaw, next Wednesday at seven p.m. Eastern!"

CHAPTER 46

Ignore them. That was Sheila's sage advice.

When paparazzi camped outside the rink and our apartment and my physical therapist's office and the drugstore where I was just trying to buy some fucking tampons, she told us to pretend they weren't there.

When reporters and sports agencies and event promoters called us at all hours of the day and night offering interviews and feature articles and endorsement contracts worth more than a whole Olympic quad's worth of prize money, she said we should let the phone ring.

Don't get distracted. You have work to do.

And when Lee got parole and started making the talk show rounds, toting our childhood photo albums and an increasingly embellished sob story about how I'd broken up our happy family to chase glory in California, Sheila said responding would only encourage him.

Focus on your training. That's the only thing you can control. Soon enough, this will blow over and they'll forget all about you.

I didn't want to be forgotten. I wanted to be remembered for the right reason: because I was a great athlete. Not because I looked lovely while bleeding all over the ice, or because my brother was white trash with a big mouth.

But I did what Sheila said, and Heath followed suit. We kept our heads down. We trained harder than we ever had before. Most mornings, I woke up so stiff Heath had to massage my legs for at least twenty minutes before I could make it across our tiny bedroom to the shower.

I didn't complain; I just set our alarm earlier so we could still be on the ice by seven.

Sometimes my body cooperated, and I could skate the same way I used to. Other times, it felt like the connection between my mind and my muscles had been severed. I had to learn to trust myself—and to trust Heath—all over again.

We were back to working with assistant coaches most of the time, while Sheila focused on whipping the twins into shape. Being sidelined stung, but I couldn't blame her. Heath and I were skating so inconsistently, we were lucky Sheila was willing to work with us at all.

Pulling out of our first two events made me that much more determined to make it to the French Grand Prix. Our withdrawal from Skate America meant we were out of the running for the Grand Prix Final in December, but I couldn't let the entire autumn go by without competing. That would mean showing up for the next National Championships untested—and, most likely, handing Garrett and Bella the title.

They were skating in the Cup of China a few days prior to our event in France. Sheila waited until the night before they left for Nanjing to drop the bombshell: due to promotional commitments for several sponsors headquartered in Asia and Australia, she wouldn't be able to make it to Paris in time, and all the assistant coaches had their own scheduling conflicts. Heath and I were on our own.

The competition got off to a promising start with our compulsory waltz, but the last time through the pattern dance, my blade hit a rut in the ice and knocked us both off balance. We ended up in second place behind Yelena Volkova and her new partner. Dmitri Kipriyanov was descended from a Bolshoi dancer and (rumor had it) a Russian mafia princess. With his boy-band hair and pillowy pink lips, Dmitri was even prettier than Yelena. Unfortunately, his skating was just as stunning.

The original dance was later the same day, leaving us barely enough time to run back to our Latin Quarter hotel for a restless attempt at a nap. As we took the ice again, I tried to swallow a yawn and smeared lipstick all over the back of my hand.

During our months in Illinois, Heath and I worked through my parents' old record collection, and he had the idea to skate to Kate Bush for our original dance. We'd pushed the furniture to the edges of the parlor so we could test out the tango steps, and he was right: it fit surprisingly well, both to the music and to our unconventional style. The rules had been tweaked to allow female skaters to wear pants for that event, and I'd envisioned us in androgynous costumes that, along with my close-cropped hair, would make us look like equals on the ice.

Sheila had other ideas. She advised a more traditional tango—"La Cumparsita," a black suit for Heath and a red dress for me, a rose pinned behind my ear. The same thing so many other teams would be doing, which meant we would have to be all the more perfect to stand out.

That evening in Paris, we were far from perfect. Heath mixed up his cross steps and nearly tripped me, then I tore a hole in his trousers with my toe pick doing a leg wrap. Our scores slipped to third place, below the French team of Moreau and Emanuel—not Arielle Moreau, who had retired several years ago, but her little sister, Genevieve.

Maybe we would have done better if Sheila had been there to coach us. But I was glad she wasn't. When we left the kiss and cry area, I didn't want to speak to anyone. Not even Heath.

"This is our first event back," he reminded me as we swapped our skates for sneakers backstage. Yelena and Dmitri were out on the ice, bringing the crowd back to life with their dramatic dance to the music of Russian tango singer Pyotyr Leshchenko. "No one's expecting perfection."

The season before, Garrett and I had won this event by a sizable margin. Now I was sitting in bronze medal position below a pair of teenagers who were *très excitée* to be competing in their first senior Grand Prix series. Perfection might have been out of reach, but that didn't mean I was willing to accept humiliation.

Heath drew me into a hug. "We've still got the free tomorrow. It's not over yet."

Our free dance was all Sheila's doing too—a classical, ballet-inspired piece, to a Mozart serenade so sedate I almost drifted off to sleep the first time I heard it. The program wasn't us, and the more we practiced, the worse we seemed to get. But Sheila insisted. *I know what the judges want,* she'd say any time we made a peep of protest. *You need to show them another side of you.* I cast aside my doubts and chose to trust her. After all, she'd always been right before.

"I think I need a minute," I told Heath. "Before the press conference."

"Sure." Heath started walking, pushing me along. "I saw a lounge this way, we can—"

"Alone."

He stopped. His hand dropped from the small of my back. "Whatever you need."

I kissed him, then turned away with my eyes still closed so I wouldn't have to see the hurt on his face. The Russians had reached the end of their program, and the applause was so loud the arena shook like an earthquake.

I kept moving until the noise faded enough for me to shut it out. I was somewhere in the bowels of the building, a long corridor lined with identical steel doors and industrial ductwork.

It was the farthest I'd been from Heath since he carried me off the ice in St. Louis.

I leaned my head back against the cinder blocks, crushing the artificial rose I'd forgotten was still there. My hair wasn't long enough to pull back, so I had to attach the flower with an elaborate grid of bobby pins. They scratched at my scalp, tugging strands out from the root every time I turned too fast.

With an exasperated growl, I seized the rose and ripped it free, pitching it to the floor. Then I stomped on it—once, twice, three times, the impact shuddering through my knee. I wished I still had my skates on so I could shred the petals into—

"What are you doing?"

The voice interrupting my tantrum was female, harsh and smoky.

With a Russian accent.

CHAPTER 47

Veronika Volkova gave the ruined flower at my feet a bemused glance.

"I think it is dead," she said. "But do not let me interrupt."

This was the first time I'd ever actually spoken to Veronika. She wasn't what I expected. Up close, a mischievous glint warmed those famous ice blue eyes.

She was still terrifying, though—and draped, as always, in her signature sable coat. Any other woman would've looked like a spoiled socialite. Not Veronika. She wore that fur as if she'd skinned the animals with her own hands.

"If you are finished," she said, "the press conference will begin soon. Yelena and Dmitri remain in first place, of course."

"Thanks for the update," I said, trying to move past her.

Veronika held her ground in the middle of the hallway. "Though I am sure the press will still have many questions to ask of you and Mr. Rocha." She sniffed. "Trust the French to privilege sex over substance."

I glared. I felt like a rabbit staring down a wolf. "We didn't ask for any of this."

She waved a hand. Her fingernails were painted a subtle nude shade but filed sharp as claws. "Save it for your adoring public. I know how Sheila operates."

"What do you mean?"

"I mean that Sheila Lin has the personal phone number of every photographer from Hollywood to Hong Kong." Veronika leaned close enough to give me a whiff of her perfume—strong and floral, with notes of bitter wintry spices. "And they always take her calls."

I scoffed. She was only trying to psych me out, set me against my coach.

My coach, who wasn't there. Who had saddled us with lackluster, ill-fitting programs this season. Who told us to ignore the paparazzi, no matter how relentless they became. No matter how quickly they seemed to find us, even after we changed our practice schedule, even after we moved to a new apartment. They always knew precisely where we'd be.

"Do not look so shocked." Veronika buffed her nails on her sable lapel. "Surely by now you must know how the game is played, Katarina Shaw."

I'd thought I knew. But Sheila was playing on a whole other level.

"When they no longer want to take your picture and ask you about your love life," Veronika said, *"that* is when you should worry."

She walked away, hips swaying as if she had a hundred suitors staring longingly after her, and she didn't give a damn about any of them. When Heath passed by her on his way to find me, she flashed him a smile. He flinched like he was afraid she might lunge.

"Are you all right?" He looked at the smashed rose petals, then back down the hall; Veronika had turned the corner toward the press room. "Why were you talking to—"

"Do you trust me?"

Heath seemed startled by the question. But he answered without hesitation.

"Of course I do."

"Good." I grinned and took his hand. "Because we can still win this thing."

VERONIKA VOLKOVA: I do not know what happened.

ELLIS DEAN: *Something* happened. They were different skaters in the free.

Katarina Shaw and Heath Rocha stand beside the boards as their names are announced at the 2006 Grand Prix event in Paris. They step onto the ice hand in hand, looking only at each other.

KIRK LOCKWOOD: Even before they skated out, you could see the electricity.

Katarina and Heath take their opening pose. Katarina gazes up, arms overhead like a ballerina in fifth position. Heath reaches out as if beckoning to her. Though they're no longer touching or making eye contact, they still seem connected, an invisible cord stretching taut between them. Their music begins: the fifth movement of Mozart's Serenade No. 10 in B-Flat Major.

KIRK LOCKWOOD: I remember being surprised when I heard they were doing something classical. I figured Sheila already had that piece in mind for Kat and her son before they split.

FRANCESCA GASKELL: No one had seen the program outside of practice. I saw them skate it a bunch of times at the Academy, though, and believe me: it was *nothing* like that.

More footage from the free dance: the choreography is formal, but the way Katarina and Heath perform it makes even the most balletic movements carnal. Anytime they're in close proximity, it looks as if they're on the verge of kissing. Anytime they separate, they look desperate to hold each other. With every glance, every touch, every step, they convey longing and desire.

JANE CURRER: Ice dance can have a certain sensuality to it, yes. Many programs express the beauty of the love between a man and a woman. But what Ms. Shaw and Mr. Rocha were doing bordered on vulgarity. It was impossible to watch them without picturing . . .

PRODUCER (Offscreen): Picturing what?

JANE CURRER: Well, you know.

Another interview with Lee Shaw, now in a brightly lit television studio. "Come on, man," he says, scowling with disgust. "I don't wanna think about my little sister that way."

ELLIS DEAN: That program wasn't figure skating, it was foreplay. Only Shaw and Rocha could make Mozart *that* filthy.

GARRETT LIN: I don't think they planned it. They just got caught up in the moment.

ELLIS DEAN: Maybe Heath got swept up in the moment. But Kat? That bitch knew *exactly* what she was doing. And it worked.

They hit their final pose: echoing their initial positions, only now they're close together at the center of the ice and his arms are around her. The crowd roars their approval, but Katarina and Heath barely seem to hear them. Katarina spins in the circle of Heath's arms and kisses him on the lips. The cheers grow louder.

JANE CURRER: I suppose that sort of display *would* appeal to a French crowd.

KIRK LOCKWOOD: Yes, they played up the sexual tension. But their technique was fantastic too. They hit every element with precision. Perfect timing, clean edges. The only obvious error was their combo lift lasting too long; anything over twelve seconds, there's a required deduction.

Slow motion footage of the penalized lift: Katarina swings up to sit on Heath's shoulder in an elegant pose, then drops down so he's holding her, one hand cradling the back of her neck. Her legs extend, held up by her core strength, creating a graceful arc as they spin.

KIRK LOCKWOOD: It didn't even look like a mistake. It looked like they couldn't bear to let each other go.

Katarina and Heath sit together, waiting for their scores. When the marks appear, they embrace again, even more passionately. They seem unaware of the cameras.

"No crying in the kiss and cry for these two!" Kirk Lockwood crows from the commentary booth. "We'll have to wait and see what the French and the Russians lay down, but those numbers will be tough to top. It's official: Shaw and Rocha are back."

CHAPTER 48

"That was quite a comeback," the reporter said, holding her audio recorder aloft. "How did you manage to turn things around in the free dance?"

Heath and I sat behind a long table on the dais at the front of the Palais Omnisports de Paris-Bercy's press room—right in the center, the place of honor.

Reserved for the gold medalists.

"I don't know," Heath answered. His hand was on my thigh, hidden by the table skirt. "We were just feeling it today, I guess."

Volkova and Kipriyanov had to settle for the silver, while Moreau and Emanuel got the bronze. Genevieve, at least, seemed ecstatic about the result. I could barely remember what that felt like, to be genuinely excited over third place.

"We had our doubts about skating to something so traditional," I said. "But eventually we worked out a way to make it our own."

The reporters hung on our every word as if the other skaters weren't even there. I'd spent so many years mired in anxiety over speaking to the media, but this was almost fun.

"Have you been in touch with your coach yet?" another reporter asked me. "She must be thrilled for you, after the recent struggles you've had."

"Not yet. But I'm sure Sheila will be proud of us."

I was sure of no such thing. If she'd been there, she would have told us to stick with what we'd done in practice, to show the judges we could be subtle and refined.

But Sheila was thousands of miles away. And people didn't want Heath and me to be "subtle" or "refined." They wanted a grand, epic love story. They wanted raw, rip-your-clothes-off passion. They didn't simply want us to be lovers—they wanted us to be *so* in love, we'd burn the whole world down to be together.

By truly connecting with each other, we finally connected with the music. It was the best we'd ever skated, and we had the gold medal to prove it.

I smiled out at the sea of reporters. Heath's hand slid higher on my thigh.

"Next question."

At the end of two grueling days of competition, plus the press conference and the medal ceremony and the endless posing for photos, I should have been exhausted. Instead, I felt ready to strap my skates back on and do the whole thing over again.

We finally left the arena well after sunset. Camera flashes still sparked in my vision against the darkened sky over the Seine.

"Let's go out," I said to Heath.

"Go out where?" he asked.

"Wherever we want."

We were young, we were in love, we were in Paris. We'd just won gold medals, plus thousands of dollars in prize money. We deserved to enjoy ourselves.

Back at the hotel, I changed into the strapless minidress I'd packed for the post–exhibition gala banquet. Usually I wore a sensible cardigan over it, and pantyhose opaque enough to cover the scar on my shin.

Not that night. Heath's eyes went wide when he saw me, and he didn't stop staring all through our romantic dinner. The maître d' sat us at a candlelit two-top in the restaurant's front window, and we ordered a charcuterie board so big it barely left enough room on the table to set our glasses of Bordeaux. As we plucked triple cream Brie and truffle crisps off the slate slab, I coiled my leg around Heath's, not caring who might see.

After dinner, we decided to go dancing—*real* dancing, unjudged and unchoreographed. We wandered through several arrondissements before a flickering neon sign beckoned us down a darkened staircase and into a space more like a cave than a nightclub. Rough brick burst through the vaulted ceilings, strobe lights and disco balls spangling the rugged surface.

Heath and I made our way to the middle of the cramped dance floor, and for the next few hours all we did was *move*. The electronic beat throbbed through my body. Heath danced behind me, hands on my hips, kissing my neck, and I was aware of nothing except heat and shadow and sound and *him*.

I have no idea what time it was when we finally stumbled back into the real world. It had started raining, but we were already drenched with sweat. My dress stuck to me like a second skin, and Heath had stripped down to his undershirt, abandoning his button-down somewhere on the dance floor. I slipped off my shoes and ran barefoot through the downpour, giddy, laughing, splashing in puddles all the way back to our hotel.

Before the suite door swung shut behind us, we were already a tangle of limbs, shedding our wet clothes, steam rising from our rain-soaked bodies, tumbling onto the red velvet love seat because we wanted each other too much to make it to the bed.

Heath fell asleep afterward, reclined on the cushions like a classical statue. I tried to sleep too, but I felt like I had lightning in my veins.

I extricated myself from under his arm and retrieved my cellphone from the nightstand. The screen lit up, casting shadows over the damask wallpaper.

Two missed calls, followed by a single text, all from the same number. Sent several hours before, while we were still out dancing—the middle of the night in Paris, first thing in the morning in China. As I read the message, my stomach clenched with dread.

Call me immediately.

CHAPTER 49

I didn't want to wake Heath, so I wrapped myself in a robe and took my phone onto the hotel room's small terrace overlooking the Place du Panthéon. The square was silent and still, but smells of baking bread wafted through the cobblestone streets.

Sheila answered on the first ring.

"I see you've been enjoying your time in Paris," she said.

She sounded even calmer than usual. My heart beat faster.

"Yes." I tried to swallow, but my mouth was too dry. "We—"

"You made a spectacle of yourself."

"We won."

Unlike Bella and Garrett, who'd barely held on to bronze at the Cup of China.

"I'm not just talking about the way you skated," she said. "What were you thinking, carrying on like that all over the city?"

By daybreak in Paris, photos of our night out were plastered all over the internet. A few days later, when our flight from Charles de Gaulle landed at LAX, we were greeted by whole newsstands full of trashy magazines trumpeting our exploits. One tabloid even published a cover story spread on our "Parisian Night of Passion," complete with quotes allegedly from other guests at our hotel who complained about being awoken by "loud cries of pleasure" and "cracking furniture." At first I was embarrassed that our private celebration had turned into a public show—but people loved it, just like they'd loved our sexed-up Mozart program. Our off-ice passion was part of the fantasy.

None of that had happened yet, though. There was only one way Sheila could have found out so much so quickly, from the other side of the world.

Veronika Volkova's voice echoed in my head. *You must know how the game is played.*

"You want to give me feedback on my skating, fine," I said. "But what I do in my free time is none of your business. This is my life, and—"

"If you want to be a champion, skating should *be* your life. And as your coach, everything you do is my business. You and Mr. Rocha are welcome to find another coach if you disagree with my methods."

I should have anticipated this, when we decided to come back to the Academy. It was naive to think Sheila would welcome Heath and me with open arms after we'd cost the twins their Olympic birthrights. She could have cut us loose, told us to go train somewhere else—but under her control, we were a threat that could be neutralized.

If tarnishing us was what it took to let her children shine brighter, Sheila wouldn't hesitate. As furious as I was, a small, mean part of me admired her for being so ruthless—and blamed myself for not seeing it sooner. When Sheila told us to ignore the media attention, I assumed it was sage advice born of her decades in the spotlight. But Sheila Lin had never in her life ignored the press. She'd played them to get what she wanted—the same way she'd played Heath and me to keep us from controlling our own career, our own story.

"I think we've learned all we can at the Lin Ice Academy."

In my head the words were nasty, forceful; when I spoke them aloud, I sounded like a lost little girl. Sheila was silent for a long moment. The breeze picked up, sending the French flag on the roof of the Panthéon rippling. I tugged my robe tighter, tears stinging my eyes.

"As you said, Ms. Shaw." Her voice was cold, but I could swear I heard a hint of sorrow in it. Maybe that was only wishful thinking, though. "It's your life."

She hung up. I snapped my phone shut, just as the terrace door scraped open. Heath stood on the threshold. He'd pulled on shorts, but he still looked half-asleep.

"I talked to Sheila," I said.

I didn't tell him the rest. I didn't need to. He could see it all over my face.

He held out his hand. "Come to bed."

I shed my robe, and we slid under the sheets together. Heath kissed my forehead.

"We don't need her, Katarina. All we need is each other."

I closed my eyes and listened to his heartbeat and, for the moment at least, let myself believe him.

PART IV

The Game

GARRETT LIN: How would I describe the next phase of Kat and Heath's career?

KIRK LOCKWOOD: All over the place. They had, what, ten different coaches in five different countries in two years?

JANE CURRER: Appalling. Parting ways with Sheila Lin may have been the worst mistake they ever made, and that's saying something.

ELLIS DEAN: The best thing that ever happened to me. Those little attention whores provided so much content, it was hard to keep up.

GARRETT LIN: I guess I'll go with "wild." In more ways than one.

FRANCESCA GASKELL: It seemed like Shaw and Rocha were *everywhere* in those days.

Katarina and Heath pose on the red carpet at a movie premiere. They pop champagne at the opening of a new dance club. They laugh on a talk-show sofa. Katarina's hair has grown out into a sleek chin-length bob, and they're both clearly being dressed by professional stylists.

INEZ ACTON: That nude shoot they did was an attack on bisexuals everywhere. Let us *live.*

Behind-the-scenes footage of Katarina and Heath's photo shoot for ESPN The Magazine's *annual Body Issue. They pose with his arm across her chest and her thigh blocking his pelvis.*

INEZ ACTON: And then there were all those YouTube supercuts. Pornographic, basically.

A snippet of a fan-made YouTube video plays: dramatically filtered clips of sexy moments from Shaw and Rocha programs, edited to match the song "Promiscuous" by Nelly Furtado.

INEZ ACTON: I heard the figure skating association tried to have the videos taken down—something about streaming rights? Big mistake on their part, if you ask me. Those were the most effective advertisements for ice dance ever made.

JANE CURRER: Mind you, Shaw and Rocha still hadn't won a major title. But the general public wasn't interested in them for their athletic skills. Katarina and Heath were *celebrities*.

GARRETT LIN: By far the craziest thing I heard about was . . . I think they call it "fan fiction"?

ELLIS DEAN: Oh my god, the erotic fanfic. Imagine having strangers on the internet write multipart sagas about you banging.

GARRETT LIN: No, of course I didn't read it. I'm just telling you what I heard.

ELLIS DEAN: *(He clears his throat, then reads from his cellphone screen.)* "Heath thrust into her hot, wet center. 'God, Katarina,' he moaned as she rode his rock-hard member. 'You even fuck like a champion.'" That's one of the better ones, if you can believe it. We did a roundup on Kiss & Cry before the 2008 National Championships.

GARRETT LIN: Bella and I were still in touch with Kat and Heath, yeah. We only saw one another at competitions, though.

FRANCESCA GASKELL: I feel bad saying it, but it was kinda nice, not having them at the Academy anymore. Everyone could relax and just focus on skating.

KIRK LOCKWOOD: Shaw and Rocha were certainly the most famous ice dance team. They were also one of the best. They were so in sync, sometimes they'd make mistakes in unison!

During the original dance at the 2007 U.S. Nationals in Spokane, Katarina and Heath stumble on their twizzles, at the same time and somehow still in rhythm to the song—which is now Kate Bush's "Under Ice" rather than traditional tango music.

GARRETT LIN: It seemed awful, if I'm being honest. All that attention. My sister and I grew up in the public eye, but what we went through paled in comparison.

ELLIS DEAN: Oh, they *loved* the attention. Well, Kat did anyway. And whatever Kat loved, Heath at least pretended to love too.

JANE CURRER: Perhaps if they'd spent more time on their training and less time posing for photographs, they would have been happier with their results. We never knew whether they'd show up to any given competition with a new coach—or no coach at all.

KIRK LOCKWOOD: The lack of coaching consistency was an issue. It's remarkable they skated as well as they did, given all the upheaval and distraction.

Katarina's brother, Lee, gives another tell-all interview: "Our father never told her no. Her eyes looked just like our mom's. Katie would fix 'em on him like a gun sight until he surrendered."

INEZ ACTON: Katarina and Heath both had this rebellious, sexy, no-fucks-given vibe. That's what people loved about them—and what they hated. But we all know a "bad boy" and a "bad girl" are treated *very* differently in our society.

JANE CURRER: Champion skaters should be role models. Perhaps it's old-fashioned of me to say so, but especially the ladies. So many young women look up to them.

Video footage immediately following the free dance at the 2008 World Championships in Gothenburg, Sweden. Ellis Dean catches Katarina and Heath as they leave the kiss and cry. He has official press credentials now, and professional recording equipment.

"How are you feeling about the silver?" he asks. "Cause if you ask me, you guys got screwed."

Heath has his hand on Katarina's elbow, like he wants to hold her back. But she's too fired up. "The results are bullshit, that's what I think. Kipriyanov almost face-planted coming out of that combo spin. The judges just didn't want to give us the gold."

JANE CURRER: I shudder to think of the influence Katarina Shaw has had on the younger generation of figure skaters. And continues to have, to this day.

CHAPTER 50

In 2009, the National Championships came back to Cleveland.

Heath and I walked through the arena doors hand in hand, same as we had nine years before. But everything else was different.

Instead of driving hours due east on I-90 in a rusty pickup truck with a busted heater, we'd flown first class, direct from a resort in Saint Lucia. We were staying at a five-star hotel rather than a roach-infested roadside motel, and a private car whisked us to the competition venue right on time for our warm-up. At our first Nationals, no one knew who we were. Now we were greeted by a horde of fans shouting our names.

When we looked up into the stands, we saw our names too: written a foot tall in glitter paint on banners and signs, collaged using Kit Kat and Heath bar candy wrappers, emblazoned on homemade shirts above screen prints of us kissing, even scrawled on faces in my signature lipstick—a vivid red shade with a subtle golden sheen called "Bold Medal Favorite," one of the many lucrative brand campaigns our sports agency had negotiated on our behalf.

Everything we wore, from our skates to our warm-up gear to our underwear, was provided via some endorsement partnership or another. Turns out that once you become rich enough to afford whatever you want, people fall all over themselves to give you things for free. Our two-week stay in Saint Lucia had been comped too, because a few photos of Heath rubbing sunscreen onto my bare back outside one of the resort's private cabanas would send bookings skyrocketing.

We had everything. Except the national title.

So far that season, we were undefeated. Gold at Skate America. Gold at the NHK Trophy. Gold at the Grand Prix Final in Goyang, where we got to stand on the top step of the podium above all of our major rivals: Volkova and Kipriyanov on the silver medal step, Bella and Garrett with the bronze.

A preview of the upcoming World Championships, I hoped. The event would be held in Los Angeles that year, and I was looking forward to trouncing the twins on their own turf.

First, though, we had to win Nationals. We'd been in first place after both the compulsory and the original dances, gaining a five-point lead over the Lins. We didn't watch Bella and Garrett's free dance, but I snuck a quick glance up at the Jumbotron as they awaited their scores. The twins looked exhausted, and Sheila's lips were set in the stiff smile she used to signal profound disappointment. They hadn't done enough.

Frannie Gaskell intercepted Bella outside the kiss and cry to give her a comforting hug—which Bella accepted with a stiff back, arms stuck by her sides. Frannie and her partner were in third, a few tenths of a point behind Bella and Garrett.

As Heath and I circled the rink, waiting for the announcement of our names, he seemed a bit distracted. More than once, he let go of my hand and bent over to adjust his skate laces. A cold stone of worry tumbled in my stomach. We were ahead, yes, but we had to skate clean, make sure the judges couldn't deny us the gold.

Once the music started, though, I realized there was nothing to worry about. Heath and I were as in tune as always. Our free dance was a total departure from everyone else in the field, set to a layered mix of moody classical piano and industrial rock Heath had arranged himself. We wore form-fitting black costumes embellished only with angular panels of mesh, and the choreography was powerful, almost aggressive, showing off our strength, the way we covered the ice together like a finely tuned machine.

Sheila Lin probably hated it. Good thing she wasn't our coach anymore.

At that point, we didn't officially have a coach. We jet-setted to training centers all over the globe, assembling a team of technical specialists and choreographers and trainers, picking up what we could from each before moving on to the next. It wasn't conventional, but it seemed to be working for us. We controlled our career. We controlled our destiny.

Sometimes it seemed as if we'd worked with every ice dance authority in the world, but there was one missing from our collection: whoever had honed Heath's technique during his three-year absence. He still wouldn't tell me where he'd been, how he'd achieved such rapid improvement. I'd become increasingly frustrated with his silence on the subject, but any time I attempted to raise it, he'd shut me down with a haunted, distant look in his eyes—a look I remembered well from childhood, any time I made even the smallest reference to his life before we met. One thing was clear: whatever he had gone through, he wasn't willing to go through it again. Or to subject me to it.

I tried to convince myself it didn't matter. Heath loved me. He shared more with me than he would have with anyone else. He would tell me his secrets someday, or he wouldn't. In the meantime, we were winning.

Our music ended with a piano glissando and a hissing electronic pulse. We held the final pose, panting in time. We'd done it, I could feel it in my bones. We were going to be the national champions. I'd won the title three times with Garrett. But winning it with Heath—and skating exactly the way I wanted to, refusing to rein in my power—meant so much more.

I started to take a bow. Then I realized Heath wasn't standing beside me. He still clutched my hand, but he'd knelt on the ice.

My first thought was that there was something wrong—a broken lace, a muscle cramp. Or worse, an injury. But when I turned to face him, he was gazing up at me, holding something pinched between his thumb and forefinger.

A diamond ring.

ELLIS DEAN: I'm a bitter bitch, but even I can admit it: damn, that was romantic!

Heath Rocha gets down on one knee to propose to Katarina Shaw at the 2009 U.S. National Championships. The energy of the crowd shifts as they realize what's happening, a few moments before Katarina herself catches on.

INEZ ACTON: Public proposals are manipulative as hell. I couldn't believe he put her on the spot like that.

GARRETT LIN: I was surprised, yeah. To tell the truth, I wasn't sure Kat even wanted to get married, however much she loved Heath. But I figured he knew her better than I did.

A close-up of Katarina's shocked face plays on every screen in the arena. She stares down at Heath, hand clapped over her mouth.

FRANCESCA GASKELL: A gold medal and an engagement ring, all in one night! What more could she have possibly wanted?

GARRETT LIN: Before Nationals, they were at some Caribbean resort for two weeks, and it'd occurred to me he might pop the question there. I actually wondered if they'd already gotten engaged in secret, and this was all for show.

INEZ ACTON: Katarina Shaw was on the verge of becoming a four-time national champ. But suddenly all anyone cared about was her becoming a *wife*.

A reporter approaches Lee Shaw outside a gas station in rural Illinois.

"Hey, Lee! Any comment on your sister's engagement?"

Lee turns. This is clearly the first he's hearing about the engagement, but he tries to play it off.

"I'm thrilled for her, of course. And for Heath. Surprised it took 'em this long."

He gets closer to the camera, looking right into the lens. His eyes are bleary, and his skin has an unhealthy pallor.

"You need someone to walk you down the aisle, Katie," he says, "you know where to find me."

CHAPTER 51

*D*on't throw up.

That was my first thought when I realized what Heath was doing.

Then I thought: *No. Please, no. Not like this.*

But with all those people watching, flashbulbs popping like fireworks, my face projected on a screen twenty feet tall, all I could say was *yes.*

I took the ring and we kissed and he spun me around and the audience cheered. When we got to the kiss and cry, the diamond was still gripped in my hand. Heath had to pry my fist open to slip it onto my finger.

More cheering. So many cameras pointed at us, I couldn't even count them.

My hand stung. I'd clenched the ring so tight, the gold prongs gouged my palm.

Finally, our marks appeared, and we were officially the national champions.

We kissed again. We stood and waved and smiled until my face hurt.

As we lined up for the medal ceremony, Frannie Gaskell grabbed my hand and squealed with delight at the way the diamond sparkled under the arena lights.

At the press conference afterward, the first question was not really a question at all: "Show us the ring, Katarina." I did what they asked, splaying my fingers so the facets flashed.

The ring was beautiful. It looked like my mother's—the Art Deco family heirloom I'd sold to pay for our first trip to Los Angeles. Heath had it custom-made, based on his recollection of that piece. That's what he told the reporters. He'd been planning this since before the season started, for when—not if—we won the championship. He had our costume designer sew a special pocket into his pants to hide the ring. He was so afraid it would fall out while we were skating, he kept checking it, making sure it was secure.

I smiled and laughed when I was supposed to, and tried not to think about how Heath's distraction could have lost us points, maybe even cost us the title. I kept my hand hooked around his elbow, so the ring stayed visible in every picture. I answered question after question. None of them were about our performance.

Afterward, Bella approached. She gave me a hug—not something she did often, even when we had been closer. I'd never told her the real reason we left the Academy, never revealed my suspicions about her mother sabotaging us. Bella and I were friendly rivals still, but I wouldn't have called us best friends anymore.

She kept her arms around me. She had to stand on her tiptoes to reach my neck.

"You okay?" she asked.

I stiffened. Then I slumped against her with relief. While everyone else was showering me with congratulations, Bella Lin saw through my feigned delight.

"Congratulations," Bella said. "On the way you skated today, and only that. Any bitch can get married, but—"

"But it takes a special bitch to be national champion?"

"Exactly." We both laughed, embracing again. "I'm coming for you at Worlds, though."

I smiled. "You better."

"And if you ask me to plan a bachelorette party or a bridal shower or any of that shit, I'm hiring a dude to whack you in the knee."

"Seems fair."

She squeezed my shoulder. "See you on the podium, Shaw."

❖

"You want to go out and celebrate?" Heath asked as soon as we were ensconced in our chauffeured car, heading back to the Ritz-Carlton. "Or stay in and celebrate?"

With a look so heated I was glad the privacy partition was rolled up, he kissed my knuckles, right above the ring. Again, my hand clenched into a fist.

Heath pulled away. "What's wrong?"

"I don't know." Truly, I didn't. I loved him. I wanted to be with him forever, as far as I could understand forever at the ripe old age of twenty-five. But every time I looked at the diamond on my finger, I felt like there were icicles puncturing my gut.

"Shit," he said. "You hated that, didn't you?"

"I just . . ." It had been so much easier with Bella. "Why now?"

"Being back in Cleveland, winning the title—it's like we've come full circle." He sighed, raking his fingers through his hair. "I thought it would be romantic."

I slid my hand across the leather seat toward him. "It *was.*"

"I'm sorry. I honestly thought this is what you would want."

Our relationship had become a public spectacle; it was no wonder he thought I'd want a spectacular public proposal too. *I* hadn't even known the line was there until he leapt over it.

"If you don't want to marry me," he said, "that's—"

I twisted toward him, seatbelt slicing into my collarbone. "Of *course* I want to marry you, Heath. You took me by surprise, that's all."

The car slowed, pulling up to the hotel.

"Let's focus on winning Worlds," I said. "Then we can figure out the wedding stuff."

Only, after Worlds we were leaving for the Stars on Ice tour. As soon as that was over, it would be time to get ready for next season. The Olympic season.

"There's no rush," Heath said. "We have the rest of our lives."

Dramatic multicolored lights strobe over a darkened ice arena.

"And now, ladies and gentlemen," a voice booms over the PA system, "please welcome to the ice reigning U.S. champions and 2009 world gold medalists, Katarina Shaw and Heath Rocha!"

Katarina and Heath skate out, illuminated by a follow spot. Cheers echo from the packed stands.

KIRK LOCKWOOD: It's an honor to be invited to perform in a major exhibition tour. Sheila and I were headliners several times back in the day; those spots are usually reserved for Olympic gold medalists. Shaw and Rocha were so popular, though, the producers made an exception.

ELLIS DEAN: It's not like they needed more money or fame. But if they wanted to go into the Olympic season as the undisputed fan favorites? Headlining Stars on Ice was a good start.

Katarina and Heath's program music begins: a cover of the Chris Isaak ballad "Wicked Game" by a breathy female vocalist. Their choreography is sensual and intimate, and their skimpy costumes leave little to the imagination.

JANE CURRER: That program was *entirely* inappropriate. Stars on Ice is a family show.

Katarina unbuttons Heath's shirt in time with the song's slinky bass line. He leans her back, his lips brushing the bare skin between her satin shorts and rhinestone-covered crop top.

JANE CURRER: The tour producers should have told them to tone it down, at *least.*

ELLIS DEAN: With every tour stop, their infamy grew—and so did the box office returns. People bought tickets to Stars on Ice, but they were there to see the Shaw and Rocha Show.

Security camera footage from the Allstate Arena in Rosemont, Illinois, shows Lee Shaw standing outside the stage door, holding a bouquet of wilted grocery store roses. There's no sound, but he seems to be trying to reason with the burly security guard.

Eventually, the guard takes the roses, motioning for Lee to move away from the door. As soon as Lee's back is turned, the guard tosses the bouquet in a nearby dumpster.

KIRK LOCKWOOD: Those tours can definitely bring out some crazies.

Katarina and Heath end their program with a dance spin. They come to a stop, mouths a breath away from meeting. For a lingering moment, they pant in unison, staring into each other's eyes.

Then, finally, they kiss. The crowd goes wild.

KIRK LOCKWOOD: Say what you will about Kat and Heath. You can't deny they were stars.

CHAPTER 52

The kiss had been spontaneous at first.

Heath and I choreographed the whole "Wicked Game" program ourselves especially for Stars on Ice, working on it whenever we had extra ice time or a spare moment in a hotel suite. Sometimes we'd get so caught up in the slow, sensual movement, we couldn't help it: more than one behind-closed-doors practice session had ended with us in bed, the song looping in the background until we were finished with each other.

On the first leg of the tour, we didn't include the kiss at every show. When we did, it was always different—sometimes a barely there brush of the lips, sometimes a hungry openmouthed clinch. After a particularly exceptional performance in San Jose, I was so charged up, it was all I could do not to drag Heath back to the dressing room and have my way with him.

As the tour wore on, though, audiences started to expect the kiss. If we ended our skate without a lip-lock, there would be cries, chants, even boos. So once again, we gave the people what they wanted.

By our final matinee in Portland, Maine, the kiss had become pure choreography. I counted the seconds until it was over, the same way I'd count steps or spin rotations.

The audience couldn't tell the difference. They cheered as loudly as they had in Tulsa and Tampa and all the other interchangeable arenas we'd performed in. They had no idea that, during the grueling months of the tour, our once scorching sex life had turned just as mechanical.

Heath took my hand. We took our bows. Beyond the spotlight, the arena was dark as the night sky, camera flashes and cellphone screens forming constellations in the stands.

Thank God we never have to do that again, I thought.

Even though the tour was over, we weren't done performing. The next night, there was a Team USA fundraising gala, and Heath and I were guests of honor.

The event was held at a historic New York City hotel, in a penthouse ballroom with panoramic views of Central Park. A storm was predicted after sunset, and wind already whipped through the park's thick canopy of elm trees. The ominous weather made a sharp contrast to the ballroom ceiling, which was painted to look like a blue sky covered in fluffy cumulus clouds.

Heath and I arrived fashionably late, and the space was already packed full of potential donors, plus plenty of once and future Olympians pretending to enjoy their company. It would be months before any of us would know whether or not we were going to Vancouver, but this was part of the game: parties and politicking, presenting ourselves as champions.

As we moved deeper into the crowd, I was careful to keep a smile on my face at all times. Heath might be able to get away with brooding, but if I appeared anything besides absolutely *delighted* to be there, I'd be branded a bitch.

The Lins were seated at the same banquet table as the president of the U.S. Olympic Committee, plus Kirk Lockwood, Frannie Gaskell, and an older woman in a power suit I could only assume was Frannie's big-deal Big Pharma CEO mother. Though Mrs. Gaskell rarely took time out of her busy schedule to attend her daughter's competitions, she was one of U.S. Figure Skating's most generous financial benefactors.

I spotted Ellis Dean too, standing next to a massive floral display in the shape of the Olympic rings. While the other male attendees played it safe with classic suits, Ellis wore a white satin jacket with marabou feathers stuck to the sleeves. He looked like some kind of unholy twink/ swan hybrid, but I had to grudgingly admit he was pulling it off.

Every two steps, Heath and I were waylaid by strangers wanting to make small talk—mostly about our much-publicized engagement. At least we had well-rehearsed answers.

"Oh, we've been way too busy to do much wedding planning." That was my line, delivered with a tinge of regret—as though I, an elite athlete, truly yearned to spend my days tasting cakes and trying on princess dresses. "Maybe after the Olympics!"

Then Heath would smile and slip his arm around my waist. "I think a gold medal would be the perfect wedding gown accessory, don't you?"

Polite laughter all around. Generic well wishes. On to the next.

People implored us to dance as well. "Please, just for one song! It would be such a treat!"

The first few times, we demurred. Finally, we wandered close enough to the stage that the string quartet caught sight of us and struck up a rendition of "Wicked Game." The whole room seemed to turn toward us expectantly.

"Shall we?" Heath said.

The storm still hadn't let loose, but a few warning drops spattered the windows. I imagined us running away, down the stairs, through the lobby and out onto Fifth Avenue. Disappearing into the park to dance under the shelter of the elms while the storm raged above us, tasting the fresh rainfall on each other's lips like we had that night in Paris.

The dance floor cleared. Heath pulled me into a tango hold, tight against his chest—to a smattering of applause, though we hadn't done anything yet. I shifted so the slit in my black dress parted, showing off the red charmeuse lining and my toned thigh muscles.

As reluctant as I'd been to perform, there was something soothing about dancing without choreography. I didn't have to think, all I had to do was drop into my body and let Heath lead me. Tango always feels like a private conversation conducted in public, every shift of weight and direction a shift in power. That night, as I hooked my leg behind Heath's knee and stared over his shoulder at the storm clouds covering the park, all I wanted to do was surrender.

The song ended, and everyone applauded.

Everyone except Ellis Dean. He hadn't moved from his spot by those ridiculous flowers, only now he was talking to some guy with an ill-fitting gray suit and a bad haircut. The man struck a dissonant note, out of tune with the rest of the room.

The quartet switched back to ballroom standards. The dance floor filled in around us. I kept watching Ellis and his friend. There was something familiar about him.

Then the man turned and looked right at me. I gasped, stepping back. Heath grabbed my elbow in time to keep me from colliding with a septuagenarian couple.

He drew me close again, but not to dance. "What is it?"

"My brother is here."

CHAPTER 53

Nearly a decade had passed since Lee and I were in the same room.

I'd seen him plenty, though. On television. On tabloid covers. Talking shit about me for a paycheck, while insisting he loved me and missed me and wanted to make things right.

Again, I thought about leaving the party, fleeing into the park, letting the trees swallow me up. But I was already walking toward Lee—slow and cautious, like he was an explosive device that could detonate at any moment.

"Katie." Lee smiled, baring tobacco-stained teeth. "It's so good to see you."

He was much thinner than I remembered. Older too—though Lee was only a little over thirty, his pallid skin and sunken cheeks made him look like our father.

"What the hell do you think you're doing?" Heath said.

He'd followed me across the ballroom. I should have been grateful for the backup, but I could feel the way his muscles coiled, ready for violence.

"I was invited," Lee said.

Heath scoffed. "Bullshit."

I looked at Ellis. "You invited him here. Didn't you?"

Before Ellis could confirm or deny his meddling, Lee turned on him. "You said she wanted to see me. You said she was ready to talk."

"I may have exaggerated. Slightly." Ellis shrugged, the marabou trim on his jacket shivering. "But now that you're both here, what a perfect opportunity to clear the air."

"Why, so you can post an exclusive scoop on your shitty blog?" I shook my head. "I always knew you were a shady bitch, Ellis, but this is *beyond.*"

"I swear I didn't know this was a setup," Lee said. "But maybe he's right, Katie. We are family after all."

This he said with a pointed look in Heath's direction. Well, as pointed as he could manage; Lee's eyes were unfocused, the pupils blown huge.

Here's one detail that's never included in the stories about my brother and me: during Lee's tour of the talk show circuit, I'd reached out to him through a lawyer, with an offer to cover the full cost of rehab if he agreed to go. He never responded.

"You need to leave," I told him. "If you want to talk, I'll give you my number, and—"

"Katarina," Heath said. I ignored him.

"—we can talk," I continued. "But not here. Not in front of all these people."

Lee's fingers closed on my arm. "Still think you're better than me, don't you, Katie?"

He was shaky and weak from whatever he was on, and I was a world champion. One twist of my arm, and I was free.

Pacifying Heath wouldn't be so easy.

"How dare you touch her." Heath seized the lapel of Lee's cheap suit. "How fucking dare you. After everything you've—"

"Let's take a breath," Ellis said. "No need for a scene."

"I thought that's what you wanted, Ellis," I said. "A scene."

People were already staring. Some edged away, others leaned closer. Bella left her banquet table and made a beeline for us.

I could picture the headlines, the mug shots. Quotes from the scandalized partygoers. Photos of the ballroom floor smeared with blood. There would be no talking Heath down, and I wasn't strong enough to hold him back.

So I did the only thing I could think to do: I turned to Ellis Dean, and I slapped him hard across the mouth.

ELLIS DEAN: Okay. I had that coming.

Grainy cellphone video taken by a guest at the charity gala shows Katarina Shaw slapping Ellis Dean. The phone shakes and tilts sideways as the person filming rushes in for a closer look.

JANE CURRER: It was appalling. There is no excuse for that sort of behavior.

Ellis reels, nose gushing blood all over the white feathers on his jacket.

INEZ ACTON: When a woman smacks a man in the face? She usually has a damn good reason.

Lee Shaw takes a lurching step toward his sister. Katarina evades him, and he stumbles, crashing into the Olympic Rings flower display beside them.

PRODUCER (Offscreen): What did you think would happen when you invited Katarina Shaw's estranged brother to New York?

ELLIS DEAN: I mean, not a heartwarming family reunion, obviously. Anyone could tell the dude was bad news. But I didn't think it'd be *that* much of a disaster.

The party devolves into pandemonium. The band stops playing, and guests stream toward the doors, holding up the hotel security guards trying to enter.

Bella Lin pushes through the crowd to get to Katarina, with Garrett Lin a few steps behind. Lee lies in a pile of crushed roses, looking dazed.

Heath puts a comforting arm around Katarina. She ignores him, staring down at her brother with a mixture of fury and contempt.

ELLIS DEAN: No, I didn't hear what she said. I was a little busy with my *broken fucking nose* bleeding all over my custom Cavalli.

More shaky cellphone footage, zoomed in on Katarina's face. She's speaking to Lee, but her voice isn't audible over the commotion.

GARRETT LIN: I'll never forget what she said to him.

PRODUCER (Offscreen): What did she say?

Katarina turns to go. Heath and the Lins follow—until Bella notices the person who's been filming. She strides closer to the camera. "Delete that, or you'll be hearing from our lawyers."

A muffled curse, the angle going wild as the person scrambles to turn off the recording. The final shot before the screen goes black shows the security guards hauling Lee to his feet. He stares after his sister with tears shining in his bloodshot eyes.

GARRETT LIN: I don't feel right repeating it. Given what happened next, though . . . I think you can probably guess the sentiment.

CHAPTER 54

Heath and I left the party before they could throw us out.

We were the only ones in the elevator car, but Heath crowded me the whole way down, asking if I was all right, examining my reddened palm, wanting to know what I'd been thinking when I slapped Ellis.

Rain obscured the view beyond the brightly lit awning outside the hotel. The temperature had fallen a good fifteen degrees, and goose bumps prickled my bare arms. Heath shrugged off his suit jacket and started to lay it over my shoulders.

"Stop," I said.

"You're shivering. I was only trying to—"

"You keep trying to take care of me, and I don't need you to. So please, just stop."

Heath slumped, letting the jacket sleeves drag on the sidewalk. "It's been a long day. Maybe we should head back to our hotel and get some rest."

"You go ahead." I folded my arms—hugging myself against the chill. Shutting him out. "I need a minute."

"What if your brother comes back?" he asked.

"Then I'll handle it."

Heath might have convinced himself his confrontation with Lee was solely for my benefit, but I knew better. I'd seen the rage contorting his face. While I'd spent the last ten years avoiding my brother at all costs, Heath had been lying in wait, hoping one day he'd have the chance to get his revenge.

"Fine," Heath said. "Take all the time you need."

He strode away from me so fast, I almost missed what he muttered next.

"You always do."

I stared after Heath's retreating form. He was headed straight for Central Park, hunched against the driving rain.

"Don't tell me you two are fighting again." Bella stood outside the gilded vestibule surrounding the lobby door. "You've got to cut this shit out, Kat."

I whirled to face her. "How was I supposed to know my brother would—"

"I'm not just talking about tonight. I'm talking about *all* the shit you and Heath have been up to the past few years. The fame whore photo ops, the flitting from coach to coach. The fighting and the fucking and the endless *drama*. You're not reality TV stars, you're world-class athletes. You're the goddamn reigning world champions."

Sheila's words from years before echoed in my head: *You're a world champion. Act like it.* But Bella's voice held none of her mother's harshness. She sounded sad, almost weary—which was so much worse.

"We have one season left," Bella said. "This is it. Our one remaining chance to go to the Olympics. You need to get your shit together and your head in the game, before it's too late."

"We were undefeated all season," I pointed out.

"Yeah, but is anyone talking about that?"

She was right. People couldn't shut up about our engagement, our sexy choreography, our scandalous reputations—which would only be bolstered by what went down at the gala. Our skills and accomplishments were an afterthought, if they were mentioned at all.

"Why are you telling me this?" I asked.

"Because I'm your friend."

"You're also my competitor."

"Which is why I want you competing at your best." Bella smiled and knocked her shoulder into mine. "So when I kick your ass, I'll know I deserved that gold medal."

We stood in silence for a moment, watching the rain. Bella sighed and shot a glance at the door. "I should probably head back in. You coming?"

"I doubt I'm welcome anymore."

"Please, they should give you a standing O. At least half the people in that room have fantasized about bitch-slapping Ellis Dean."

She hugged me, her familiar white peony perfume cutting through the petrichor.

"You're my best rival, Katarina Shaw. You better not back down now."

I thought about following Heath into the park. But he had too much of a head start, and the weather was getting worse, so instead I hailed a taxi and headed back to our hotel suite alone.

Hoping to avoid attention, we'd checked into a Lower East Side boutique hotel under assumed names. The rooms were obnoxiously trendy, all sleek and monochrome with furniture that looked like it belonged in a modern art gallery. The views were impressive, though: floor-to-ceiling windowpanes wrapping around the corner opposite the bed.

I left the lights switched off so I could watch the storm. Lightning crept closer and closer, flaring against the steel-and-glass skyscrapers.

Surely Heath wasn't still out in that. Any minute I'd hear his keycard in the door, and there he'd be, soaking wet and sheepish.

But an hour passed without any sign of him. The storm clouds started to recede, the rain slowing from sheets to a steady drizzle. Maybe he'd gone somewhere else. Out for a drink, by himself or with some of the other skaters from the tour.

Or maybe he'd gone looking for Lee.

I climbed under the covers with my cellphone, as if I were hiding what I was about to do even from myself. A quick search established that our showdown at the gala hadn't shown up on any major news sites yet, but Ellis had wasted no time writing a lengthy post for Kiss & Cry, complete with bystander video.

"Ice Queen Melts Down" read the headline, above a screen cap of me looking unhinged. Ellis's breathless firsthand account of the incident barely mentioned Heath, focusing instead on my fraught family history, and the "sudden, unprovoked" way I'd lashed out at Ellis himself.

I kept scrolling, down to the comments section.

> Kat Shaw is one crazy bitch! I don't know why Heath puts up with
> her tbh
> he's probably scared of her, she's had her claws in him since they
> were little kids u know
> Her poor brother . . . did anyone else watch that interview where he
> talked about how his dad loved Heath Rocha more than him? It
> seriously broke my heart.

Each word was like a fingernail digging under a scab, drawing fresh blood. When I finished all the comments on the gala post, I clicked back through the archives.

> realized who KS reminds me of: my ex, same sort of narcissistic
> drama-seeking missile
> she tries so hard to be sexy so no one will notice what a shitty
> skater she is
> someone should teach that cunt a lesson

I scrolled and scrolled, until my thumb hurt, until my eyes felt like sandpaper. When the door lock finally clicked open, I startled, dropping my phone on the bleached white duvet.

Heath was back.

CHAPTER 55

"Where have you been?" I demanded.

Heath shrugged. "Walking around." His suit was sopping wet, dripping onto the faux-wood flooring, and his hair was plastered to his skull.

"You're shivering." The same thing he'd said to me, before I snapped at him and told him to leave me alone, to stop trying to take care of me.

He must have walked the whole way from the park.

I led him into the bathroom and turned on the shower. While the water heated up, I took off his wet clothes—slowly and gently, nothing like the practiced passion we acted out on the ice.

Heath wouldn't look at me. He hung his head as I finished undressing him, cold droplets falling from his hair to sting my bare toes.

I took off my clothes too and joined him in the shower stall. With the steam curling around us, fogging the glass, I could almost pretend we were back by the lake, watching sea smoke roll in with the tide.

Then he pushed me against the wall, gripping my hips hard enough to bruise, and I wrapped my legs around his waist. My nails scraped his shoulders, making new marks on his back, and I thought: *finally*. After all those months of choreography, something real, some *heat* to drive away the cold wind that had stolen through the hairline cracks in our connection.

But we both felt the moment it shifted. When we slipped back into the performance, even though our only audience now was each other.

Heath pulled away. The water had begun to cool.

"I'm pretty tired," he said.

"Of course," I said. "We should get some rest."

I stepped out of the shower and knelt to gather my clothes.

We would be fine, I told myself. We were just stressed, after the season, after the tour, after the altercation with my brother. We needed some time to decompress, some time at home.

Except I had no idea where home was anymore. Since leaving The Heights after my post-injury idyll in 2006, I'd only seen my childhood house as a backdrop for Lee's media blitz—for the few seconds I could stand anyway, before I slammed the *off* button or threw the magazine down in disgust. We couldn't go back, not while he lived there.

For the past few years, Heath and I had stayed in a patchwork of hotels and short-term rentals spread across multiple continents. The Olympics were in less than a year, and we didn't have a coach or a guaranteed place to train. We didn't even have a permanent address.

The shower switched off. I picked up my phone to check the time—a few minutes after midnight, earlier than I'd assumed. But still late for anyone to call, and the screen showed multiple missed within a few minutes of one another, all from a New York number I didn't have saved in my contacts.

Lee, I thought. Probably drunk-dialing me from some dive bar, or whatever roach-infested hotel he'd found to hole up in. I hadn't given him my number, but Ellis could have.

The phone started to buzz again in my hand. Same number. I knew I should decline it, but I was so full of unspent energy, I almost *wanted* to argue with my brother.

I accepted the call.

"Kat."

It wasn't Lee after all. It was Ellis Dean. Not calling from his usual number, no doubt to trick me into answering.

"Fuck off, Ellis," I said, finger poised to hang up.

"Wait! I need—I have to tell you, before someone else—"

"Tell me what?"

Ellis sounded different than I'd ever heard him before—panicky, uncertain, desperate.

And one hundred percent sincere.

"I'm so sorry, Kat," Ellis said. "This is all my fault."

Video footage of a news report: "Last night," the anchorwoman says, "during a charity gala at the St. Regis Hotel in Manhattan, controversial figure skating star Katarina Shaw was seen arguing with her estranged older brother, Lee Shaw.

"A few short hours later, Lee Shaw was dead."

ELLIS DEAN: Lee was a troubled person.

The next morning, Katarina and Heath walk through the terminal at LaGuardia Airport, both wearing sunglasses. Reporters swarm them, shouting questions about Lee.

"Katarina, how are you holding up?"

"What happened between you and your brother, Katarina?"

"You don't seem that broken up, are you happy he's dead?"

At that last question, Katarina flinches, but she doesn't break her stride.

GARRETT LIN: Lee's death was a tragedy, but it wasn't her fault.

ELLIS DEAN: It wasn't anyone's fault. He was an addict. He overdosed.

INEZ ACTON: By all accounts, Kat's brother was an abusive piece of shit. Why did people expect her to be grief-stricken by his death?

FRANCESCA GASKELL: She did seem to move on awfully fast. But I guess we all grieve in our own ways, right? Besides, with the Olympics coming up, there was no time to waste.

Aerial stock footage of a snow-covered alpine mountain range.

JANE CURRER: In the summer of 2009, Katarina and Heath relocated to Germany, to train with Lena Müller, a former ladies champion who'd coached several Olympians during the 1990s.

Photographs of Müller, first from her competition days, then covering her coaching career. She's a stern woman with a strong jaw and a shock of white hair.

KIRK LOCKWOOD: I knew they were serious when they started working with Lena. She wasn't an ice dance specialist, but they didn't need help with their dance skills. They needed someone who was going to kick their asses every day and refuse to put up with any bullshit. That was Frau Müller. People didn't call her "The Valkyrie of Old Bavaria" for nothing!

GARRETT LIN: Müller's training center seemed like a good fit for them. Quiet, remote, no distractions. We didn't see Kat and Heath again until the Grand Prix Final, but the difference in their skating was clear. They seemed more focused. Not that they *totally* avoided controversy . . .

Practice footage of Katarina and Heath working on their free dance: they're both in striking red and black costumes, and Katarina wears a choker with beads that look like blood dripping from her throat. Their music is from the score of the 1992 film Bram Stoker's Dracula.

KIRK LOCKWOOD: The vampire program? It was memorable, I'll give 'em that.

JANE CURRER: For an exhibition, fine. But for the Olympic season?

ELLIS DEAN: I loved it, personally. What are the Olympic Games if not a giant theatrical production where the whole world pretends to get along for two weeks?

GARRETT LIN: The fans loved it—and the technical level was so high, even if the more old-school judges docked a few presentation points, Kat and Heath were still tough to beat.

At a ceremony following the 2010 U.S. National Championships in Spokane, Washington, Shaw/Rocha and Lin/Lin are named to the Olympic team. The bronze medalists, Frannie Gaskell and Evan Kovalenko, are relegated to the alternate spot again, in favor of more experienced skaters Tanya Fischer and Danny Chan, who finished in fourth place.

FRANCESCA GASKELL: I'm not gonna lie: we were disappointed. But those other teams—it was supposed to be their last-ever chance to go to the Games, you know?

KIRK LOCKWOOD: It had been years since the U.S. had legitimate ice dance medal hopes at the Olympics. Now we had two teams in serious contention. We had to capitalize on that.

A television spot for the 2010 Winter Olympics: "Shaw and Rocha. Lin and Lin. Two teams, but only one gold medal. Don't miss the ultimate showdown of America's ice dance superstars!"

GARRETT LIN: They made it look like we were about to go head-to-head in a boxing match.

ELLIS DEAN: Oh, the rivalry was *delicious*. I even made T-shirts: *Team Katarina* or *Team Bella*. The Bella ones sold the most, but I think some *Twilight* fans might've skewed the results.

GARRETT LIN: It made me uncomfortable. We had enough pressure from the Russians.

Flashing back to the medal ceremony at 2009 Worlds in Los Angeles, where Shaw and Rocha get the gold; Volkova and Kipriyanov, the silver; and Canadians Pelletier and McClory, the bronze.

VERONIKA VOLKOVA: Yelena came down with a terrible flu before that free dance.

Close-up of Yelena on the Worlds podium with glazed eyes and a sweat-sheened forehead.

VERONIKA VOLKOVA: She skated with a 101 degree fever, and *still* she and Dmitri only lost the gold by two points. Had she been healthy, they would have defeated the Americans.

KIRK LOCKWOOD: Pelletier and McClory were looking strong too. They'd just come off their fifth Canadian title, and with the Games in Vancouver, they had a hometown advantage. But there was zero doubt in my mind: Shaw and Rocha were the gold medal favorites.

VERONIKA VOLKOVA: Perhaps it was better for everyone to assume Shaw and Rocha would take the gold. After all, when you are on top, you have nowhere to go but down.

CHAPTER 56

All my life, the Olympic Games had been my dream—but those first few days in Vancouver, I felt like I was sleepwalking. We marched in the opening ceremony, sweating through our Ralph Lauren reindeer sweaters and ski pants, waving at the crowd until our arms were sore. We marveled at the simulated snowfall, the looming lit-up bear puppet, the flurry of fake maple leaves, the fireworks. We posed in front of the Olympic flag, the Olympic rings, the chain-link fence surrounding the frosted-glass Olympic cauldron, smiling in our matching Team USA clothing, Heath's arm tight around my waist.

I wanted to savor every moment. Instead, I stood outside myself, evaluating. Did I look happy? Did I look confident? Did I look like an Olympian? Did Heath and I look madly in love even though we hadn't slept together in months?

Our room in the Olympic Village had a pair of twin beds, but even on the king-sized mattress in the cozy private chalet we'd been renting in Germany, most nights we rolled to the outer edges like repelling magnets.

After so many years of performing intimacy for all the world to see, the fire between us had guttered out. And I had no idea how to reignite it.

No one watching our compulsory dance would have guessed at the growing distance between us, though. We took the lead with a passionate Tango Romantica, all sharp movements and snapping eye contact in time with the crisp snare drum beat under the bandoneon. Yelena Volkova's blade caught in a rut during their second pass through the pattern steps, and the Russians plummeted to third place behind the Canadians.

Bella and Garrett were in fourth, after leaving points on the table with a few minor mistakes. We'd steered clear of one another so far, preserving the narrative that we were bitter rivals battling it out to boost the ice dance broadcast ratings.

Despite the media frenzy, I knew the Lins didn't pose a serious threat. They hadn't beaten us all season. Bella was as ambitious as ever, but after their time skating with other people, the twins had never quite gelled as a team. If we lost the gold, it wouldn't be to them.

Bella and I had managed to steal a moment of solidarity at the opening ceremony, when we were sure no cameras were pointed at us: a quick squeeze of our gloved hands as the U.S. delegation started walking into the stadium, and a shared glance that said, *We really did it. We're really here.* For that one moment, I truly felt like an Olympian.

There was a day off between the compulsory and the original dance, and our publicist—a terrifyingly poised woman who'd exclusively represented movie stars and pop idols before adding Heath and me to her client roster—booked us on a morning show.

Morning on the East Coast, which meant a middle-of-the-night hair and makeup call out in Vancouver. Our coach didn't come with us; *I'm an old woman, I need my rest* was her excuse, though Lena Müller was probably the most vigorous person I'd ever met, at any age.

Kirk Lockwood was supposed to be interviewing us, but while we were getting primped and mic'd, a production assistant informed us that Kirk had felt a cold coming on and canceled all media appearances, in the hopes of recovering in time to call the rest of the skating events. When the substitute host approached to introduce herself, I thought she was another PA. She was young—maybe even younger than we were—with frizzy curls and thick-framed glasses.

"Inez Acton," she said. "I'm so excited to be chatting with you guys today!"

It was barely five a.m., and Inez sounded as if she'd already downed six espressos. As Heath and I settled on the love seat in the studio, her feet jiggled anxiously, heels pistoning in her plain black pumps.

The set was built to resemble an upscale ski lodge, with a fireplace and a mantel made of gray stones that would have reminded me of home if they weren't so spotless and uniform. A plexiglass wall behind the line of cameras looked out on the plaza where, even at this early hour, fans pressed behind the barricade to watch the taping.

Well, not all of them were fans: in the center of the crowd, I spotted a middle-aged white woman waving a poster board with a drawing of me sporting devil horns and a blood-soaked ice pick in my fist. Points for creativity, at least.

The producer counted us down. Heath waited until the last second before we went live to shift closer and slip his arm around my shoulders.

Inez started the interview, reading off a stack of note cards she held so tight, her knuckles turned white. She tripped over her words, punctuated her sentences with *ums* and *uhs,* and referred to the compulsory dance as the "compulsive" dance. The network seriously didn't have anyone more experienced to take over in Kirk's absence?

"You two got engaged at last year's National Championships, right?" she asked.

"That's right," Heath said.

"Let's see a picture."

Inez turned to look at a monitor, which displayed a photo of Heath kneeling on the ice in Cleveland. The crowd outside let out a long *awwww.* Right on cue, Heath squeezed my shoulder and smiled at me. I smiled back and felt nothing. It was only a reflex, muscles contracting to pull my face into a pleasing shape.

The monitor dissolved to another image of us: ten years old, on the beach by Lake Michigan. My father had taken the picture, with my mother's old Polaroid camera. It was only public because Lee had handed our family photos over to the press without my consent.

"So cute!" Inez exclaimed. "From childhood sweethearts to possible Olympic champions. You two are serious couple goals. When's the big day?"

"The big day?" I repeated.

Inez gave a nervous giggle. "Your wedding! Have you picked out a dress yet? I know everyone's dying to see what you choose."

Our wedding was just some stupid party. February 22, the day of the Olympic ice dance final—*that* was our big day.

"Not yet," Heath answered when I failed to. "We've been focusing on the Games. Once that's over, I'm sure we'll have more to share."

"What about after the Games?" Inez asked. "Will you be taking time off from skating to start a family?"

Heath's smile turned coy. "We'll have to see about—"

"What the hell kind of question is that?"

Katarina Shaw and Heath Rocha are interviewed by rookie NBC correspondent Inez Acton at the 2010 Winter Olympics. As the subject turns to their romantic relationship, Katarina is visibly rankled. Finally, she can't take it anymore.

"What the hell kind of question is that?" she snaps.

Inez pales. The studio audience gasps.

INEZ ACTON: That was my first-ever on-air interview. And my last.

"I'm an Olympic athlete," Katarina continues, "and all you want to ask about is my wedding dress and when I'm going to start popping out babies?"

"I'm—" Inez fumbles with her notecards. "I'm sorry, I—"

KIRK LOCKWOOD: I watched the whole thing live back in my hotel room. If I hadn't been on strict vocal rest, I would've been screaming at the television.

FRANCESCA GASKELL: Okay, the questions were a little on the personal side. But Kat didn't have to go off like that. I felt so bad for the poor reporter!

"I don't even want kids," Katarina says. Heath stiffens, fingers digging into the American flag patch on the sleeve of Katarina's jacket. "Not that it's any of your business."

INEZ ACTON: Olympic athletes, female ones especially, are expected to follow a certain script. To be respectful and humble and *so* grateful to be representing their countries.

"I'm not some pretty little ice princess or blushing bride." Katarina leans forward—away from Heath, who still hasn't said a word. "And I don't want to be. I want to win."

INEZ ACTON: Kat Shaw shredded that script and set it on fire. I looked at her and thought: that's the kind of woman I wish I could be. I know I wasn't the only one.

CHAPTER 57

After the interview, Heath and I had less than two hours before our morning practice session. Not enough time to go back to sleep but, as it turned out, plenty of time to argue.

"Well." I sat on my bed. The flimsy metal frame screeched in protest. "That was—"

"You don't want kids?" Heath said.

I laughed. The wrong response, but I couldn't believe *that* had been his takeaway from our train wreck of a TV appearance.

"You *do* want kids?" I asked.

Heath frowned and turned toward the windows. The shades were still pulled down since we'd left so early, but slivers of sunrise wrapped around the edges.

"I don't know," he said. "It just seems like something we should have discussed privately before you announced it on live television."

I hadn't thought we needed to discuss it. Heath knew me better than anyone, so he should have known there wasn't a single maternal thing about me.

We had discussed moving back to Illinois; Lee's death meant the house was wholly mine, and we had the funds to fix it up however we wanted. I'd imagined hanging our gold medals above the parlor fireplace. I'd imagined gutting Lee's toxic waste dump of a room and turning it into a state-of-the-art home gym. I hadn't imagined anyone there apart from the two of us—and definitely not a squalling infant.

Heath sunk onto the other bed, head in his hands. "I don't know if I can do this anymore."

"It's just a few more days."

"A few more days, and then the next competition, and the next and the next. Where does it end, Katarina?"

"If this is about the wedding," I said, "then—"

"I don't care about the wedding!" Heath stood up again and started pacing. "We could elope today, for all I care. I just want to know we're going to be together forever, even after . . ."

He didn't finish his sentence, but we both knew where it was headed: after I no longer needed him as a skating partner.

"I love you," I said. "You know that."

"You're so good at pretending now. It's hard for me to—"

I shot to my feet too. "You think I'm *pretending* to love you?"

"That's not what I said."

"Which is it, Heath? I'm too fake, or I'm too honest? Cause I told the truth in that interview, and you didn't like that either."

"The problem is that I can't tell the difference anymore. Can you, Katarina?"

There was a glint of pity in his eyes. I preferred the contempt.

"When Lee died, you didn't cry," Heath continued. "You wouldn't even talk about it."

"You of all people should understand why I wasn't especially devastated by his death."

You're not my family, Lee. You're nothing to me. I used to wish you'd died instead of our father, but now I'm glad he's not alive to see you like this.

Thank God none of the videos from the gala had picked up what I'd said to Lee in our final moments together. Even without that damning evidence, there were plenty of people convinced I was a coldhearted bitch with my poor brother's blood on my hands.

Heath had been the first to assure me that it wasn't my fault. So how could I tell him that when I found out about Lee's untimely demise, *my* first thought was to wonder where Heath had gone for all those hours after the gala?

When we learned Lee had died of a drug overdose, with no signs of foul play, I was relieved—and sad, and furious with myself for mourning someone who'd given me only misery, and guilt-ridden over my knee-jerk suspicion of the man I loved. My feelings were too unwieldy to contain, too dangerous to express.

So I packed them away and shoved them into a dark corner inside myself, one more thing I could deal with after I became the Olympic champion.

"Let me in, Katarina." Heath touched my face, tender now. "That's all I want."

Let me in? I didn't know whether to laugh or scream at him. Lee's death was the *least* of the things we didn't talk about. Why should I be the one to open up and make myself vulnerable, when Heath's past was still a sealed vault?

We were less than seventy-two hours from victory. I couldn't lose control. I thought back to that night when we were sixteen, when I climbed through his bedroom window.

Convince him. That I could do. The rest we could figure out later.

I kissed him, hard. He kissed me back harder. I pulled his hair, he pulled me down to the floor. Every second of contact felt like a dare, a challenge, a step closer to the edge of oblivion. We were punishing each other, telling ourselves it was passion.

It frightened me, but I was more frightened of what might happen if we tried to have this conversation with words instead of our bodies. We might burn down to ash. We might explode.

By the time it was over, when we lay sweat-soaked and scraped raw in the narrow space between our beds, bright morning sunbeams stabbing through the shades because we'd blown right past the start time of our practice session—I don't know if I'd convinced Heath of anything.

But somehow I convinced myself that I had won.

INEZ ACTON: Everyone was talking about the interview.

ELLIS DEAN: It wasn't just Kat going full Bad Bitch Mode. It was also the way Heath looked at her—and the way she *didn't* look at him. They let the mask slip for a second.

KIRK LOCKWOOD: Whatever was going on behind closed doors, they didn't bring it onto the ice during the original dance. That program shut everyone's mouths.

JANE CURRER: The required rhythm for the original that season was folk dance. The International Skating Union assumed most teams would choose traditional dances from their own countries, to celebrate their culture on the Olympic stage.

INEZ ACTON: As you might expect in such a blindingly white sport, it turned into a carnival of cultural appropriation.

ELLIS DEAN: There were Hungarians dancing the hula and Brits doing bhangra and Germans in geisha getups. This was in the Year of Our Lord 2010!

INEZ ACTON: You could not get away with this shit today. At least, I fucking hope not. Amazingly, though, the U.S. couples all managed to choose relatively inoffensive themes.

GARRETT LIN: Bella and I did a modern take on a Chinese sword dance. It was the first time we'd ever performed something inspired by our heritage. We even spent a few weeks working with a *jian wu* master in Tianjin. I loved that program, but it was more avant-garde than our usual style. The judges didn't get it.

ELLIS DEAN: Fischer and Chan did a country-western line dance, complete with cowboy hats and bedazzled gingham. Let's just say it did *not* make me proud to be an American.

Katarina Shaw and Heath Rocha take the ice for the original dance event at the 2010 Winter Olympics in Vancouver. She wears a black dress with a sequin-covered tartan sash. He wears a shirt with a lace-up collar and, instead of trousers, a pleated leather kilt. Their music begins with a blast of accordion and fiddle: the traditional Scottish social dance tune "Strip the Willow."

KIRK LOCKWOOD: The Scottish ceilidh style made perfect use of their strengths. It was energetic, technically challenging, but also full of attitude.

Katarina and Heath perform an intricate step sequence with multiple changes of direction as they speed from one side of the rink to the other. The music transitions to a driving punk rock cover of the same song. They clasp hands and swing each other in a circle, the hem of Heath's kilt flaring out to show the skintight shorts he's wearing underneath.

ELLIS DEAN: Don't get me wrong, it was a ton of fun. I'm just disappointed Heath didn't *fully* embrace his inner Scotsman, if you know what I mean.

FRANCESCA GASKELL: That program was infectious. You wanted to get up and dance right along with them.

As they launch into a gravity-defying combination, the camera zooms out to show the crowd in the Pacific Coliseum. They're up on their feet, clapping along with the beat.

KIRK LOCKWOOD: All Shaw and Rocha had to do was hold on to their lead from the compulsory dance, and they'd be in the ideal position going into the free.

Instead of losing steam toward the end of their program, Katarina and Heath seem to be building momentum. The final note plays, and they raise their arms in triumph.

FRANCESCA GASKELL: They didn't just hold on to the lead. They increased it.

KIRK LOCKWOOD: After the original dance, Volkova and Kipriyanov were a distant second, and the Lins were basically tied with Pelletier and McClory for third.

Heath lowers his arms after a second, but Katarina keeps hers up as she soaks in the adulation of the crowd. She lifts her chin, looking supremely confident—or cocky.

FRANCESCA GASKELL: The gold medal was theirs to lose.

CHAPTER 58

"Skate well. Do not embarrass me."

This was what passed for a pep talk from our extremely German coach.

Lena gave us each a bracing slap on the shoulder and left us to finish our warm-up routine alone. The free dance was late in the evening; we would be the final team to skate, so we had plenty of time to prepare. As the lowest-ranked group took the ice, I moved through my usual flow of stretches, breathing into the lingering soreness in my legs and hips.

During the original dance the day before, my inner thighs had ached as if they were bruised—but apparently I'd hidden it well enough to score a season's best and leave the Russians in the dust. Now four minutes of skating stood between me and everything I'd ever wanted, and I was sure nothing could shake my focus.

After stretching, we went to the dressing rooms to get into costume. I applied my makeup—pale foundation contoured to emphasize my cheekbones, bloodred lips, dark sweeping eyeshadow with a crimson haze at the edges—and put on my dress. I needed Heath's help to fasten the choker that set off the sweetheart neckline, so I carried it out with me, closed in my hand to protect the delicate beading.

The necklace was a custom piece, designed to look like a slash across my throat with a few drops of blood dangling from my jugular. Though we were using music from *Dracula*, the story our program conveyed was nothing like the literary classic. I was the ancient, powerful vampire, and Heath was the young man caught in my thrall. For most of the choreography, I was the aggressor: seducing him, tormenting him, and finally tempting him to taste my blood so we could be together for all eternity.

Heath's costume and makeup were far simpler—trousers and a tailcoat with red lining, a faint smudge of gray around his eyes to make him look sleepless and ashen—so usually by the time I finished getting ready, he was waiting for me. When I emerged from the dressing room, though, there was no sign of him.

I wandered the backstage area, worrying the red beads between my fingers. Every person I passed—skaters, coaches, staff—seemed to make a point of not looking directly at me. Genevieve Moreau, who'd skated in the first group, did glance my way, but quickly averted her gaze, whispering something to the Czech girl beside her.

Were people seriously *still* talking about the damn interview? Well, soon Heath and I would be Olympic champions, and they could talk about *that*.

Bella walked out of the ladies' restroom. Her makeup was done, but she was in her warm-up clothes, hair only half styled. She had time still, but considerably less than Heath and I did, since she and Garrett were earlier in the order.

When she saw me, her steps quickened.

"Hey," I said. "Have you seen Heath?"

"No. Not since—"

I held out the choker. "Can you help me with this, then? The clasp is tricky, but if you—"

"Kat, I have to tell you something."

Bella's eyes darted back and forth, and she pressed her cellphone to her chest. She looked anxious. Bella Lin never looked anxious. Certainly not backstage at an event where all the other competitors could see her.

"What is it?" I asked.

"I'm sorry." Bella held up her phone. "But you need to see this."

CHAPTER 59

Bella's phone screen showed a Kiss & Cry post with a picture of Heath at the top—not a recent photo, but one from years before, when his hair was buzzed short. The way he looked when he reappeared in my life after his three-year absence.

I took the phone and scrolled down to the article below the image. No matter how many times I read the words, my mind refused to make sense of them.

"No." I shook my head and handed the phone back. "This isn't true."

"I didn't want to believe it either. But—"

"It's not true." I kept shaking my head. Back and forth, back and forth. A flag whipping in the wind, unable to settle until the storm passed. "There's no way."

I caught a flicker of red in my peripheral vision: Heath, jogging around the corner, jacket flaring behind him.

He'd seen those outrageous lies too, and he was coming to reassure me of what I already knew: none of it was true, because if it was, he would have told me.

He'd had so many chances to tell me.

Looking out over the canyon in Los Angeles, when I first asked what happened to him during his time away. All those months alone in Illinois. The years we'd spent together since, skating and sleeping side by side, partners in every possible way.

Heath would clear up this misunderstanding, and we would win the gold, and later we'd laugh about this. I knew it, like I knew him.

Then I saw the look on his face, and I realized: I didn't know Heath Rocha at all.

"Katarina," he said. "Let me explain."

"No." I turned away. The choker fell out of my hand. I heard Heath pick it up, the scrape of beads on the floor. His footsteps following me as I fled down the hall. "No."

The article claimed that after Heath left me in Nagano, he traveled to Moscow and begged Veronika Volkova to coach him. He was willing to do anything.

Anything. Enduring training methods so harsh they left him bleeding. Skating with Yelena Volkova, pursuing Russian citizenship so he could officially become her partner after Nikita Zolotov's retirement. And worst of all, telling the Russians everything he knew about me, about the Lins, about the Ice Academy, so they could use it to beat us.

Training with our competitors, I could understand. We'd spent years sharing the ice with sworn rivals—including each other. But to actually *conspire* with the Volkovas—to share my secrets, my weaknesses, my insecurities? To take the years of history and trust we'd shared and trade them as currency? That was true betrayal.

"I should have told you," Heath said. "I know I should have told you, but don't you see what's happening here? This was released *today,* right before the final. Whoever did this, they're trying to turn us against each other. We can't let them."

He took my hands, the choker pressed between our palms like a rosary.

"Please, Katarina. You have to know it was all for you. I did it all for you, to—" He blinked back tears, but it was too late, his eye makeup was already blurring. "Please. I love you. I never stopped loving you, not for one second."

Heath had been hurt. He'd been desperate. In his own twisted way, he'd done it all out of love. I could have forgiven him for that.

What I couldn't forgive was how he'd allowed his secrets to fester, so they could be used against him—against *us*—at the worst possible time. He kept begging me to let him in, to open up and be honest, and all the while he'd kept me locked in the dark for years. Heath had *always* kept me in the dark. It was one thing when we were young, when he was a traumatized little boy who lacked the words to express what had happened to him. But we weren't children anymore.

"I can't deal with this now." I pulled away from him, snatching the choker too. My fingers trembled, but after a few tries I managed to clasp it myself. "We can talk about it later."

"Katarina, you can't just—"

I was already walking away. We were minutes from the introduction of the final group. We had to focus. We had to win.

I don't remember lacing up my skates or removing my blade guards or stepping onto the ice. I don't remember the group warm-up or the waiting period that followed as the other teams performed their programs. I don't even remember skating out for the start of our free dance. In my memory of that night, I'm walking away from Heath, and the next second I'm skating with him in the Olympic final.

One thing I can't forget, though: how fucking furious I was.

ELLIS DEAN: A journalist never reveals his sources.

KIRK LOCKWOOD: No way was I going to discuss claims from some two-bit gossip blog on the air. Not until the network fact-checkers confirmed the allegations.

In the stands prior to Shaw and Rocha taking the ice, spectators stare at their phone screens and share whispered conversations about the shocking contents of the blog post.

KIRK LOCKWOOD: Not that it made any difference. Back in my day, you had to wait for the evening news or the morning papers. Now everyone has breaking headlines in their pockets.

FRANCESCA GASKELL: Kiss & Cry could be entertaining, but it could also do real damage. Ellis Dean didn't seem to care either way, as long as he made money.

ELLIS DEAN: If I posted something that wasn't true, by all means correct me. I'll wait.

VERONIKA VOLKOVA: I had nothing to do with it. As I said at the time.

Backstage before Volkova and Kipriyanov's free dance, Yelena and Veronika Volkova argue in hushed, rapid-fire Russian.

PRODUCER (Offscreen): Did your argument with Yelena have anything to do with—

VERONIKA VOLKOVA: I cannot recall.

Tears stream down Yelena's face, and she points an accusing finger at her aunt. Subtitles translate the few words the backstage mics picked up clearly: "—your fault. You lied to me!"

VERONIKA VOLKOVA: Yelena could be quite sensitive. She gets it from my sister.

ELLIS DEAN: There was clearly more to the story. A *lot* more.

VERONIKA VOLKOVA: It is ridiculous. The very idea of I, or anyone else, tearing Katarina Shaw and Heath Rocha apart. No, that they could only do to themselves.

CHAPTER 60

At first, I convinced myself I was just getting into character.

As sepulchral strings echoed over the sound system, I slithered around Heath, clutching at his costume like I could tear him apart with my bare hands. I was a creature of the night. I wanted to bend him to my will. I wouldn't stop until I'd consumed him, body and soul.

Our opening twizzle sequence hit on a crescendo of choral wailing, and we whipped around in unison, left legs extended straight out, slicing the air like swords. The closer you spin, the higher the level of difficulty, and we were so close my toe pick snagged Heath's tailcoat.

A brief bobble, but he saved it, throwing himself into our next dance hold like he couldn't decide whether he wanted to rip my clothes off or wring my neck. He was furious too.

Good, I thought. We could use it—channel our rage, our love, our hate, our lifetime of simmering resentments and jealousies and secrets, spill it all out onto the ice and leave it there.

So when he spun me so hard I heard my spine crack, and I dug my nails in under his jaw until I left marks, I told myself this was what it took to be a champion. You had to be willing to inflict pain and to take it, to sacrifice everything on the altar of your ambition.

Only when it was over did I realize what we'd done.

Our performance had been unhinged—all passion, no precision. I wasn't even certain we'd completed all the required elements. Heath and I hadn't competed together during that skate, we'd warred against each other. With the whole world watching.

In our final position, he held me in his arms, dipped so low my hair brushed the ice, and buried his face in my neck as if he were drinking my blood. At every other competition, applause had roared in our ears while he pressed a soft kiss below my earlobe before setting me back on my feet so we could take our bows.

On February 22, 2010, there were over fifteen thousand people in the Pacific Coliseum, and we heard nothing but silence. Then, finally, a smattering of tepid, uncomfortable applause.

I couldn't stand it a second longer. The pressure of Heath's hand on the back of my neck. His breath on my skin. All those eyes staring at us, wondering what the hell they'd witnessed.

So I scrambled upright and shoved him away from me. He was still gripping my neck, fingers tangled in my hair, caught in the clasp of the choker.

Red beads scattered over the Olympic rings. I had a momentary manic urge to bend down and try to gather them up—perhaps the only way I could've made the situation more humiliating.

Instead I left the broken necklace behind, and we skated off without bowing.

Lena waited at the boards. "What was that?" she demanded, her thick German accent turning the question even more severe.

I said nothing. Heath said nothing. What could we say? Four minutes before, we had been the gold medal favorites. Now we had almost certainly fallen the whole way off the podium.

Lena stalked away, letting out a stream of what I could only assume were German expletives. She refused to join us in the kiss and cry, and I didn't blame her. I had no desire to see our scores either. Until the numbers appeared, I could pretend this was all a bad dream, and I was about to wake up in my uncomfortable Olympic Village bed with a chance to do it over.

Heath and I sat on opposite ends of the kiss and cry bench. I hadn't bothered to put my Team USA jacket back on, so sweat chilled my bare arms. I grit my teeth to keep from shivering. Heath stared at the floor. A few feet away, Veronika Volkova stood with Yelena and Dmitri, waiting to see what color their medal would be.

"The scores, please, for Katarina Shaw and Heath Rocha of the United States of America."

GARRETT LIN: Their free dance was a bit . . . intense.

KIRK LOCKWOOD: It was unforgettable, that's for sure.

ELLIS DEAN: It looked like they were trying to kill each other.

The empty podium sits in the center of the ice at the Pacific Coliseum, awaiting the ice dance medal ceremony at the 2010 Winter Olympics in Vancouver.

GARRETT LIN: Everyone goes to the Olympics dreaming of a gold medal, but you have to be realistic. There can only be one winner.

KIRK LOCKWOOD: Shaw and Rocha had such a big lead coming into the free, and they'd been skating so flawlessly all season, anyone would've thought they had it in the bag.

Over the loudspeakers, an announcement, first in French and then in English: "Bronze medalists, representing the United States of America . . ."

KIRK LOCKWOOD: But that's why we love this crazy sport, right?

"Katarina Shaw and Heath Rocha!" Their free dance program music plays as they skate out. They mount the lowest platform of the podium, without touching or looking at each other.

VERONIKA VOLKOVA: After that free dance, it was a travesty for Shaw and Rocha to stand on any step of the podium.

FRANCESCA GASKELL: Do *I* think they deserved a medal? Well, that's not for me to say, is it? That's why we have officials.

VERONIKA VOLKOVA: Worse still, their dramatics distracted other athletes from skating their best that day.

The announcer introduces the silver medalists: "Representing the Russian Federation, Yelena Volkova and Dmitri Kipriyanov!" Yelena looks miserable, her eyes and nose red from crying.

GARRETT LIN: No one could have predicted it would turn out the way it did.

"Gold medalists," the announcer says, but the names of the winning skaters are drowned out by wild cheering.

GARRETT LIN: Bella and I . . . well, we were both stunned. The whole thing felt surreal.

Canadians Olivia Pelletier and Paul McClory skate out to greet their adoring hometown crowd. Thanks to stumbles by the Americans and the Russians, they pulled off a surprise upset and clinched the gold.

GARRETT LIN: We stayed in fourth. Less than a point between our total score and Kat and Heath's. Between us and the Olympic podium.

Katarina and Heath receive their bronze medals and bouquets. Katarina positions her flowers over the medal, like she doesn't want anyone to see it.

JANE CURRER: You would have thought someone died, from the looks on their faces. Most athletes would be thrilled to win an Olympic medal, no matter the color.

KIRK LOCKWOOD: Sure, Shaw and Rocha could've been more gracious.

JANE CURRER: Frankly, bronze was better than they deserved. The only reason they made it onto the podium at all was their stellar scores from the first two events.

Katarina and Heath stare straight ahead as the Canadian, Russian, and American flags rise.

KIRK LOCKWOOD: You can't understand what it's like, unless you've been there. Metaphorically speaking—obviously *I've* never been on the bronze medal step at the Olympics.

GARRETT LIN: When expectations are that high? Anything but the best feels like failure.

CHAPTER 61

The last thing I felt like doing that night was celebrating.

But we returned to the Olympic Village to find a party already in progress. The U.S. women's hockey team had trounced Sweden in the semifinals, and they seemed to have invited half the athletes at the Games to toast their victory.

Heath and I pushed through the crush of muscular women in red, white, and blue to reach our room. Not for the first time, I wished we'd booked off-site housing like the Lins; they were staying at a hotel on the waterfront, several kilometers removed from the chaos of the Games.

Though the official athlete accommodations were far from luxurious, they did offer one major perk: members of the press were banned from the premises. I couldn't face another question about *what went wrong* or *how I was feeling*.

I was feeling like shit. Like a complete failure. Like my entire life had been a waste and now, at the age of twenty-six, it was over.

Heath took his medal off and lay it gently on the nightstand. I kept mine on. The blue ribbon hung like a noose around my neck.

"Can we talk?" he said.

The flowers they'd given us on the podium were hideous, green and leafy like a bouquet of salad. I tore at the petals, scattering them on the industrial gray carpet.

When I didn't respond, Heath continued. "I should have told you. I wanted to, so many times, but—"

"No, you should have fucking *talked* to me instead of running away in the first place!"

I thrashed the bouquet against the wall. Heath flinched.

"And how dare you claim you did it all for me," I said. "I never asked you to."

"All you care about is winning." Heath spoke calmly, evenly, like he was trying to gentle a wild animal. "So I turned myself into someone who could win. Someone worthy of you. But I guess that wasn't enough either. Nothing's ever enough for you."

"That's really what you think of me?"

"That's who you've always been, Katarina. And I've always loved you anyway."

There was no anger in his voice. No thorn of cruelty. Only exhaustion and resignation.

Somehow that made it hurt more.

"Sorry it's been such a hardship for you." My voice was solid ice.

Finally, his temper flared. "This is exactly what I'm talking about! I tell you I love you, and you throw it back in my face. I suffer for *years* to get back to you, and—"

"You wanted to get back *at* me. You wanted me to suffer too. That's not love, Heath."

"My love isn't good enough for you either. Got it."

"That's not what I meant, and you know it."

"Then tell me, Katarina." He sunk to his knees in front of me. "Tell me what you want from me. Tell me what to do, and I'll do it."

Despite the contrite posture, his expression was defiant. I buried my hands in his curls.

"There's nothing you can do," I told him.

Heath started to rise. I seized his hair at the roots and held him there. He reached for the medal around my neck, trying to pull me down with him.

So I ripped off the medal and threw it to the floor. Then I tore my engagement ring off too. The diamond bounced off the bronze, ricocheting into the shadows under the bed.

This time when I stormed away, Heath didn't follow.

Out in the common area, I picked up the first bottle I found and chugged straight from the neck. One of the hockey players, a ruddy brunette with braided pigtails, let out a long whistle.

"Rough day, Ice Queen?"

I wiped my mouth, smearing the remains of my lipstick. "Don't fucking call me that."

CHAPTER 62

The next hour passed in a blur. I gulped down plastic cups of Molson while grinding to Lady Gaga songs until I was simply one more sweaty body moving to the music.

Most of my life, I'd been working toward a single goal: winning gold at the Olympics. That was the bright light that guided my every move, my every decision. Now? Everything had gone dark. I couldn't picture my future. Allowing myself to think even as far ahead as dawn sent dread surging around me like murky floodwater.

If I stopped dancing, I feared I'd drown.

Around midnight, the Lins showed up. Garrett scanned the crowd, looking for someone. Bella zeroed right in on me.

"What are you doing?" she shouted over the bobsledders belting out "Bad Romance."

"What are *you* doing?" I shot back. "Thought you were staying at that fancy hotel so you wouldn't have to mix with the common folk."

"We were invited," Garrett said. "Are you okay, Kat?"

I know how I must have looked: hair plastered to my neck, breath reeking of cheap beer, stripped down to my sports bra to dance with strangers. And Heath nowhere to be found.

"I thought alcohol wasn't allowed in the Village," Bella said.

Technically, she was right; the U.S. delegation had rules against alcohol consumption. But other countries weren't as strict, and for a bunch of adrenaline-junkie high-performance athletes, rules were more like suggestions. The party hadn't devolved into the orgiastic bacchanal I'd heard rumors of from past Olympics, but as the night wore on, it turned wilder. The darkest corners were full of people making out up against walls or balanced on the edges of furniture, and I'd noticed quite a few couples—and bigger groups—disappearing behind closed doors.

"You wanna go eat some carbs?" Bella offered. "I heard about this place with incredible poutine, over by—"

"Oh, *now* you're concerned about my well-being." I rolled my eyes and took another drink of room-temperature lager.

"What's that supposed to mean?"

"Why did you show me that article?"

She rocked back on her heels. "What?"

"Why did you show it to me," I repeated, "right before we skated?"

Bella glanced at her brother, but he was preoccupied, peering out over the sea of faces.

"I thought you needed to know," Bella said.

"You could have waited until afterward."

"Everyone was talking. It was only a matter of time before you found out, and I figured you'd rather hear the news from your best friend than from—"

I laughed. "My *best friend*? We've barely spoken in years, Bella."

I knew how nasty I sounded. I saw the way she shrunk from me. I didn't care.

Garrett was watching us now, too—gauging whether he needed to get involved or if he could stand back and stay neutral.

"You didn't have a chance in hell of getting on that podium," I said, "unless you found a way to knock me down. Well, guess what, it still wasn't enough."

Bella's eyes sparked with anger. "If you'd *really* wanted to win, that story wouldn't have stopped you. Nothing would have stopped you."

As far as I was concerned, that was a confession. I wasn't even surprised. Our friendship had been real once, but I always knew it could only go so far where competition was concerned.

"I need a drink," Bella muttered. "Come on, Garrett."

"In a minute," he said. She stalked off without him.

"Can you believe her?" I said. "She purposely messes with my head before the biggest competition of my life, then has the audacity to act like—"

"You won an Olympic medal today. You know that, right?"

I blinked at Garrett, caught off guard by the harsh edge in his voice. He'd never spoken to me that way before. I'd never heard him speak to *anyone* that way.

"And yeah, okay, Heath did some screwed-up things. But he loves you so much. The way you two torture each other, it's . . ." Garrett trailed off with an exasperated shake of his head. "Do you know what I'd give for even a *taste* of what you've got together?"

I threw my hands up, sloshing what was left of my beer onto the floor. "Oh my god, Garrett, *no one cares* that you're gay!"

A few of the partygoers closest to us turned to stare. Garrett glanced back and forth, panic building behind his eyes.

"Shit." I set the cup down and reached toward him. "I'm sorry, I didn't mean t—"

"Of course you didn't mean to, Kat. That would require thinking about someone other than yourself for one goddamn second."

He turned his back on me and walked away, in the same direction Bella had gone.

Garrett's words sobered me up like a splash of cold water. The loud music, the cacophony of voices, the stench of spilled beer and smashed-together bodies—it was all too much.

I retrieved my sweatshirt—at least I hoped it was mine, they were all identical, team uniforms meant to make us feel united, patriotic, like something bigger and more important than ourselves—and stepped out onto the patio.

The night air was cool and brisk, a steady breeze blowing across the False Creek inlet. The American athlete housing was near the top of the building, so we had panoramic views of downtown Vancouver and the mountain ranges beyond. The North Shore Mountains. How strange that they had the same name as the area where Heath and I grew up, where we first skated together. That night, as I stared out at the hulking peaks blending into the blackness beyond the city skyline, I'd never felt farther from home.

The door opened, and out stepped Ellis Dean. He certainly had a talent for showing up at the worst possible moment.

"Well, if it isn't 2010 Olympic bronze medalist Katarina Shaw."

"I'm not in the mood, Ellis."

He strolled past me to lean against the railing enclosing the patio. He'd dressed in accordance with the red, white, and blue theme, except Ellis's idea of patriotic attire involved stripes of faux fur that looked like he'd skinned several Muppets.

"If it's any consolation," he said, "that performance will certainly be remembered forever. Maybe not for the reasons you wanted, but—"

"How did you get in here anyway? Press isn't allowed in the Village."

"Technically, I'm a former Olympian." He clocked my bare ring finger. "Don't tell me you crazy kids called it quits."

Had we? I wasn't sure.

"For what it's worth," Ellis said, "and I know it's not worth much: I genuinely thought you knew already. Don't you and lover boy tell each other everything?"

"Apparently not. So who the hell told *you* all that stuff?"

"A journalist never reveals his—"

"Cut the crap, Ellis. You're a gossip blogger, not an investigative reporter for *The New York* fucking *Times*."

I gripped the railing next to Ellis, cold metal searing my skin. Despite the late hour, the square below the building still teemed with people. Laughing, celebrating, walking close so their shoulders touched.

Ultimately, it didn't matter who had discovered Heath's secrets, or how, or when. He still hadn't chosen to confide in me. And now I'd lost him and the gold, in the same damn day.

No, not lost him. Thrown him away.

"It's not supposed to feel like this, is it?" I wasn't sure whether I was talking about skating, or the Olympics, or my relationship with Heath. "It's not supposed to hurt this much."

"You're a skater," Ellis quipped. "You love pain." He shifted to face me, suddenly serious. "You want my advice?"

"Not especially."

"Too bad, you're getting it." He laid his hand over mine. "Don't let

Heath disappear on you again. Not without at least trying to work things out. You two are a total disaster, but anyone can see how crazy you are about each other."

"Thanks, Ellis. That was almost sweet."

He turned away. Moment over. "Oh no, I meant *literally crazy*. You and Heath Rocha deserve each other. Maybe at your wedding you can rock matching straitjackets."

I rolled my eyes and laughed.

"Time to mix and mingle," Ellis announced. He offered me his arm, like he had all those years ago at Sheila Lin's Red, White, and Gold Party.

"I'll see you in there," I said.

I stayed on the patio alone for a while, savoring the fresh air on my skin. Much as I hated to admit it, Ellis was right: Heath and I drove each other crazy sometimes, but I hated to imagine any version of my future that didn't somehow include him. I couldn't let him go without at least telling him so.

Back inside, the party had settled into a mellower rhythm, though there were still plenty of people entwined on the furniture scattered around the common area. Including Garrett.

He was fully horizontal on one of the sofas, having a feverish make-out session with Scott Stanton, a men's singles skater who'd been on the Stars on Ice tour with us—and had seemed remarkably indifferent to the gaggles of female fans who crowded around him after every show. I still felt awful about blurting out Garrett's secret earlier, but it looked as if the closet door was blown off the hinges now. Good for him.

When I reached my room, I eased open the door as silently as possible, in case Heath was sleeping. The lights were out, but he'd left the window shades open, so I could just make out the shape of him under the comforter. The spot where I'd flung the flowers was bare; Heath must have cleaned them up. He'd picked up my medal and ring too, placing them on the nightstand.

I was trying to decide between getting into my own bed or breaking the ice by sliding under the covers with him when I heard them.

Heath was in bed all right. But he wasn't alone.

A jerky, low-resolution cellphone video taken by another athlete at the Olympic Village party shows Katarina Shaw rushing past.

GARRETT LIN: Kat was upset. Who wouldn't be?

Heath Rocha follows, half-dressed, trying to pull his shirt on as he hurries after her. A few steps behind him comes Bella Lin, also frantically tugging her clothing back into place.

Heath says something to Katarina, inaudible on the recording, and she screams at him.

ELLIS DEAN: She lost her *shit*. She threw a freaking chair at his head.

GARRETT LIN: No, Kat did not throw a chair.

A dark object blurs past, colliding with Heath. In the background, a voice says, "Oh shit*!"*

GARRETT LIN: It was a stool. A small one. At least I think so. I was a little . . . distracted.

ELLIS DEAN: I stayed out of the way. I'd learned my lesson at the gala.

Katarina and Heath stand in the middle of the common area, shouting at each other. With the buzz of other voices and music in the background, their words are unintelligible, but they appear on the verge of coming to blows.

JANE CURRER: I'm not aware of any incident, but violence or other inappropriate behavior between Team USA athletes would of course be dealt with swiftly.

Katarina turns on Bella. Heath steps between them—which seems to enrage both women.

GARRETT LIN: I wish I could say that was totally unlike my sister. But I know her too well. On the ice or off, she'd do anything to win.

ELLIS DEAN: If they gave out gold medals for revenge, Bella Lin and Heath Rocha would've been undisputed champions that night.

Heath takes a step closer to Katarina. She shoves him away, raking her nails across the bare skin above his half-fastened shirt.

GARRETT LIN: Maybe I should have done something. But I was so tired of always being the peacemaker, the reasonable one. I figured they'd work it out themselves.

"Fuck both of you," Katarina says, loud enough to spike above the background noise. "We're done." She storms out, slamming the door behind her.

GARRETT LIN: That was the last time any of us saw Kat Shaw for years.

CHAPTER 63

I didn't see them together. Not really. The lights were out. As soon as they realized I'd caught them, they stopped. As soon as I realized what they'd been doing, I ran.

But my imagination was all too willing to fill in the gaps. Every time I so much as blinked, I saw them: Bella straddling Heath, the dark fall of hair down her bare back. Heath's hands on her slender waist, drawing her closer, closer, closer.

The next thing I knew, I was outside. Running across the square, tears burning in my eyes, throat raw from screaming. I couldn't remember anything I'd said, except my final words, meant for both my fiancé and my friend: *we're done.*

I had no idea where I was headed. Just: *away.* I didn't have a coat, cash, ID, anything. Not even my athlete credentials, which meant I was going to have a hell of a time convincing them to let me back into the Village.

I didn't care. I didn't want to go back. I didn't want to see Heath or Bella ever again.

So I kept walking, following the waterfront. No one gave me a second glance. With my makeup faded and the hood of my Team USA sweatshirt flipped up, I no longer looked like the infamous Katarina Shaw. I could have been anyone.

The shoreline dropped off, giving way to a metal bridge that arced over the still, dark water. Glowing on the opposite shore was the stadium where the opening ceremony had been held. Only ten days before, but it felt like an eternity.

Eventually, I realized I wasn't walking aimlessly any longer. I had chosen a destination.

The Lins' hotel was a striking modern structure stacked on the shore near Vancouver Harbour. I walked into the lobby and straight to the elevators. I didn't need to know the room number. Sheila would be in the best suite: top floor, northeast facade for the grandest, most panoramic vista of the water and the mountains.

I rapped lightly on the door. There was no answer. So I pounded it like a beat cop and shouted her name until she let me in.

Sheila was in nightclothes—elegant white satin pajamas with a matching robe—but she seemed wide awake. I'd seen her in passing—at the Pacific Coliseum during the Games, and during other events where we'd competed against the twins over the past several years. But I hadn't really *looked* since before our falling out in 2006.

She was frailer than I remembered, with sunken cheeks and shadows under her eyes. Sheila had always been ageless and perfect to me, forever frozen in her moment of triumph back in Calgary. For the first time, she looked like a real person.

"Ms. Shaw," she said, as if she'd been expecting me. "Come in."

I followed her into a sitting area with cream-colored furniture and a view of the glowing sails of Canada Place. Several miniature bottles sat empty on a side table. I'd never seen Sheila Lin drink more than a glass of white wine, and even then only with dinner.

"Please." She took two more bottles out of the minibar and offered one to me. "Sit."

The last thing I needed was another drink, but I took a sip anyway. It was some sort of sickening-sweet liqueur, like maple syrup mixed with lighter fluid. I coughed and set the bottle down next to the empties.

For a few moments, we gazed out the windows. I had no idea where to begin.

"You had so much promise," Sheila finally said. "All four of you." She took a deep pull from her bottle without so much as a wince. "What a waste."

I spun to face her. "You know, all I ever wanted was to be like you."

Sheila turned toward me too—slow, deliberate, eyes sparking the same way Bella's had.

"Then you should have listened to me," she said.

"So it's all my fault? You were my coach."

And you wanted me to fail. Even after everything, I couldn't bring myself to voice my suspicions about Sheila throwing Heath and me to the wolves so we'd pose less of a threat.

"No," she said. "It's my fault—for allowing you into the Academy in the first place. I let my children convince me that training with you and Mr. Rocha would drive them to greater heights. Instead you dragged them down to your level."

"Sorry to be such a disappointment," I spat.

"I'm sorry too." She stared out the window again, but her eyes were unfocused, no longer taking in the view. "This was my last chance."

Even if the twins managed to qualify for the next Olympics, it was unlikely they would be medal contenders. And to Sheila, competing was pointless if you couldn't win.

"At least I did everything I could for them." This Sheila said so softly, I almost thought she was speaking to herself. "I hope they appreciate that."

The realization clicked into place, a key in a lock.

All this time, I thought I understood what she was capable of, how ruthless she was, how far she would go to win. All this time, I'd had no idea.

"It was you," I said.

Sheila gave me a look that was not quite a smile. Not quite a confirmation.

Dropping a tell-all article right before the Olympic final seemed like a classic Sheila Lin chess move. But there was only one way she could have known so much about Heath's lost years. Only one reason she would have passed over her Rolodex full of reputable reporters in favor of Ellis Dean, who was more than happy to post first and ask questions later.

She was the one who had sent Heath to Russia in the first place.

CHAPTER 64

"That night in Nagano," I said. "Heath came to see you. Didn't he?"

I pictured him showing up at a fancy hotel suite like this one, dripping wet after running through the freezing rain. Shivering, lost, desperate. After I said he was holding me back. After I broke his heart.

"He was upset," Sheila said. "He told me he wanted to be good enough for you, that he'd do anything. I told him I couldn't help him. But I knew someone who might be able to."

"Why?" I choked out.

"I figured a few days under Veronika's medieval training methods and he'd give up for good. Turns out Heath was the toughest competitor of you all. If only he wanted to win as much as he wanted you."

Heath hadn't run away from me. Sheila had *driven* him away. He'd gone to her for guidance that night, and instead she poured poison in his ear. And of course he had listened—how many times had I implored him to *trust Sheila, she knows what she's doing*.

She certainly did. It disturbed me how easily I could parse Sheila's logic: get rid of Heath, pair Bella with Zack Branwell and Garrett with me, and overnight she'd neutralized her children's biggest competitors and secured her control over the top two teams in the country.

"You were our *coach*," I said. "You were supposed to help us, to—"

Sheila slammed the bottle down on the table. "I let you live in my house, skate with my son, ingratiate yourself to my daughter. I gave you all the things I had to scrape and claw and *earn* for myself, and you threw them back in my face. For *love*."

She said it like a curse.

"What the hell do you know about love?" I shot back.

"Everything I've ever done has been out of love. For my children, for—"

"*Your children* are convinced their father must have been a gold medalist, because otherwise you would have aborted them."

Sheila got up and walked toward the window, tugging her satin sash tighter.

"He was," she said. "Downhill skiing champion in both Lake Placid and Sarajevo."

"So why not tell them that? Don't you think they deserve to know?"

"We spent one night together, and I never saw him again. I don't even remember his name. Though I suppose I could look it up."

She couldn't remember the name of the man who'd fathered her children, but she knew exactly how many Olympic golds he'd won.

To Sheila, he'd merely been a means to an end. That's what the twins were to her, too—a means to extend her legacy, to keep winning when she could no longer compete herself. And look what it had done to them: Garrett, burying his true self to protect the family brand. Bella, willing to betray anyone to gain the upper hand, no matter the damage she left in her wake.

Heath's words echoed in my mind. *All you care about is winning.*

He was right: that's who I was. But it wasn't who I'd always been.

It was who I'd *become*, after a lifetime spent striving to be just like Sheila Lin. Like her, I'd discarded my past, my home, my family. I'd convinced myself if I became the best, it didn't matter who I hurt, because in the end, it would be worth it. Even if I hurt myself most of all.

For all the years I'd spent obsessing about Sheila—first watching her on television, then skating for her, pushing myself to extremes for crumbs of praise—I'd never truly seen her. Not until that night, drinking in the dark in a Vancouver hotel room.

And all I saw was misery.

You can always be better, she'd said to me when we first met. But what was the point if you had everything and enjoyed nothing? Sheila's whole life had been spent grasping for more—more medals, more money, more power—and it would never be enough.

Nothing's ever enough for you, Heath had said. He was wrong about that.

I'd finally had enough, of the striving and the pain and the heart-break. I didn't want to be Sheila Lin anymore. I didn't want to be Katarina Shaw either.

I wanted to disappear.

PART V

The Last Time

GARRETT LIN: After the Olympics, there were all sorts of rumors.

INEZ ACTON: People said Kat suffered a nervous breakdown and had to be institutionalized. Because any woman who dares to show anger in public must be "crazy."

FRANCESCA GASKELL: She joined a cult, or she changed her name and started shooting adult films, or she married some rich stockbroker and moved to Connecticut.

ELLIS DEAN: Yeah, I heard that one about the finance bro. If you ask me, the porn star rumor was *way* more plausible.

GARRETT LIN: As far as I know . . . she just went home.

Blurry photographs show Katarina Shaw picking up a grocery delivery at the entrance to her family home in The Heights, Illinois. She's dressed down in a flannel shirt, ripped jeans, and muddy work boots. She glares in the photographer's direction like she's daring them to trespass on her property, then turns and disappears down the tree-lined driveway.

NICOLE BRADFORD: When I heard she was back in the area, I sent her a note, telling her she was welcome to skate at North Shore whenever she wanted. She never responded.

GARRETT LIN: I think she needed peace and quiet and time to process everything that happened. I could certainly understand.

Sustained shot of a rolling green lawn on a sunny day. The only movement is the breeze stirring the blades of grass—until a taxi pulls up, and the backseat door pops open.

PRODUCER (Offscreen): So when was the next time you saw Katarina after Vancouver?

ELLIS DEAN: The same time the rest of the world did.

Katarina emerges from the car wearing a black dress. Her hair is long again, in a low ponytail.

FRANCESCA GASKELL: Three years later—January 2013.

Flashbulbs go off, reflecting in the lenses of her sunglasses. She walks past, ignoring them.

GARRETT LIN: When she showed up at my mother's funeral.

CHAPTER 65

I'd forgotten how bright the sun shone in Los Angeles.

The locals wore light jackets to ward off the mid-January chill, but coming from the Midwest, the California weather felt sweltering to me. As I walked into Hollywood Forever Cemetery, sunlight heated my skin like a follow spot, and whispers trailed in my wake.

Is that—oh my god, it is.

What is she doing here?

I thought she was dead.

"Kat!"

I turned to see Garrett Lin walking across the well-manicured grass, hand raised in a friendly wave. So at least one person was pleased to see me.

The second he was close enough, Garrett wrapped me in a hug. The first time anyone had touched me since . . . I didn't want to think about it. He'd put on weight, enough to soften the planes of his face; it looked good on him.

"This is Andre," Garrett said, gesturing to the man beside him. "My boyfriend."

"Pleasure to meet you, Kat." Andre looked to be a few years our senior, handsome with dark skin, dorky glasses, and a deep, soothing voice. He shook my hand, then took Garrett's.

"I'm so sorry for your loss," I said. "I had no idea she was sick."

"None of us did," Garrett said.

Cancer, I'd read in the news, though the reports didn't specify what kind. Apparently Sheila had been battling the disease for years, in secret. So Vancouver really had been her last chance at the Olympics—and the last words I'd ever spoken to her were in anger.

The ceremony was scheduled to start in a few minutes, and people had begun to migrate toward the white chairs lined up on either side of a rectangular reflecting pool. I drew more than a few curious looks—including from Frannie Gaskell, now all grown up and going by her full name, Francesca. She and her partner had wasted no time taking over the spot Heath and I once occupied as the top American ice dance team.

Ellis Dean lurked around the perimeter, soliciting comments from passersby with a microphone bedazzled to match the rhinestones on his bowtie. When he tried to wave us over, both Garrett and I pretended not to see him.

"I hope it's all right that I'm here," I said.

"Of course it is!" Garrett said. "I meant to call you, but everything's been so hectic and—wait, how *did* you find out about the service?"

"Heath told me."

Garrett's eyes widened, and he exchanged a look with Andre.

My less-than-glamorous lifestyle over the past several years had bored the media into leaving me alone for the most part; it was rare I received a call not from a telemarketer. When the phone rang on the night Sheila passed away, I hadn't even bothered to glance at the screen. It wasn't until the next day, when I went to select a playlist for my morning run, that I noticed the voicemail.

I know I'm the last person you want to hear from. But I thought you should know.

I felt like the wind had been knocked out of me, and I couldn't tell whether it was from hearing Heath's voice again or from the shocking news he broke.

I didn't cry. I didn't think. I swept the dust off my old carry-on suitcase and started packing. A couple of hours later, I was at O'Hare, boarding the first available flight to LA.

"So Kat," Andre said, changing the subject, "do you still skate?"

Garrett stiffened. "Babe, let's not—"

"It's okay." I smiled. "I do, but it's just for fun now. What about you, Garrett?"

"Not for years," he said. "After Vancouver, I had . . . well, there was an accident."

"A fall?" I asked. I thought I'd noticed a new hitch in his step when he approached.

"I'd stayed super late at the Academy, trying to—" He shook his head. "It doesn't matter. Anyway, I fell asleep at the wheel and flipped my car over a median on the freeway."

I gasped. Andre gave Garrett's hand a supportive squeeze.

"Holy shit," I said. "Are you—I mean, are you okay? I'm so sorry, I didn't know, or I—"

"I'm fine," Garrett said. "At least I am now. But yeah, I figured that was as good a sign as any that my skating days were done."

Perhaps it was a strange thought to have at a funeral, but I'd never seen Garrett look happier or healthier—which forced me to realize just how tense and miserable he'd been before.

"I'm back in school, actually," he continued. "Or, well, I guess it's the first time I've *gone* to school like a regular student."

"He's studying psychology at Stanford." Andre looped his arm around Garrett's waist and beamed at him with supportive pride. "Top of his class."

"That's amazing, Garrett," I said. "Congratulations."

The minister, a gray-haired woman in a pantsuit, took up her position behind the podium. There was no casket, only a portrait of Sheila in her prime—the gold dress, the gold medal around her neck—and an elaborate spray of white orchids and lilies to match the smaller arrangements in pedestal bowls along the edge of the pool.

"You can sit with us," Garrett offered, gesturing to the section reserved for family. Bella sat alone in the front row, her intricate braided chignon and impeccable posture unmistakable.

"Oh no, that's all right," I told him. "I'll see you after the service."

I took a seat in the back, a still empty row that everyone steered clear of once they spotted me. As the rest of the chairs filled in, I scanned the crowd and told myself I wasn't looking for Heath.

Seconds later, I spotted him coming down the stairs beside the mausoleum. He'd grown a full beard, and he took the steps two at a time with the rhythmic grace of a trained dancer. I held my breath, hoping he wouldn't look at me or acknowledge me in any way, and also longing to spring out of my seat and run toward him.

I needn't have worried. Heath didn't notice me, and he sat in the front.

Right beside Bella.

The ceremony got under way with a brief, secular eulogy, before the minister brought Kirk Lockwood up to charm the crowd with a few stories from Sheila's skating career. Garrett took the stage next, delivering a moving speech about how much he had always admired his mother, and how glad he was she had gotten the chance to know the real him—and the man he loved—before her death.

"Finally," the minister said, "Sheila's daughter, Isabella, would like to say a few words."

I held my breath, bracing myself for my first look at Bella Lin's face since the night she'd betrayed me. But she didn't move from her seat.

Garrett leaned down to say something to her. Bella shook her head, and her shoulders trembled. She was crying, or trying hard not to.

Heath put his arm around her, and her shuddering stopped. Bella still made no move to rise, though. Instead, she leaned into him, resting her head on his shoulder.

The minister tried to smooth over the awkward moment. "Let's move on to the—"

"I'd like to say something."

KIRK LOCKWOOD: I still couldn't believe Sheila was gone.

Close-up of the flowers and portrait at Sheila Lin's funeral, slowly panning back to show the mourners gathered around the Fairbanks Reflecting Pool at Hollywood Forever Cemetery.

FRANCESCA GASKELL: She was at the Grand Prix Final with me and Evan in December, fierce as ever. And then a few weeks later . . .

GARRETT LIN: It was sudden, but I think that's how my mother would have wanted it, if she'd had a choice in the matter.

VERONIKA VOLKOVA: You want me to say something sweet about Sheila, because she is dead? Please. What do you think she would say about me if I were the one in the ground and she was sitting here with you?

ELLIS DEAN: It was a lovely service. And then Katarina Shaw showed up.

Katarina's voice comes from behind the camera: "I'd like to say something."

The shot swings around to show her, standing in the last row, then follows as she walks up to the podium. The bewildered minister moves out of frame, ceding the floor to her.

Katarina takes off her sunglasses and holds them clenched in her fist.

"The first time I saw Sheila Lin," she says, "I was four years old. And my mother had just died."

Cut to another camera angle, focused on Bella Lin, who is seated between her brother and Heath Rocha in the front row. Her mirrored sunglasses reflect the blue sky.

Katarina continues: "She'd been sick for a long time—so long, I don't have any memories of her healthy. I don't remember her funeral either. But you know what I'll never forget?"

A beat, as she looks out over the black-clad audience. No one moves.

"After the service, I couldn't sleep, so I snuck out of my room to watch TV—volume turned low so I wouldn't wake up my father or brother. And the Calgary ice dance final was on."

Katarina looks at the photograph of Sheila on the stand beside her.

"I saw Sheila win her second gold medal, and she was so strong, so confident, so completely perfect, I couldn't take my eyes off her. Her strength gave me strength, when I needed it the most. The next morning, I asked my dad for skating lessons."

Cut to the Lins again. Garrett is crying. Bella's face remains unreadable. Only Heath's hand is in the shot, his fingers making slow circles on Bella's shoulder.

"When I was older, I was lucky enough to train with Sheila Lin for several years. I thought I wanted to be exactly like her. But the truth is . . ."

Katarina's voice breaks, and she blinks away tears. Cut to a close-up of Heath, who watches her with hard, unblinking eyes.

"I don't think I ever really knew her," *Katarina says.* "Maybe no one did. Here's what I do know about Sheila: she was a gold medalist and a devoted mother and a successful businesswoman. And she was the most ruthless, calculating person I ever met."

A few gasps and murmurs of dismay from the crowd. Katarina keeps going.

"She changed my life for the better, and she also tried to ruin it on multiple occasions. She was strong—she had to be, to survive our fucked-up sport—but that's not all she was. She could be weak. She could be cruel. She could be human, no matter how much she tried to hide it."

Another shot of Bella, closer this time. A single tear tracks down her cheek. She wipes it off with a flick of her fingertips.

"Sheila Lin wasn't perfect," *Katarina says.* "But she was a champion."

CHAPTER 66

Despite what you may have heard, my speech at Sheila Lin's funeral wasn't planned.

Until the whole crowd swiveled to stare at me, I didn't even realize I'd stood up and volunteered to speak. I had no idea what to say. I barely recall what I *did* say.

I remember squinting into the sun, gripping my glasses to keep my hands from shaking, sweat creeping down my spine under my black dress.

And the way Bella and Heath looked at me. She seemed hostile at first—muscles tensed, dreading the scene I was surely about to cause—but as I spoke, she softened. When I stepped away from the podium, she gave me a nod of acknowledgment, so swift and subtle I thought I might have imagined it.

Heath, though—he stayed so still, he could have been another monument in the cemetery. I felt his eyes on me, but I couldn't bring myself to meet them. I was afraid of what I'd see—pure loathing, smug satisfaction. Or worst of all, total indifference.

I left Hollywood Forever without saying another word to anyone and changed my flight so I could leave LA as soon as possible. By the time the plane lifted off the tarmac, my visit to California already felt like a strange dream.

That was it, I figured. I would never see Heath or the Lins again.

I returned to my solitary life in Illinois. Weeks passed, every day the same as the last—until a blizzard swept through overnight, brushing a coat of glittering white over everything.

The next morning, I walked out my front door and found Bella Lin standing in the snow.

Bella was dressed all in white, and she looked so much like her mother, for a moment I thought I'd been visited by a ghost.

"Hi," she said. The compact car behind her was white too, nearly invisible against the snowdrifts and the pale cloud cover.

I walked down the icy steps, stopping on the final tread. "What are you doing here?"

"I was in the area."

She'd been at the U.S. National Championships, which were held in Omaha that year—at least a six-hour drive. Even for Midwesterners, calling that *in the area* was pushing it.

"What are you really doing here, Bella?"

"I wanted to see you."

"You just saw me at the funeral."

"Yeah, and you left without saying goodbye." She folded her arms. "Without saying anything, actually, aside from your big speech about what a bitch my dead mother was."

I shifted my weight. "I'm sorry, I didn't—"

"Don't apologize. That speech was the most honest thing anyone said all day."

She looked me over, noting my layered workout clothes and the tote I carried.

"Going skating?"

I nodded, tucking the bag closer against my fleece jacket.

"Mind if I join you? I've got my skates in the trunk."

I gave her suede ankle boots, already stained with slush, a dubious glance. "You have different shoes in there too? It's a bit of a walk."

"I'll be fine," Bella said with a familiar smile. *Challenge accepted.* "Lead the way."

She kept pace with me as I headed into the woods, an occasional heavier huff of breath the only sign that the slippery terrain gave her any trouble. I kept expecting her to ask where we were going, but she didn't say a word—until we reached our destination.

"Holy shit," Bella said. "You have your own *ice rink?*"

About a year into my self-imposed exile, I'd had the old stable building where Heath used to hide out converted into a private skating facility. The ice surface was small, and I had to spend a good hour a day dragging a rake-like tool back and forth to keep it smooth enough to skate on, but it was all mine.

I hauled open the sliding barn doors and switched on the fairy lights strung across the rafters. The east-facing wall was all windows, looking out on the forest and the lakeshore beyond. The panes retracted so I could skate in the open air when the weather was better, a refrigeration system keeping the ice frozen even in the summer heat.

Bella spun around in awe.

"I knew it," she said. "I knew you could never give it up."

I'd certainly tried. The first few weeks after Vancouver, I did nothing except sleep and eat and seethe with rage. Then I decided I needed a project to occupy my time, so I vowed to fix up the house. If I couldn't reach my full potential, at least my home could.

For months, I stripped paint and steamed wallpaper and scrubbed woodwork. I piled trash on the beach and lit a bonfire. I cleaned out my brother's room and finally let myself cry about his death—and his life—gasping in dust and stale smoke until my lungs burned.

No matter what I did, though, my body roiled with restless energy. When it was warm outside, I walked in the woods until my feet blistered. When the weather turned, and the silence became too much, I played my parents' records—*Hounds of Love* and *Private Dancer* and *Rumours*, volume turned as loud as it would go—but that only made me want to move, to dance.

To skate.

Money can't buy happiness, but for me it bought the next best thing. I found a contractor who specialized in at-home hockey rinks—and who, thankfully, had never heard of Olympic ice dancer Katarina Shaw. Several months and a significant chunk of my savings later, the stable had been transformed.

At first I'd been clumsy on my blades, my limbs pathetically uncoordinated from disuse. I fell on my ass over and over and over again, until my backside was one big blue-purple bruise. But there was no one there to see, no one to judge. For the first time in my life, I was skating only for myself.

"We need music," Bella announced after lacing up her skates.

"There aren't any speakers."

"You built yourself a whole damn rink and didn't bother to install a sound system?"

"I'm usually alone."

Some days, I skated with headphones in and a playlist blasting, but most of the time my only accompaniment was the meditative scrape of my blades.

Undeterred, Bella took out her iPhone, starting up a pop song with a lively drumbeat and propping the device against the boards to make the most of the tinny speakers.

She did some basic footwork in time with the tempo, singing along— something about traffic lights and busy streets. When she saw my blank look, she laughed.

"Oh my god, you really have turned into a hermit, haven't you? This has been all over the radio for months. One of my junior teams wants to skate to it next year."

I joined her on the ice, and we circled each other, tracing overlapping ellipses.

"The younger skaters still talk about you, you know," Bella said.

"What, as a cautionary tale?" *Katarina Shaw, the Wicked Ice Queen Who Destroyed Her Own Career in a Single Day.* Sounded about right.

"No," Bella said. "They talk about you the same way you talk about my mother."

"So they think I'm a bitch?"

"Mm-hmm. And they want to be exactly like you when they grow up." She did a graceful pirouette, arms above her head. "This is amazing. I want a skating rink in my backyard."

"It used to be a stable. It'd been on the verge of falling down for years, but—"

"Wait." Bella stopped, blades spraying snow. "*This* is where your brother made him sleep? In the middle of *winter*?"

So Heath had told her about Lee's abuse. I wondered what else he'd told her.

My fury over finding Heath and Bella together had long since cooled, but the thought of him confiding in her about the childhood trauma that bonded us stung like a fresh scald.

"So." I'd put off the subject as long as I could. "You and Heath."

"It's not like that," Bella said—a little too quickly.

"What's it like, then?"

"Well, at first, it was revenge."

Hearing her admit it was almost a relief. They'd both been furious that night, and they couldn't have found a better way to wound me than jumping into bed together.

"Then after Vancouver," Bella continued, "I was assisting my mother, and Heath started choreographing programs for some up-and-coming teams at the Academy."

"Really?" I'd assumed Heath would want nothing more to do with the skating world.

"He's great with the younger kids. Especially the boys who don't have formal dance training; they really look up to him. But anyway, Garrett moved away, and my mother . . ." Bella shook her head. "I don't know why I thought working with her would improve our relationship. She treated me like I was just another junior coach. So Heath and I ended up spending a lot of time together."

I thought of the way she'd leaned toward Heath at Sheila's funeral, seeking solace from him instead of her twin. Part of me—the part that loved them both, in spite of everything—was happy they had each other to rely on, in whatever capacity.

The rest of me wanted to rip Bella's hair out at the root and use it to set the building on fire with her locked inside.

At least a hint of that impulse must have shown on my face, because Bella quickly added, "We're just friends."

"Friends with benefits."

"*Friends*," she insisted. "Until . . . well, there was this one night. I had an extra ticket to see Adele at the Palladium, and Heath offered to go with me."

I wasn't sure which was more shocking: Heath willingly attending an Adele concert or Bella taking a night off to have some fun for once.

"I swear," Bella said, "it was purely a physical release. It meant nothing."

"So that was it?" I fought to keep my face neutral, to keep any hint of hope from sneaking into my voice. "Just that one time, and then—"

"What, you want an exact count?" Bella's eyes flashed. "You left, and Garrett left, and Heath and I stayed. All we had was each other."

And I had no one. But that was my own fault, wasn't it?

For the next few songs on the album—which later, after I'd officially rejoined society, I learned was Taylor Swift's *Red*—we skated in silence, improvising to the music. Eventually we turned toward each other and clasped hands in a dance hold, switching off lead and follow roles.

By the end of "We Are Never Ever Getting Back Together," Bella was bent double, breathing hard, while I'd barely broken a sweat.

"Jesus," she said. "This whole time I thought you were, like, sitting on the sofa watching soap operas, and instead you've been secretly training for Sochi."

I laughed and performed a few one-foot turns around her, showing off. "Sure. Me and my imaginary partner. Put us in, coach!"

"If you want a real partner, I have a pretty good idea where you could find one."

I laughed again. Bella didn't.

"Heath hates me," I said. Yes, he'd called to tell me about Sheila's funeral, but the message had been brief, businesslike at best.

"Plenty of skating partners hate each other," Bella said. "Pretty sure Heath is incapable of hating you, though. He misses you."

"He said that?"

"I mean, not in so many words. As I'm sure you're aware, words are not that man's strong suit. But I can tell."

If Heath missed me so much, surely he would have contacted me long before Sheila's death forced his hand.

Then again, I hadn't attempted to get in touch with him either. And I'd fled the cemetery the second the service ended, like I was being chased by rabid coyotes.

"Why don't you two team up for Sochi?" I asked. "Since you're such good *friends.*"

"Because I'm a better coach than I ever was a skater—and I was a damn good skater." She paused. "I don't know if Garrett told y—"

"He did." I hadn't been able to stop thinking about it: Garrett, stretched so thin by stress and guilt and self-flagellation that he'd frayed apart. He'd almost *died,* and I'd had no idea.

"I should have seen it," Bella said. "The way the pressure was eating him alive. I had myself convinced he thrived on it, like us."

"Thriving? Is that what we were doing?"

"Probably not." She shook her head. "How messed up is it that it took seeing my twin brother in traction to get me to rethink my life and my choices?"

I didn't want to admit it, but I'd watched a bit of the Omaha Nationals. During Gaskell and Kovalenko's gold medal–winning free dance, the broadcast kept cutting to Bella, standing behind the boards. Sheila had always been still and stoic when her skaters were on the ice; Bella was the complete opposite. She performed the program along with them, bouncing and smiling and swinging her arms. Seeing her so animated, so joyful, I couldn't help but smile.

"I'm sure you're a fantastic coach," I said. "But you can't seriously think Heath and I could make the Olympic team. We're practically senior citizens."

"You're *experienced.* The U.S. ice dance program has been struggling since you split. Aside from Francesca and Evan, it's a bunch of baby skaters who've never come anywhere near an international podium."

Back in 2010, I had been so sure the Olympic Games would be the pinnacle of my existence. It was as if I'd nearly summitted a mountain, only to tumble down right before reaching the top. And now I was standing at the base, staring up at that distant peak again. Could I really be crazy enough to consider another climb?

"My mother left the Academy to me," Bella said. "But the Lin name only goes so far. Now that Nationals are over, skaters are already talking about leaving to work with more experienced coaches. Having Shaw and Rocha on our roster, especially if you made the Olympic team again—well, it would go a long way."

"And you've spoken to Heath about this?" I knew even asking the question was declaring some level of interest. But of *course* I was interested. As restorative as my just-for-the-hell-of-it skating regimen had been, I missed competing. I missed skating with a partner.

And yes, I'll admit it: I missed Heath. I missed him the way a soldier misses a severed limb. Seeing him with Bella had hurt, but it was nothing compared to the phantom pain of his absence.

"I haven't talked to him yet," Bella said. "I didn't want to get his hopes up, on the off chance you told me to go fuck myself. So are you telling me to go fuck myself?"

A soft ballad wafted from her phone speakers now, the album winding down. The sun had started to dip beneath the waves, and the fairy lights shone above us like golden stars.

I could have let Bella leave. She would have started up her rental car, driven to whatever boutique hotel she'd booked for the night, ordered room service, and flown back to California in the morning. We would have continued to go our separate ways, diverging further and further until the gap was too broad to bridge.

But she was right. I could never give it up, no matter how hard I tried.

"I'm starving," I said. "Wanna eat some carbs?"

Bella grinned. "I thought you'd never ask."

ELLIS DEAN: When I heard Kat and Heath were considering a comeback, I thought they were crazy. Which is how I knew it was probably true.

JANE CURRER: I was no longer involved in the day-to-day operations of U.S. Figure Skating, having moved on to a position with the International Olympic Committee. But news of their reunion certainly came as a shock to the entire athletic community.

ELLIS DEAN: And with Bella coaching them! Talk about messy.

GARRETT LIN: I kept my opinions to myself. That wasn't my world anymore. If my sister wanted to coach them, that was her business. If she and Heath Rocha wanted to keep on . . . Like I said, none of my business.

PRODUCER (Offscreen): You and Evan moved to a new training facility that season, correct?

FRANCESCA GASKELL: That's right. And before you ask, no, it wasn't because of Kat and Heath. We just needed a change.

PRODUCER (Offscreen): Sure, but you have to admit, the timing was—

FRANCESCA GASKELL: We'd lost our coach. We were *grieving*, okay?

ELLIS DEAN: Of *course* Gaskell and Kovalenko left the Academy. Sochi was supposed to be *their* Olympics, after they'd been stuck in the alternate slot twice in a row.

FRANCESCA GASKELL: We were really excited to compete against Kat and Heath again, believe it or not. Even as old and out of practice as they were—no offense—we figured having them in the mix would push us to be our best.

ELLIS DEAN: Staying at the Academy would've meant staying in Kat and Heath's shadow. And Frannie was ready for the spotlight.

CHAPTER 67

I imagined my official reunion with Heath Rocha a thousand different ways.

He would run toward me like a third-act rom-com hero in an airport terminal. He would give me a cordial smile and a firm handshake as if we were rival CEOs negotiating a merger. He would stare in shock, then refuse to skate with me, because this had been some elaborate scheme on Bella's part, and he *did* hate me after all.

The reality was far less dramatic. On a Tuesday afternoon in early February, a taxi dropped me off at the Lin Ice Academy. Heath and Bella were finishing up a session with one of the junior teams, who looked like babies to me but were probably around fourteen or fifteen.

The girl spotted me first. Her eyes went wide like a cartoon kitten, and she made a strangled sound of surprise. Heath turned.

"Hello, Katarina," he said.

He didn't seem happy to see me. He didn't seem disturbed by my presence either. His expression was like the lake on a still night: placid on the surface, shadows below.

"Right on time," Bella said. "Let's get started."

The two young skaters exited, the girl still staring at me. I smiled at her, and she almost tripped over her skates.

I'd become so accustomed to my compact private rink, the regulation-sized ice surface felt vast. Bella stood off to the side while Heath and I looped the perimeter, picking up speed with each circuit. On the fourth time around, he took my hand.

His palms were slick with sweat. So he was nervous too.

As soon as our fingers interlocked, our blades fell into a steady rhythm. Our breathing synced. Heath drew me into a dance hold, and we moved through our standard warm-up sequence without a single misstep, as if we'd been doing it every day.

Bella switched on a low-key bluesy instrumental, and we began to improvise, seamlessly blending old choreography with spontaneous new elements. I'd worried skating with him again would be awkward, stilted, difficult. Instead, it was easy. So easy it terrified me.

When Bella started calling out guidance from her spot beside the rink, that felt easy too. Heath could respond to her feedback before she'd even finished the sentence, and his experience as a choreographer had turned him into an even stronger lead. The slightest pressure of his hands, and I could sense exactly how he wanted me to move.

Eventually the music stopped, and so did we. Center ice, chests pressed together, close enough to kiss. Eyes locked, my entire world shrunk to the deep brown of his irises.

"I think that's enough for today," Bella said.

I felt like Heath and I had been on the ice for ten minutes, tops, but it had been over an hour. We were both covered in sweat—our own, each other's. As we unlaced our skates and chugged from our water bottles, we avoided eye contact like we'd woken up after a regrettable one-night stand. *There* was the awkwardness I'd been expecting.

Bella had more work to do, so Heath and I walked out together, still silent. He held the door open for me as we stepped into the golden hour light.

"I guess I'll see y—" I started, just as he said, "Katarina, I—"

Another voice interrupted us both. "Ms. Shaw?"

The young girl he and Bella had been working with earlier waited at the curb.

"Yes?" I said.

"Would you—I mean, if it's not too much trouble . . . could you please sign this for me?"

She thrust something into my hands. A program from the 2009 Stars on Ice tour, with Heath and me on the cover.

"Sure," I said. "Do you have something to write with?"

"Oh! No, I'm so sorry, I—"

"Here." Heath took a pen from his bag and passed it to me.

"What's your name?" I asked the girl.

"Madison. Madison Castro. My older sister took me to see the tour for my birthday. In Dallas, that's where I'm from. Well, like twenty miles outside of Dallas."

Once Madison conquered her fear of speaking to me, she couldn't seem to shut up. Heath didn't bother trying to hide his amusement, but she was too enraptured to notice.

"Seeing you skate is what made me want to become an ice dancer. I'm going to go to the Olympics one day, and—" She caught herself. "I mean, I hope I will."

"I'm sure you will. And hopefully you'll do much better than I did." I handed the program back, my signature scrawled under her name. "Good luck this season, Madison."

"Thank you!" She bounced off, beaming, the program clutched to her chest.

"Well, well," Heath said. "Guess you're a role model after all, Katarina Shaw."

I rolled my eyes, but I was smiling; if nothing else, Madison's enthusiasm had shattered the uneasy silence between us.

"Where are you staying?" Heath asked. "Around here?"

"I found an Airbnb over by the beach."

"Marina del Rey?"

I shook my head. "Playa."

"Oh, thank God."

"Don't tell me Heath Rocha, committed hater of Los Angeles, has turned native enough to express sincere and deeply held neighborhood beliefs."

"Hey, I'm just looking out for my skating partner's safety and well-being," he said. "Wouldn't want you to get mowed down by a double stroller. It's wild out there in MDR."

"Next you'll tell me you've gotten into hot yoga and juice cleanses."

"Hot yoga is so last year. It's all about SoulCycle now." Heath smiled, and a stray curl fell across his forehead, shining in the waning sunlight. "So you want a ride home?"

"Don't tell me you drive some obnoxious sports car now."

"Worse."

He gestured toward a small motorcycle parked alongside the curb. A black helmet with gold racing stripes hung from the handlebars.

"Seriously?" I said. "You're a *biker dude*?"

"You want a ride or not?"

I hesitated. But what was the issue? We were colleagues. Colleagues could engage in friendly banter. Colleagues could give each other rides home.

Heath handed me the helmet and climbed onto the bike. I mounted the seat behind him, cinching my arms around his waist. We'd touched far more intimately during the training session, but that was work. This was . . . I wasn't sure what it was.

He took the scenic route along Vista del Mar. The day had been calm and cloudless, so the setting sun poured over the ocean like molten metal. Suddenly I wasn't in such a hurry to get back to my small, starkly furnished rental.

I tugged on Heath's sleeve. He nodded and turned toward the coast.

The weather was chilly by California standards. Aside from a woman tossing a Frisbee to her chubby pit bull farther down the shoreline, we had the beach to ourselves.

"Where are you living these days?" I asked as we trudged toward the water, shoes in hand. "Somewhere better than that shitty studio over on Higuera, I hope. Remember that dump?"

"How could I forget?" Heath looked down. "No, I'm over in the Palisades now."

"An apartment?" I said. "Or—"

Heath's jaw ticked. Oh.

"We each have our own space," he said. "But Bella was all alone in that huge house, and we're—"

"Friends. Yeah, she told me."

At the Academy, I'd been on the lookout for any simmer of attraction between them. What I saw instead might have been worse: Heath and Bella had an easy rapport, a relaxed intimacy that made it impossible to ignore how close they'd gotten while I was gone.

Heath turned to face me. All that golden light reflected in his eyes.

"What else did Bella tell you?" he asked.

I met his gaze. "She told me you were a choreographer now. And that you missed me."

"Of course I miss you, Katarina." He stepped closer, stumbling in the sand. I had to rock back, or we would have collided. "And I'm so sorry, about what happened in Vancouver. If I could go back, I—"

Click.

We both stiffened at the all too familiar sound of a camera shutter, slicing through the crashing waves and seagull cries.

"Behind you," Heath said. "On the bike path."

"Just like old times."

"What do you think?" He smiled, leaning in. "Should we give 'em a show?"

CHAPTER 68

If there was one thing Heath and I were good at, it was putting on a show.

We pretended to be oblivious to the paparazzo's presence, the same way we used to in the days when they followed us everywhere. We held hands. We laughed and smiled. I teasingly pushed Heath away, then let him pull me back in again and tangle his hands in my hair.

As the sun sunk past the horizon, we stared into each other's eyes, and Heath canted his chin, moving closer and closer, until he was so close I was sure he would kiss me.

At the last second, he deflected to my cheek, his beard scraping along my jaw. I was relieved. I was disappointed. I was more confused than ever before.

"I think the guy's gone," he whispered in my ear. I was painfully aware of every point where our bodies touched, from his palm cradling the back of my head to my bare toes brushing against his as our feet sunk deeper in the sand. "Do you want to—"

"I think we should keep things professional," I blurted out.

Heath pulled back. "Okay."

"I'm sorry too." I swallowed. "About Vancouver. But you know the problems between us didn't start in Vancouver, our personal feelings have always been a distraction, and if we're going to try this again—"

"Is that what you want?" he asked. "To try this again?"

"Do you? Bella said—"

"I don't want to talk about Bella right now. This is about you and me, Katarina."

"I understand it's a long shot," I said. "Us making it to Sochi, let alone winning."

"You know I've never cared about medals as much as you and Bella do."

"You're still skating, though," I said. "I have to admit, that surprised me."

"Yeah?" Heath buried his hands in his pockets. "It surprised me too. Did Bella tell you I worked in a record shop in West Hollywood for a while?"

She hadn't. "Let me guess: dealing with hipsters all day made you run screaming back into figure skating's frigid embrace?"

"That might've been a factor. But mostly, I missed that *feeling*—of becoming part of the music, instead of just listening. There's nothing quite like it, is there?"

I thought back to our practice session that afternoon, the effortless sensation of swirling across the ice in his arms. "No. There isn't. And if we don't do this, if we don't at least try . . ."

Heath smiled, but there was a hint of sadness in it. "We'll always wonder."

Dusk had fallen, casting our faces in shadow. Heath looked so different from the boy he'd been—not only because of the beard, but also the lines creasing the corners of his eyes, cutting across his forehead. He would turn thirty in July; I'd follow him in October. Young by the standards of the real world but pushing obsolescence in our sport. As smoothly as our practice session had gone that afternoon, my knees and back ached, and I knew I would be hobbling like an old lady come morning.

"So I'll see you tomorrow?" I asked.

He nodded. "See you tomorrow, Katarina."

Even after all our talk of keeping things professional and the distraction of personal feelings, when Heath dropped me off after our detour to the beach, it took tremendous restraint to resist inviting him inside.

My temporary home was an unassuming A-frame on one of the hilly, winding streets east of the beach. It had a security system and tall hedges—which, given my diminished public profile, I hoped would suffice, but getting papped on my first day back wasn't the best omen.

The lightbulb beside the front door was burnt-out, and I fumbled in the dark for the keys. My foot hit something on the stoop.

Flowers. A dozen yellow roses in a ceramic vase.

I carried them inside and set them on the knockoff midcentury modern console table in the entryway. I had no idea who could have sent them; only Heath and Bella knew the address, and why would they have sent flowers here instead of giving them to me at the rink?

Finally, I located the card, tucked between the stems. As I pulled it out, a thorn nicked my fingertip, drawing blood. I stuck my finger in my mouth as I read the message.

Two words. No signature.

Welcome back.

ELLIS DEAN: Obviously they were fucking. Did you see those pictures on the beach?

A montage of paparazzi photos of Katarina Shaw and Heath Rocha at Playa del Rey Beach in Los Angeles. They look like a happy couple who can't keep their hands off each other.

ELLIS DEAN: My best traffic since the Olympic Village furniture-throwing incident, by *far*.

GARRETT LIN: I think it's nice they were able to remain friendly after everything.

INEZ ACTON: Who cares whether they were fucking or not? They were attempting a major athletic feat together, trying for another Olympics after years away from the sport. *That's* way more interesting than their sex lives. At least to me.

FRANCESCA GASKELL: I wasn't paying attention to them. I didn't have time, quite frankly. The Games were a year away, and I had a lot of work to do.

ELLIS DEAN: Canoodling on the beach at sunset is all well and good. But if they were serious about making a comeback, they had to *skate*.

KIRK LOCKWOOD: They kicked off the season with a lower-level competition, as a trial run.

Katarina and Heath skate their free dance, to a dramatic Philip Glass piano piece frequently used in movie trailers, at the 2013 U.S. International Classic in Salt Lake City, Utah.

KIRK LOCKWOOD: They won, but not by much—and the field wasn't that competitive. The old Shaw and Rocha would've crushed them all.

ELLIS DEAN: The real test was Skate America, where they had to face off with Gaskell and Kovalenko for the first time.

During the free dance warm-up at the 2013 Skate America competition in Detroit, Michigan, Katarina Shaw and Francesca Gaskell eye each other from opposite sides of the rink.

ELLIS DEAN: Kat and Heath had the lead going into the free, but Francesca and Evan pulled ahead and got the gold.

JANE CURRER: Shaw and Rocha's free dance felt a bit unfinished. Their scores reflected that.

FRANCESCA GASKELL: Maybe they should've listened to the officials' preseason feedback like the rest of us, instead of thinking they knew best. I mean, that's what people were saying anyway. Like I said, I had more important things on my mind.

On the Skate America podium, Katarina and Heath wave and smile, concealing any disappointment over their second-place finish.

JANE CURRER: Still, I was pleasantly surprised by their performance level—and their behavior, both on the ice and off. I hoped perhaps they had matured, and their days of courting drama were behind them. Then they went to Russia.

CHAPTER 69

Heath and I hadn't set foot in Russia since 2005—when I won my first world title, and he haunted me like a specter from the stands.

We were both surprised to receive an invitation from the Russian skating federation for their annual Grand Prix event, the Rostelecom Cup—though we knew damn well it wasn't a gesture of goodwill. Volkova and Kipriyanov were headlining the competition, and no doubt wanted to warm up for Sochi by humiliating us on their home turf.

Moscow was even colder and gloomier than I remembered. I found it difficult to imagine Heath living there, even as he slipped effortlessly between Russian and English with clerks and cabdrivers and gestured to landmarks. He pointed out the tumbledown apartment block he used to live in, and the old church—converted to a skating rink back in the Soviet era—where he'd once trained, but his breezy tone belied the hardships he must have faced. Still, it was more than he had ever willingly shared about that time in his life before, at least with me. Holding back the flood of questions I wanted to ask in response to each new drop of detail took all my willpower.

The Rostelecom Cup was held in a smaller venue at the same sporting complex where Worlds had taken place eight years earlier. In contrast to the frigid weather, the heat inside the arena was cranked so high white steam rose from the ice, and sweat pooled at the small of my back before I'd even finished lacing my skates. The space felt claustrophobic, plain concrete walls and glaring faces everywhere we turned. During team introductions, the crowd of Moscow locals shook the rafters with raucous cheering for the young Russians right before us, then reverted to stony silence when our names were announced.

"Don't let them get to you," Bella told Heath and me after the warm-up. "This is a good thing. You two have been out of the game for years, and they still consider you a threat."

Since Vancouver, Yelena and Dmitri had faced few serious rivals, at home or abroad. They'd moved to a brand-new purpose-built training center, rumored to have been subsidized by the Kipriyanov family's shady business interests. After racking up four consecutive world titles and countless other medals during our absence from the sport, they were widely expected to walk away with the next Olympic gold.

When you're so dominant for so long, though, it's easy to rest on your laurels, to stop pushing yourself. Whereas for the past several months, Heath and I had done nothing *but* push. Working with Bella felt less like being coached and more like a collaboration among equals— although sometimes I felt like the least crucial member of the team. Bella called the shots, Heath selected the music and created all our choreography. All I did was skate.

Win or lose, though, we were in this together. We might not beat our rivals this time, but we could make them worry.

The International Skating Union had finally done away with the stuffy, repetitive compulsory dance event, and rebranded the original dance as the "short dance." For the Olympic season, everyone had to skate the Finnstep—a fast, complicated style requiring swift edge and direction changes that could trip up even the most experienced skaters. One wrong step, and it was almost impossible to catch up with the tempo again. But you couldn't go *too* fast either, or you'd run rough-shod over the precise choreography.

That's exactly what happened to the rookie Russian team skating first: they rushed through their program like they couldn't wait to get it over with, and all nuance was lost. By the end, they were both panting, the guy's face so flushed you could hardly make out the acne scars on his cheeks anymore. He folded over and put a hand down on the ice, trying to catch his breath, while his partner—a teenager wearing heavy blue eyeliner that made her look even younger—skated to the boards without him.

As Heath and I awaited our turn, I kept smoothing my skirt, palms scraping over the sequins until I'd nearly rubbed my skin raw. When I first saw a sketch of the design, I thought the gunmetal-to-white ombre effect was gorgeous. The finished dress, though, made me think of dirty snow on a city curb, and the fabric felt too heavy for the light character of the Finnstep.

We took the ice second—supposedly due to our lack of world ranking from the previous season, but everyone knew it was a deliberate slap in the face. Right before our music—a swingy, upbeat cover of "Crazy in Love"—kicked in, Heath sucked in a breath. I had to wait until well into the opening promenade section before I could catch a clear glimpse of what had startled him.

Though Yelena and Dmitri wouldn't skate until the end of the event, Veronika Volkova stood at the boards, watching us. She'd taken up a position right beside Bella, so if we wanted to look to our coach for help or reassurance, we couldn't avoid seeing *her* too.

"Eyes on me," I said, just loud enough for Heath to hear.

He nodded and refocused, and we pulled off a dizzying series of turns in such perfect synchronicity, we even coaxed a few claps from the unfriendly crowd.

The next part of the dance required every team to stop on the exact same spot of the rink for an exuberant display of stationary footwork—legs swinging back and forth like tolling bells, then quick, bouncing steps balanced on toe picks. Smiling wide all the while, despite the sweat streaming into our eyes.

We were in a close hold, so I felt it the second Heath started to fall. His right leg seemed to glitch, as if his skate had snagged on something. Then his foot flew out from under him.

Instinctively, I grabbed onto his shoulder to stabilize him, but he was already going down. Worse, he'd twisted out of the hold to avoid hitting me with his blade, so he struck the ice at an angle, torquing his back.

Our bubbly music still blared as I knelt beside him, steam rising around us. He hadn't cried out, aside from a low groan only I was close enough to hear. But I knew what Heath was capable of enduring without making any complaints at all. This was bad.

"My blade," he said through gritted teeth. "It hit something."

I glanced frantically at the spot where we'd been performing our stationary steps. Later in the event, I might have suspected a rut in the ice, but we were only the second team to skate.

At first I saw nothing through the haze. Then I looked closer. A scatter of tiny dots glinted under the arena lights, barely distinguishable from the ice surface. I pressed my finger to one, and it stuck to my skin.

A sequin.

ELLIS DEAN: Ah, yes: GlitterGate.

During the short dance at the 2013 Russian Grand Prix competition in Moscow, Heath Rocha takes a hard fall in the midst of a stationary footwork sequence.

ELLIS DEAN: I came up with that name. The hashtag was trending on Twitter for days.

VERONIKA VOLKOVA: "GlitterGate." What does this word even mean?

ELLIS DEAN: The whole GlitterGate saga was my top-performing post of the season. Until . . . well, you know.

Medical personnel rush onto the rink to examine Heath. Bella Lin motions Katarina over to the boards, and Katarina holds up her hand, showing Bella something.

VERONIKA VOLKOVA: Shaw and Rocha did not stand a chance competing against my skaters. So what did they do?

As the medics work on Heath, Bella and Katarina speak with the officials. Veronika Volkova stands off to the side, arms folded over her fur coat, looking exasperated.

VERONIKA VOLKOVA: They caused a scene. Over a *sequin.*

KIRK LOCKWOOD: I know it might not seem like a big deal, but even the smallest object on the ice can be dangerous. Your blade can't glide over it, so you just *stop.*

JANE CURRER: The rules regarding point deductions for program interruptions differ based on whether the skaters stop because of a problem with their own equipment, or due to an issue that was no fault of their own.

The conversation with the officials begins to devolve into a heated argument.

JANE CURRER: In either case, the team has a maximum of three minutes to resume their skate, or they are automatically withdrawn from the competition.

VERONIKA VOLKOVA: The sequins were from Katarina's dress.

ELLIS DEAN: Those sequins were there before Shaw and Rocha skated out.

Following their short dance a few moments earlier, young Russian skater Ilya Alekhin lags behind his partner Galina Levitskaya. He bends at the waist and brushes his right hand on the surface of the ice.

ELLIS DEAN: He touched the *exact* spot where Heath tripped. The same spot where every team had to perform the stationary footwork in the Finnstep. You think that's a coincidence?

VERONIKA VOLKOVA: It was unfortunate that her partner tripped, but they had no one to blame but themselves—or perhaps their tacky Hollywood costume designer.

ELLIS DEAN: Levitskaya and Alekhin were a brand-new team, and they'd only recently started training in Moscow. Wanna make a wild guess who their coach was?

VERONIKA VOLKOVA: Galina and Ilya were so excited to compete in their first senior Grand Prix event. It saddens me that their experience was tarnished by this shameless attempt to cast aspersions and create a scandal.

The crowd around Katarina and Bella has grown, with camera operators pushing in to get better angles. Katarina looks directly into the lens and glares. The camera pushes even closer. "Get out of my face," she snaps.

VERONIKA VOLKOVA: The whole thing was a pathetic ploy for sympathy, straight out of the Lin playbook.

ELLIS DEAN: It was flagrant sabotage. Typical Veronika Volkova.

Bella continues trying to reason with the Russian referee. He shakes his head.

VERONIKA VOLKOVA: The rules are clear, no matter how loud a tantrum you throw: three minutes, and you are out.

"Katarina Shaw and Heath Rocha of the United States have withdrawn," comes the official announcement, which is repeated in Russian.

The medics help Heath off the ice. He refuses the stretcher, instead looping his arms around Katarina's and Bella's shoulders. The three of them hobble backstage together.

CHAPTER 70

When Heath and I decided to attempt a comeback, I knew we would face our fair share of obstacles: better teams, biased officials, bad press, all the unresolved personal tensions between him and Bella and me.

But I never guessed we'd be brought down by fucking *sequins*.

Back in my Moscow hotel suite, I checked every square centimeter of that costume ten times over. No sequins were missing. Besides that, the ones I found on the ice were subtly different from the ones on my dress: brighter white, with sharper edges.

I *know* we were sabotaged. I also knew if we pushed the issue, we would only bolster our reputations for courting drama and scandal. Ellis Dean's gossip rag ran the GlitterGate story into the dirt, while every reputable news outlet treated it as a joke.

Back in Los Angeles, my rental property began to draw swarms of paparazzi like flies to rotting meat, so I retreated to the Ice Palace. Though Heath had been telling me the truth—he and Bella slept in separate bedrooms and behaved more like roommates than lovers—it was still strange, the three of us living together after everything we'd put one another through. The house was over ten thousand square feet, and it didn't feel big enough to contain our fraught triangle.

Heath's doctors were optimistic his back would be sufficiently healed for the U.S. National Championships in January. In the meantime, though, he was on a strict regimen of rest, physical therapy, and World Anti-Doping Agency–approved pain medication. I kept up my training as best I could without him, running through the choreography with my arms embracing empty space, like I was dancing with a ghost.

During the Grand Prix Final in December, we set alarms to wake us up at half past midnight so we could watch the live broadcast from Fukuoka, Japan. Volkova and Kipriyanov had to settle for silver, after Gaskell and Kovalenko pulled off an upset for the gold. Those two teams would be the favorites going into the Sochi Olympics. Heath and I would be lucky to make it to the Games at all.

I fell into bed sometime around four, but I couldn't sleep. Every time I closed my eyes, I saw Francesca Gaskell's Disney-princess face gazing up at the American flag. Maybe we'd made a mistake, trying to come back. Maybe we were too old, too tired. Even Bella had seemed wrung out lately—dark circles under her eyes, pushing food around her plate at dinner.

Down the hall, I heard Heath's door open. I tracked his footsteps down the corridor.

Past my room. Stopping at Bella's. She slept in her childhood bedroom still, leaving the sprawling main suite vacant. A whisper of wood across carpet as the door swung open and shut.

Then silence.

Whatever they were doing, I told myself, it was none of my business. I closed my eyes and tried once again to fall asleep.

That lasted about ten minutes, before I got up and crept across the hall to shamelessly eavesdrop. I held my breath and pressed my ear to Bella's door, bracing myself for an encore of what I'd interrupted in Vancouver.

But I only heard their voices, low and familiar. Too low to make out what they said. So familiar, so thoroughly at ease with each other, my chest ached with envy.

I went back to my room. Heath stayed with Bella until morning.

A week before Christmas, Heath finally got the okay to return to the ice. He wasn't allowed to lift me, though, until the new year—only a few days before Nationals.

The first time we tried it, even off-ice with crash pads on the floor, was terrifying. His arms shook and his back spasmed and his face screwed up with agony. But he refused to give up. We'd come too far to stop now.

By the time we flew to Boston, he could lift me without my heart leaping into my throat, and we were back to doing full program runthroughs. Our free dance still felt a bit lackluster, our performance not fully meshing with the music, but we didn't have time to try any significant changes. I did get a new dress for the short dance, though: pleated purple with a kicky skirt and eye-catching lime accents—and absolutely *no* sequins.

Our Finnstep was far from perfect, but thanks to a few uncharacteristic errors from Gaskell and Kovalenko, Heath and I took the lead. Another national title was within our grasp.

Four years before, getting gold had felt like life or death; now I knew from experience that failure wouldn't kill me. Even if we fell to second, our chances of an Olympic berth were solid. But I still wanted to win, to show Frannie, Evan, and everyone else that they couldn't write us off. Heath and I had come back for a reason, and we were going to fight for every point.

The free dance started in the late afternoon. By the time we arrived at the TD Garden arena, the sky was already pitch black, snow flurries shimmying across the frozen Charles River. Bella wore a down coat that looked like a sleeping bag, and she kept it zipped up to her chin even once we were inside.

Ellis Dean had been awarded a special backstage pass to record preskate interviews with the competitors. Before my stretching routine, I put in headphones, hoping he'd take the hint. But when I straightened out of my first forward fold, there he was with that stupid sparkly microphone in my face.

"Congrats on being in the lead going into tonight's final," he said, practically shouting to make sure I could hear him over my music.

I took out one earpiece, leaving the other one blasting the warm-up playlist Heath had curated for me. *Damned if she do, damned if she don't,* moaned Alison Mosshart.

"Although," Ellis continued, "it's easy to exceed expectations when they're low to begin with. How are you feeling about the free dance?"

"I'm feeling *fantastic* about the free dance. Thanks so much for asking, Ellis."

"Where's the lovely Ms. Lin? I'd be thrilled to get her take on your performance too."

"I haven't seen her."

Not since we arrived—which was odd. Usually Bella stuck close while we stretched, and gave us a pep talk before the group warm-up. When I stopped to think about it, she'd been making herself scarce the whole time we'd been in Boston. Our first day, she slept through an early morning practice session, then begged off breakfast to go back to her hotel suite. If I didn't know her better, I would have thought she was sneaking around with some secret lover.

Ellis moved on to Francesca, who flipped her ponytail and grinned, more than happy to serve up sound bites. I went over to Heath, who was on a floor mat completing some physical therapy exercises.

"Have you seen Bella?" I asked.

He shook his head. Even that small motion provoked a wince.

I bent down beside him. "Your back?"

"It's just this cold weather," he said. "Guess California's turned me soft."

He needed more rest, more time, more treatment, but we didn't have it.

"Bella should have some muscle rub in her bag." I straightened up. "I'll go find her."

I figured she was in the bathroom or something, but I checked every stall and there was no sign of her. Maybe she'd gone to get something to eat? Come to think of it, I hadn't seen her consume more than a granola bar in the past forty-eight hours, and that was only after Heath pressed it into her hand.

I remembered seeing some vending machines down a different hallway, so I headed in that direction. Sure enough, there she was, leaning against the wall, still wearing her winter coat.

"Hey," I called out. "Heath's back is acting up, and he was wondering—"

Bella didn't seem to hear me. She didn't even turn her head.

I watched in horror as she slumped to the floor.

CHAPTER 71

I ran to Bella and crouched at her side.

She was conscious, but barely—head sagging limp against the wall, eyes squinted like she couldn't bear the brightness of the fluorescent lights.

"Bella?" I pressed the back of my hand to her forehead. "What's wrong?"

"Shit, is she all right?"

Ellis. He'd followed me.

"You better not fucking write about this," I said.

He pressed a hand to his gold lamé ascot. "What kind of monster do you think I am?"

"You really want me to answer that? Make yourself useful and go get the medics."

Bella let out a soft whimper and clutched at the bottom of her rib cage. Her coat zipper was halfway down, like she'd tried to take it off and given up.

"Find Heath too," I shouted after Ellis. He nodded before scurrying out of sight.

I'd never seen Bella so weak. In all the years we'd known each other, that bitch had never even caught a cold, and now she looked like she was dying. She'd been fine an hour before.

Hadn't she? I reassessed the past several weeks—her oversleeping, her listlessness, her lack of appetite. All the symptoms I'd assumed were due to stress from our punishing training schedule, the uncertainty of Heath's recovery. More than once, I'd had the uncharitable thought that Bella had no right to be so exhausted, when we were the ones doing the real work.

Heath jogged around the corner. When he saw us, he broke into a sprint.

"What happened?" he asked.

"I don't know. I found her like this."

He knelt beside me, dust blurring the knees of his black pants.

"It's okay," he murmured, cupping Bella's sallow cheek. "You'll be okay."

"Heath."

Bella's voice broke across the sound of his name, and it was so vulnerable, so intimate, I felt like I had no right to witness it.

I peered down the hall. Where were the medics? What the hell was taking so long?

When I turned back, Heath was embracing Bella, his face buried in her hair.

His palm pressed to her abdomen.

Before I could fully process the moment, the medical team rushed in.

"Her blood pressure is extremely elevated," the lead medic reported after a few minutes of ministrations. "She needs to go to the emergency room."

Bella seemed to flare back to life. "No, no, they're skating soon. Can't it wait?"

We'd missed the introductions and the warm-up. The first skaters in the final group were already on the ice, the muffled melody of their One Direction program music providing a strangely cheerful counterpoint to the drama unfolding backstage.

"I'm afraid not, dear. The ambulance is on its way."

I glanced at Heath. He didn't take his eyes off Bella.

How had I missed it, all these months? The connection between them. The love. Maybe not the same love he and I had felt for each other, but love all the same.

"You should go with her," I said.

Now he looked my way. But Bella was the one who spoke.

"I'll be *fine*. You have to skate. This is your last chance."

Applause rumbled as the team finished their free dance. Then, in the silence afterward: the wail of approaching sirens.

I knew we were thinking about eight years before in St. Louis, another ambulance racing toward another arena. Another difficult choice that wasn't really a choice at all.

Maybe Bella was right. Maybe it *was* our last chance. All I knew was, I couldn't ask Heath to choose me this time.

"Go," I told him. "I'll be right behind you."

KIRK LOCKWOOD: I assumed their sudden withdrawal was due to Heath's injury. They were real tight-lipped about it, but anyone could tell he was struggling.

NBC's coverage of the 2014 U.S. National Championships cuts away from the competition to show an ambulance pulling up to the TD Garden arena in Boston, Massachusetts.

KIRK LOCKWOOD: Then I got a report that Bella Lin was being rushed to Mass General.

Bella is wheeled out on a stretcher and loaded into the ambulance. Heath climbs in beside her.

ELLIS DEAN: I said I wouldn't write about it on the blog, and I didn't. Well, not right away.

The ambulance drives off, leaving Katarina standing alone, snowflakes swirling around her.

GARRETT LIN: Andre and I were watching the broadcast back in the Bay Area. As soon as we saw Bella, I started packing, and Andre got on the phone to book airline tickets.

FRANCESCA GASKELL: I didn't know what was going on until after Evan and I had already skated. That was probably for the best. Maybe that sounds heartless—but I know Bella, and she would have wanted me to focus on competing, not worrying about her.

JANE CURRER: The Olympic team selection was scheduled to take place immediately following the competition. And once again, at the last possible second, Katarina Shaw and Heath Rocha threw everything into doubt.

Katarina emerges from the dressing room in casual clothes with her hair back in a messy knot, though she hasn't washed off her free dance makeup. A horde of reporters waits for her.

"Katarina! What happened tonight?"

"Why did Heath leave with your coach?"

"Are you planning to petition for a spot on the team? Or is this it for Shaw and Rocha?"

Katarina ignores all the questions, trying to push past. She's visibly struggling under the weight of both her bags and Heath's, which slows her down. Another voice pipes up.

"Hey, Kat."

It's Ellis Dean. Katarina stops.

"Tell me," Ellis says, "why do you and Heath deserve to go to the Games again?"

CHAPTER 72

"Why do you and Heath deserve to go to the Games again?" Everyone fell silent, cameras at the ready to record my response to Ellis.

The question seemed like a blatant provocation—bait dangled to entice me into an arrogant, scorched-earth speech proclaiming that Shaw and Rocha were the best, that they'd be idiots to leave us off the team, that we were sure to wipe the floor with our competition in Sochi.

But Ellis wasn't holding a microphone or a camera. He wasn't trying to set me up to spark some easy clickbait. He was giving me a chance—to remind the world of our past accomplishments, to plead for understanding about our coach's medical emergency, to make a sincere case in favor of sending us to Sochi despite everything.

The perfect opportunity to defend myself, and I couldn't come up with a single point in my own favor. All I could think about was whether my best friend was all right.

"We don't," I said.

Ellis raised his eyebrows. "Excuse me?"

"Heath and I don't deserve to go. No more than the other teams competing tonight."

The space around us exploded with shutters, flashbulbs, more shouted questions. Ellis smirked. Then he stood aside with a sweep of his arm, making me a narrow path to the exit.

✿

The staff at Massachusetts General couldn't stop staring. I wasn't sure whether they recognized me, or were simply taken aback by my heavy makeup, which no doubt looked even tackier after my mad dash from the arena to the hotel to the hospital.

Bella had a private room. She was sitting up, and she appeared brighter and more comfortable than before, even with all the wires and tubes attached to her.

"Hey," I said. "How are you feeling?"

"I'll live."

"Glad to hear it."

"I might have to kill you, though. Why the *hell* didn't you skate?"

Yes, Bella was definitely feeling better. "Because Heath—"

"Heath would have stayed if you asked him to."

I wasn't so sure about that.

"Where is he?" I asked.

"He went to find something to eat that isn't watermelon Jell-O." She made a face. Then her expression turned serious. "Listen, I hate that you have to find out like this, but—"

"You're pregnant."

Bella took a breath in. "How did you know?"

"I didn't, until tonight."

"Then I guess you also know that Heath's the father."

I nodded, though my stomach sank. I hadn't realized how much I'd wanted to be wrong.

"Are you mad?" she asked.

I was feeling many things—so many I couldn't find clear threads to label *anger* or *heartbreak* or anything else.

"I don't have any right to be mad," I said. "Heath and I are just skating partners now."

"Please. You two will never be *just* anything."

"Is that why you decided not to tell me?"

"I'm not due until May. I thought I had plenty of time." Bella laid her hand on the blanket-covered swell of her stomach. "Obviously, none of this was planned."

I attempted some mental math about when she must have conceived, how long she'd been keeping this secret. During the Team USA skating camp we'd been required to attend last August, maybe? She and Heath had disappeared several nights that week, but I figured they were just avoiding all the icebreaker activities and other mandatory fun that crowded the schedule.

"So you're keeping the baby?" I asked.

"I wasn't sure at first," Bella said. "I even made an appointment for an abortion, then canceled it at the last minute. And now . . ."

I sank into the uncomfortable chair beside the bed. "What did the doctors say?"

"I have signs of severe preeclampsia. They want me to stay on bed rest until I deliver."

"Shit." For a woman like Bella Lin, used to working and striving every second of every day, bed rest might be a fate worse than death.

"Tell me about it." She rubbed slow circles over her belly. "Heath says he'll support me, no matter what. But I don't know if he's up for all this. Especially since we're not exactly . . ."

"Not exactly what?"

"Together," she said. "I mean, it's not like I *love* him."

"Bella."

"I don't! Not the way you do. The way you did."

"Bullshit me all you want, but stop bullshitting yourself."

She gave me a wry smile. "You know how much I hate being stuck in second place."

"It isn't a competition." I reached for her hand. "There are lots of different kinds of love."

Love like a steady, warming campfire that keeps you alive in the cold. Love like a raging blaze that burns down everything in its path until nothing but ash remains.

"Do you . . ." Bella twisted the edge of the blanket. "Do you think I'll be a good mother?"

"Are you kidding? You'll be a wonderful mother. The best."

A smile teased at Bella's chapped lips. "So you're saying I'll win at motherhood."

"Absolutely. All the other mothers will wish they could be half as good as you." I squeezed her fingers. "You scared the shit out of me today."

"Yeah, yeah. I still think you should have sucked it up and skated. You might have won."

"We might have. Or Heath might've been so distracted by worrying about you that he dropped me on my head, and I'd be in the hospital too."

We both laughed, right as Heath came through the door. He looked at the two of us apprehensively, an armful of vending machine snacks clutched to his middle.

I stood up and hugged him, plastic wrappers crinkling between us. "Congratulations," I said. Then, whispering so only he could hear, "You'll be a great dad."

Heath's shoulders dropped. "Thank you," he whispered back.

I meant it. Heath's shortage of good parental role models would make him work all the harder to give his own child the love and stability he'd never had himself.

His *child*. It sounded strange. Somehow, though, it also sounded right. And it was something he would've had to give up if he'd stayed with me.

Heath arranged the snacks on the bed for Bella to peruse. She took a sleeve of Oreos. I helped myself to some sourdough pretzels.

"Do you know who won?" Heath asked.

"Francesca and Evan, I assume." I snapped a pretzel in two and offered him half. "I left before they skated."

The competition was over by now. Most likely, the committee was already behind closed doors, deciding our fate. I'd submitted the official petition paperwork on our behalf, though I knew it was a long shot. Heath and I were former national and world champions, past Olympians with more international competition experience than all the other top American teams put together. But that experience came with a lot of baggage too. We might simply have too many strikes against us.

For the time being, there was nothing any of us could do except wait. A prenatal specialist was supposed to come examine Bella as soon as possible, but every question we asked the nurses was answered with some variation on *Just a little while longer, hon.* We found a mindlessly soothing home renovation show on the TV set bolted in the corner and continued working our way through the snack pile.

Finally, someone came to check on us, but it wasn't a doctor.

Ellis Dean stood in the doorway, holding a Get Well Soon balloon emblazoned with a cartoon face that could have been smiling or grimacing.

"Bella," Ellis said. "How are you feeling?"

She scowled. "No comment."

Ellis lifted his hands. The balloon bumped against the low ceiling. "I come in peace. And to tell you to check your goddamn phones already."

Heath and I both retrieved our iPhones, keeping a wary eye on Ellis all the while. Mine was still in silent mode, but several new messages displayed on the screen.

"Holy shit," I said.

"What?" Bella demanded. Heath passed his phone to her.

We were on the Olympic team, along with Gaskell and Kovalenko. The 2014 U.S. silver and bronze medalists had been bumped to the alternate spots.

We'd done it. Shaw and Rocha were going back to the Olympics.

"Don't you dare," Bella said.

"Of course not." Heath sat on the bed beside her. "We would never even consider leaving you, not while—"

"Oh my god, *stop*." Bella's heart monitor beeped faster. She flopped back on the pile of pillows and shot me a weary, exasperated look.

"Ellis, could we have a minute?" I said.

He nodded and slipped into the hall, shutting the door behind him. That damn balloon stayed behind, leering at us from above.

I turned back to Bella. "You want us to go to Sochi."

"Obviously. So don't you *dare* even think about giving up the fucking *Olympic Games* to stay here and play nurse. I'm a Lin, I can afford to hire real nurses. Besides, Garrett's landing at Logan in a few hours, and he's way more nurturing than the both of you put together."

Fair enough. Heath and I looked at each other. I could tell he was torn—which meant that however much he cared for Bella, and for the child they were about to have together, a part of him wanted to see this through. With me.

In the past, I would have done anything to convince him, to bend him to my will. I wanted to go to the Games, of course. The desire flared in my chest—yet another kind of love, the furnace that had been powering me all my life.

But this was a decision we had to make together.

"I'm in," I told Heath. "But only if you are."

He took Bella's hand. "Are you *sure* this is what you want?"

She smiled and held out her other hand, reaching for me.

"I'm sure," she said. "Screw baby showers and push presents. All I want is gold."

JANE CURRER: I had reservations about Shaw and Rocha representing the United States at the Olympics, given their . . . reputations. But it wasn't up to me.

During the official Sochi Olympic figure skating team announcement at the 2014 National Championships, Katarina Shaw, Heath Rocha, Francesca Gaskell, and Evan Kovalenko wave and smile in front of a backdrop covered with the U.S. Olympic team logo.

ELLIS DEAN: I *may* have put in a good word with some friends on the selection committee. Whether or not they ended up on the podium, Kat and Heath competing in Sochi was solid gold content for Kiss & Cry.

FRANCESCA GASKELL: I was just thrilled to finally—*finally*—be going to the Olympics.

GARRETT LIN: Bella's doctors advised her not to fly, so we were stuck in Boston.

KIRK LOCKWOOD: After Nationals, I reached out right away.

GARRETT LIN: Kirk really came through for us. He arranged ice time for Kat and Heath at his family's rink, and put Bella and me up in his guest house.

KIRK LOCKWOOD: It was the least I could do, for Sheila's kids.

GARRETT LIN: I thought competing in the Olympic Games was the hardest thing I'd ever done in my life. Until I tried to keep my sister on strict bed rest.

Cellphone video shows Bella Lin sitting in a plush recliner chair beside the rink at the Lockwood Performance Center while Katarina and Heath run through their short dance. Bella has a microphone, so she can give them instructions without raising her voice.

"Those edge changes were sloppy as hell," she says. "Run it again."

"Don't you think it's time for a break?" comes Garrett's voice from behind the camera.

Bella sticks her tongue out at her brother, then says into the mic, "Again!"

ELLIS DEAN: They went on a total media blackout. No photo shoots, no interviews, no heartwarming NBC Sports packages.

KIRK LOCKWOOD: My bosses at the network were pissed off, but I had to respect it.

INEZ ACTON: As far as I know, I was the only reporter they spoke to, and that was just to contribute a quote for a story I wrote about Russia's anti-LGBT legislation.

A screenshot from feminist blog The Killjoy shows an image of Katarina and Heath, with the headline "Shaw and Rocha Say Russia Should Be 'Ashamed' of 'Bigoted' Anti-Gay Laws—So Why Are Their Teammates So Tight-Lipped?"

ELLIS DEAN: Saying homophobia is bad is literally the *least* they could do, but it was more than most of the American skaters were willing to say.

Francesca Gaskell and Evan Kovalenko are interviewed by NBC. When asked about the controversy, Francesca says, "We don't think it's our place as athletes to get political." Evan nods and adds, "We're just really looking forward to competing in Sochi."

FRANCESCA GASKELL: Once and for all, let me be clear: I have *plenty* of gay friends.

GARRETT LIN: Usually athletes travel a week or more before the Games start, so they can get acclimated and recover from jet lag. But Kat and Heath wanted to maximize their training time with Bella, so they kept pushing their departure.

KIRK LOCKWOOD: They missed the whole first week, including the opening ceremony. Up until the day before they left, they were changing things—in the free dance especially. They must have tried twenty different musical tracks for that program.

Another cellphone video. Katarina and Heath take the opening positions for their free dance.

GARRETT LIN: Kat was the one who finally found the right song. Though I guess Bella had played it for her first, almost a year before.

Low piano chords play: the opening of "The Last Time" by Taylor Swift and Gary Lightbody.

GARRETT LIN: With that music, everything finally clicked—the choreography, the emotion, their connection with each other. But going to the Olympic Games with a program they'd never done in competition before . . . it was a big risk.

The tempo increases, orchestration joining the harmonizing vocals. As the music swells, Heath flips Katarina onto his shoulders for an impressive rotational lift, no sign of pain or hesitation.

The video goes blurry, and there's the sound of whoops and applause.

GARRETT LIN: I think they felt like, why not take the risk? Because we were all well aware, no matter what happened at the Games . . . this *was* the last time.

CHAPTER 73

"It should be under *Lin*," I told the dour-faced hotel clerk. "L-I-N."

Heath and I had been traveling for over twenty-four hours by that point—two planes, a train, and then, once we finally set foot in Sochi, a surprise visit from doping control, who escorted us to an unmarked building and made us drink watered-down fruit juice until we were rehydrated enough to provide samples, even though we'd both repeatedly submitted to random drug testing back in Boston.

By the time we made it to our hotel, it was well after dark—and our rooms, apparently, were no longer available, even though Bella had made the booking months earlier, before the damn building was even finished, and confirmed it before our departure. Twice.

The place still looked under construction, with sawdust covering the lobby furniture, loose wires hanging from light fixtures, and the clerk wearing a handwritten tag that proclaimed, in crooked Sharpie strokes, that his name was *BORIS*.

"No Lin," Boris said. "No room."

Heath stepped in, addressing the man in Russian. No matter how many times I heard him speak the language, it never ceased to be both sexy and unsettling.

But Boris was unmoved. He kept repeating a series of guttural sounds I could only assume were Russian for *Go away stupid Americans, we are fully booked.*

"There's one room open," Heath relayed after a bit more back and forth. "But he says it's quite small."

"As long as it has a bed, I don't give a damn."

I was so exhausted, I felt almost envious of the stray dogs snoozing on the street outside. We had agreed we were too old for the raucous Olympic Village party scene this time around, but I would have happily accepted one of those uncomfortable ultra-long twins if it meant I could get off my feet.

There was no one available to help with our baggage, or even a luggage cart on hand, so we trudged down the dimly lit hallway dragging everything behind us like pack animals. The lobby decor and customer service left a lot to be desired, but I thought surely the room itself would be better.

I thought wrong. The space was a shoebox, with a tiny bathroom bulging off to one side like a tumor and a coatrack in lieu of a closet. The tang of fresh paint was overwhelming, yet somehow the walls looked grungy. There was indeed a bed, but only one—a double, though the shadows made it appear even narrower.

I hung up the garment bags containing our costumes, doing my best to balance the weight so that the flimsy rack wouldn't topple over or snap right in half. Heath's costumes were mostly black, but my free dance dress was delicate sea-foam satin, and I didn't want the fabric touching *anything* in this room.

Heath dropped the rest of our luggage on the greige carpet. "Is it just me, or is this even worse than that motel back in Cleveland?"

"Hey now," I said. "This place has all sorts of amenities that motel in Cleveland didn't offer." I nodded to the only decor on the walls. "For example, this glorious portrait of President Vladimir Putin, here to watch over us while we sleep."

Heath snickered. "What about this light fixture with not one but *two* dead flies inside? Can't find that just anywhere, now can you?"

We both shook with laughter, on the verge of fatigue-induced hysteria. Then the light burned out with a loud pop, and we lost our shit completely, collapsing on the bed, holding our stomachs, tears streaming down our faces.

A few moments passed before I realized how close we were. Our fingers brushed together on the thin comforter, and one of my legs was flung over his. He seemed to realize too, and we both tried to extricate ourselves—only to end up closer, eyes shining inches away from each other in the dark.

A heavy *thump* rattled the door. We sat up.

"What was that?" I asked.

Heath switched on the standing lamp beside the bed. "I don't know."

I slid off the mattress. There was no peephole in the door, so I opened it a few inches, peering out.

A vase filled with red roses sat on the floor outside our room. I looked up and down the hall, but whoever had delivered them was already gone.

I picked up the flowers and shut the door. "These from you?" I asked.

In my jet-lagged stupor, I'd almost forgotten it was the fourteenth of February—though even when we were a couple, we'd never cared much about Valentine's Day. Maybe he'd ordered the flowers for Bella in advance, and forgotten to cancel?

"Nope, not from me." Heath looked down. "Katarina, your shoes."

Something red dripped from the vase, spattering the toes of my sneakers. The stuff was on my hands too, oozing over my knuckles.

I dropped the flowers. The glass shattered, covering the floor in sticky crimson shards. In the center of the mess, there was something white.

"Careful!" Heath said as I bent to pick it up.

A small rectangle of card stock, printed with a short phrase in Cyrillic script.

с возвращением Катарина

My hands shook as I handed the message to Heath. "What does it say?"

He studied the card. "Well, this last word is your name. And the first part—the literal translation would be 'to your return.'"

The corners were stained red, oozing toward the center. Paint, I told myself, or some sort of dye. Except it gave off the copper tang of real blood.

"What it really means, though," Heath said, "is *welcome back.*"

CHAPTER 74

W *elcome back, Katarina.*

  The same message as the bouquet of yellow roses I'd received upon my return to Los Angeles—which I hadn't told Heath, or anyone else, about at the time. The flowers had wilted in a day or two, and I'd tossed them in the trash, along with the cryptic card.

Receiving a dozen roses, Heath informed me, had a very different meaning in Russian culture. Even-numbered flower arrangements were used only for funerals. Yellow blooms, instead of indicating love or friendship, symbolized betrayals and breakups.

As for filling a vase to the brim with blood? No translation necessary there; that was a clear *fuck you* in any country.

Our first full day in Sochi passed without further incident. We ran our programs during our allotted time on the practice rink, then went straight back to our room and tried to sleep—no easy feat with the hotel's paper-thin walls and creaky innerspring mattress.

Bella had been horrified when we told her about the accommodations during our post-practice Skype debrief. But every other hotel in the area was either booked solid or even seedier, so we were stuck.

The ice dance competition started on Sunday evening at the Iceberg Skating Palace, the brand-new skating venue right off the plaza where the Olympic torch burned. On the way there, I was even more exhausted than when we first arrived in Sochi. As soon as we walked inside, though, excitement took over.

The whole building vibrated with energy—the buzz of anticipation from spectators already in the stands, the giddy nerves of the other competitors getting ready to take the ice, the potent mix of pride and awe that only the Olympic Games could provoke.

Before starting our warm-up, we ducked into the arena and snapped a selfie to send to the twins. It was early morning in Boston, but they were awake already, settling in to watch the live stream of the event. Garrett texted *good luck you two!!,* followed by a string of American flag emojis, while Bella's reply was more ominous:

Watch your back.

We couldn't prove the Russians were responsible for my special deliveries, or for Heath's injury at the Rostelecom Cup. But I was sure as hell going to keep a close eye out in case they tried anything else.

I didn't run into either of the Volkovas until Heath and I went our separate ways to get into costume. When I walked into the dressing room, Yelena was already there, busy applying crystals along her lash line to match the rhinestone-encrusted bodice of her dress. Our eyes met in the mirror, and she dropped one of the stones. As she was patting the floor in search of it, I swept past without a second glance.

She looked innocent as ever, all fluttery and delicate like some gossamer-winged blond butterfly, but I wasn't fooled. Yelena was a wolf in sparkly clothing, same as her aunt. She wouldn't have lasted this long in the sport otherwise.

By the time I emerged in my dress, Yelena was gone, and two German girls were vying for her spot at the mirror. I found an empty bench and sat down to lace up my skates.

I'd spent an hour after our morning practice session cleaning and polishing them until the white leather was spotless and the steel blades gleamed. I ran my thumb over the engraved letters of my name and thought of the carving Heath and I had made all those years ago.

Shaw & Rocha. The way our names would be written in the record books.

Some skaters have superstitions about which skate they put on first.

They have to do it in the same order every time, or risk casting a pall of bad luck over their performance. I've never given it much thought; whichever one I grab, right or left, that's the one I step into.

Before the short dance in Sochi, it was the left. I slipped my foot into the boot, savoring the feel of the custom-fit leather molding around my ankle, cradling my instep.

Then something stabbed deep into my arch, and all I could do was scream.

VERONIKA VOLKOVA: Yes, I heard the scream. Everyone did.

Before the short dance event at the 2014 Winter Olympics, Katarina Shaw bursts out of the backstage dressing room. She's holding her skates, and she looks livid.

Other skaters, including fellow team USA ice dancer Francesca Gaskell, rush over to see what's the matter. Katarina ignores them, frantically glancing around—until she spots Heath Rocha, sitting on a bench several yards away, about to step into his own skates.

"STOP!" Katarina shouts.

ELLIS DEAN: I was backstage doing interviews, minding my own damn business. Then all hell breaks loose. Luckily my camera was already rolling.

Heath looks up, confused. Katarina hurries past—leaving a trail of bloody footprints.

VERONIKA VOLKOVA: She seemed to have a little cut on her foot. That is all.

ELLIS DEAN: Kat was bleeding everywhere. It was like a murder scene.

FRANCESCA GASKELL: I just tried to stay out of the way. You know what she could be like. *(She shakes her head.)* That *temper.*

Veronika Volkova stands nearby, talking with Yelena Volkova and Dmitri Kipriyanov. Katarina stalks up to them and turns her skates upside down. Several small objects tumble out.

ELLIS DEAN: There were *thorns* in her skates.

Katarina hurls accusations at the Russian coach and skaters. Only a few words are audible on the video—"flowers," "blood," and "sabotage."

VERONIKA VOLKOVA: I had no idea what she was going on about.

ELLIS DEAN: Not like little tiny ones either. Big jagged motherfuckers.

Heath checks his own skates. Sure enough, when he turns them over, more thorns fall out.

ELLIS DEAN: First GlitterGate, now this. Her foot was all ripped up, and if she hadn't warned Heath in time, his would've been too.

The camera moves in closer as Katarina continues her tirade. Yelena shrinks away, while Veronika stands her ground, seeming vaguely amused by the situation. Dmitri stands off to the side, looking dumbfounded—until Heath comes to stand by Katarina's side.

"This is low," Heath says. "Even for you."

Dmitri gets in Heath's face, growling something in Russian. Katarina moves between them, but not to keep the peace. She shoves Dmitri so hard he stumbles back, hitting the cement floor.

VERONIKA VOLKOVA: She should have been disqualified, then and there. But the Americans allow their athletes to get away with anything.

ELLIS DEAN: For once, Kat and Heath had every right to throw a fit. Someone had sabotaged them. And let's be real: we all knew who the most likely culprits were.

Medics arrive to look at Katarina's cuts—and now Dmitri's bruised tailbone too.

Heath takes some first aid supplies, but waves off the medics so he can tend to Katarina's foot himself. As he kneels in front of her, dabbing disinfectant on the gouges left by the thorns, Katarina continues to glare daggers at the Russians.

ELLIS DEAN: One thing's for sure: when they took the ice, they were out for blood.

CHAPTER 75

I survived the short dance on adrenaline, spite, and a dry-swallowed dose of ibuprofen.

By the end of the night, we were in first place, a full two points ahead of the Russians, and my foot was so swollen I could barely get it out of my boot. Heath offered me some of his prescription painkillers to take the edge off, then realized he'd left the bottle back at our hotel—which we couldn't return to until we sat through a barrage of questions from event officials about the "incident," as they insisted on calling it.

Why hadn't I checked my skate before putting it on? Why didn't we report the bloody flowers right away, if they disturbed us so much? Had our bags been unattended at any point? Where? For how long?

As if it was somehow our fault. As if we didn't know better than to leave our skates lying around in a place swarming with professional rivals.

Between practice and the short dance, our equipment hadn't been out of our sight—with the exception of a ten-minute span where I'd taken a shower and Heath had gone to get us some food. He was adamant that he'd locked the door behind him. Which meant whoever did this had access to our room, or they'd bribed the hotel staff. The Kipriyanov family's mob connections would've made that easy. Actually proving the Russian team was behind the sabotage would be much harder.

The officials pulled sympathetic faces and swore to conduct a "thorough investigation." But the damage was done. The most important competition of my career was less than twenty-four hours away, and my foot was full of puncture wounds.

Clearly the hotel wasn't safe, but we had nowhere else to go. We'd have to barricade the door and hope for the best. As we made our way back, Heath shouldered all our bags himself and let me lean on him to take the weight off my injured foot. No matter how slowly and carefully I walked, every limping step ended in pure agony.

The hotel lobby was deserted. The lights flickered as we made our way down the hall, turning the ambience that much more apocalyptic.

We reached our room. Heath dug into his pocket for the key.

"Wait," I said.

The door was open, a sliver of darkness between the edge and the frame.

Fresh adrenaline flooded my body, washing away the exhaustion. We had closed and locked it before leaving for the venue. Someone had broken in again, and this time they wanted us to know.

"Stay here," Heath said, but I was already pushing past him, nudging the door open the rest of the way. I threw the light switch, but the burnt-out bulb hadn't been replaced.

There was enough illumination from the hallway to outline the stain the broken vase had left on the carpet, the shapes of our luggage next to the coatrack in the corner, the crooked stem of the lamp beside the bed—and something else.

A still, dark shadow spread across the mattress. Shaped like a body.

CHAPTER 76

Red and blue lights flashed over the freezing pavement. I sat on the curb with my knees pulled under my chin and tried not to think about it.

But the smell was all over me. That thick, metallic reek, blended with the aroma of roses.

This time, there had been no flowers. No thorns. Only petals—ripped out and scattered like in a honeymoon suite. My free dance dress was draped over the bed, covered in rose petals.

And soaked through with blood.

Animal blood, the Sochi City Police thought. Maybe cow or pig, from a butcher shop. A tasteless prank, certainly, but no one had been hurt. Nothing had been stolen either. Two officers stood and watched as Heath and I searched every compartment in every piece of luggage; all our possessions were there, undamaged, including Heath's costume for the free dance. It was a shame about my pretty dress, but couldn't I wear another one?

We tried to tell them about the rest of it, to explain the pattern, the escalation from the strange flowers to the wounds on the sole of my foot to this horror show in our hotel room. I quickly reached the limit of my patience, but Heath kept appealing in Russian to the cops, the night shift clerk, the hotel security guard, even a few other guests who'd ventured out to see what was causing all the commotion. None of them had witnessed anything suspicious.

"Seriously?" I said when he relayed this to me.

"So they say."

"And the police, what are they going to—"

"What do you think?"

They weren't going to do any more than the Olympic officials. Ask a few questions, write up a report, send us on our merry way.

Heath offered his hand to help me up. The pain in my foot thrashed like a live wire, searing the entire left side of my body. A ruined dress was the least of my problems. How the hell was I going to make it through the free dance like this?

"You'd better get some ice on that," came a voice from behind us.

Ellis Dean stood under a streetlamp, looking uncharacteristically subdued in a black wool overcoat. He ambled toward us, hands in his pockets, casual as can be.

"How are you doing?" he asked. "I heard what happened."

The Olympics were a glorified small town, and Ellis knew everyone. I was just surprised he'd managed to make it here fast enough to scoop the other media outlets.

"Ellis," Heath said. "We've had a long day."

"I just wanted to—"

"What, take a picture for your stupid blog?" I said. "Maybe a whole fucking slide show? Sorry I don't have blood all over my face, I bet that would make the header image *really* pop."

Ellis sighed and slipped something out of his pocket: a small black plastic card. Heath and I both looked at it like it might bite.

"The key to my hotel room," Ellis said. "They have actual security there. And working deadbolts. And a pretty bomb breakfast buffet."

I eyed him suspiciously. "What's the catch?"

"No catch. I'm sleeping elsewhere tonight, and there's no sense in letting a perfectly good room go to waste."

"You got a hot date or something?"

"Did I mention the buffet?" Ellis waved the card back and forth. "Not one, not two, but *three* different kinds of blini."

I stared at him until he rolled his head back with a groan.

"Fine, yes, I have a date. A certain silver fox with a golden voice *may* have invited me over for a vodka martini nightcap."

I made a face. "You and *Kirk*?"

"He's old enough to be your father," Heath said.

"Which makes him the perfect age to be my *daddy*." Ellis waggled his well-groomed eyebrows. "And I don't want to keep him waiting, so could you two *please* set aside your pride and accept this gesture of simple human kindness before I change my mind?"

I glanced at Heath. His posture was tense, but he didn't protest. Wherever Ellis was staying, it had to be an improvement on the actual crime scene that awaited us inside.

"You know, Ellis," I said. "You're a pretty good guy when you want to be."

"Yeah, yeah." He slapped the keycard into my palm. "You better not tell anyone, bitch."

ELLIS DEAN: I'd never seen Kat like that. She looked scared.

VERONIKA VOLKOVA: How many times must I repeat myself? I had nothing to do with it.

KIRK LOCKWOOD: The Russians tried to hush up the whole thing. The Sochi Games had enough bad press already, what with all the unfinished construction and the corruption. Not to mention the Russian government's blatant homophobia.

VERONIKA VOLKOVA: Wild accusations, without proof. Still to this day you have no proof, and yet you continue to ask me about this. It is insulting. Tell me why I should not get up and leave right now.

ELLIS DEAN: When I let Kat and Heath stay in my hotel room the night before the free dance, I really thought that would be enough. I thought that'd be the end of it.

Katarina Shaw and Heath Rocha emerge from a taxi outside the Radisson Blu Resort hotel in Sochi, Russia. As Heath pays the driver, Katarina catches sight of the camera filming them from across the street, but she seems too weary to summon a glare.

ELLIS DEAN: Unfortunately, it was only the beginning.

CHAPTER 77

Ellis's room at the Radisson was so generic, we could have been anywhere in the world.

It was absolute heaven. I took my first hot shower in days, then rigged up a cold pack for my throbbing foot with the plastic bag from the ice bucket, while Heath figured out how to connect his phone to the Bluetooth speaker on the nightstand. We both availed ourselves of his painkillers before he hopped in the shower too. He was on the same pills I'd been prescribed after my fall at 2006 Nationals, and I was already looking forward to the warm-bath sensation that would wash over me once they kicked in.

He came out of the bathroom wearing a towel around his waist, beads of water clinging to his back. The hot water had made his scars stand out in sharp relief.

"How's your foot?" he asked.

"Better. The ice is taking the swelling down."

I moved over on the memory foam mattress to make room for him, and he lay back against the pillows, shoulder touching mine. His moody folk-rock playlist wrapped around us like a soothing sonic blanket, but I still wasn't feeling anything from the medication.

"Let me see," Heath said.

"It's gross."

"Katarina."

With a sigh, I twisted around to lay my foot in his lap—careful to hold my hotel bathrobe shut, since I wasn't wearing anything underneath. Not that he hadn't seen it all before.

Heath examined my wounds, the heat of his hands grazing my skin. I flinched.

"Sorry," he said. "Did that hurt?"

"No." Yes, but I didn't want him to stop.

"Want me to bandage it up again?"

"Probably better to let it breathe."

Heath nodded and set my foot gently down on the comforter, then reached behind him to adjust the pillows for more support.

"Your back?" I said.

He nodded. I stood on my knees and gestured for him to sit up.

"You don't have to—" he started.

"I want to." I smoothed my palm over his trap and dug my thumb under his scapula. "Unless you don't think you can take it?"

Heath smiled. "Do your worst."

For the next twenty minutes, I worked my way through every major muscle in his back. He melted under my touch, eventually stretching out flat on his stomach so I could get more leverage. I straddled his legs and ground my knuckles into his lumbar spine until he groaned.

"You are *evil*," he mumbled into the pillows.

"Oh, come on. You've had worse."

I was only teasing. But with my fingers brushing his scarred skin, it didn't seem so funny.

"I'm sorry," I said.

Heath flipped over underneath me. "For what?"

"That you had to go through . . . everything you went through. That I wasn't—"

"Like you said." His voice rumbled against my bare thighs. "I've had worse."

"Still." The belt of my robe was starting to come undone. Heath's towel had slipped too, exposing his hip bones. "No one deserves—well, whatever the hell Veronika did to you."

"It wasn't Veronika."

I froze.

"She never touched me," he continued. "Although she did scream a lot, whenever we did something wrong in practice. She said it was so we wouldn't make the same mistake twice."

My hands had come to rest on Heath's chest. His fingertips skimmed the hem of my robe.

"If it wasn't Veronika," I said. "Then who—"

My phone buzzed on the nightstand. We both turned to look.

Bella Lin's smiling face lit up the screen.

CHAPTER 78

"Is everything okay?" Bella said as soon as I picked up the Skype call. "You didn't contact me after the short, and I—"

She stopped, taking in the scene on her phone screen: my flushed cheeks and messy hair, Heath's bare chest, the different decor behind us. The Civil Wars in the background, crooning mournfully about *the one that got away*.

"Where are you two?"

"Ellis gave us his hotel suite for the night," I explained.

"Ellis *Dean*?"

We gave her a rundown of our eventful evening. The tampering with our skates had been mentioned on the broadcast, accompanied by backstage footage of me flipping my shit at the Russian team—though Kirk had shied away from outright accusing them of sabotage on air. But this was the first Bella was hearing about the hotel room break-ins, my ruined dress, or the dismissive response from Sochi law enforcement. Guess Ellis was too busy enjoying that nightcap to get a new Kiss & Cry post written.

"What are you going to wear tomorrow?" Bella asked.

"My short dance dress again, I guess." The bright colors clashed with the character of our free program, but it was my only option unless I wanted to compete in the Olympic final in my warm-up gear.

Bella never once questioned *whether* we would take the ice for the free dance. We were Shaw and Rocha. Swollen feet and bad backs and bloody dresses weren't anywhere near enough to scare us away.

"How are you feeling?" Heath asked. I opened my mouth to answer him—then realized he was addressing Bella.

"I'm fine," she said. "Garrett's taking good care of me."

Garrett popped into view behind her, holding a mixing bowl. He waved to us with the pancake batter–covered spatula.

Bella shot her brother a look. "Maybe *too* good."

"You're welcome." Garrett kissed the top of her head and looked down at the phone. "Good luck tomorrow, guys! Show those Russians who the real champs are."

"Try and get some rest," Bella said. "And until we know for sure who's behind all this: don't trust anyone."

Heath and I nodded. The screen went dark. We were alone again in the bed, sitting even closer since we'd had to squeeze together to both fit in the video frame.

I shifted away from him, clearing my throat. "She's right. We should get some rest."

We took turns in the bathroom, changing into proper pajamas and brushing our teeth.

"You want another one before bed?" Heath asked, shaking the orange painkiller bottle. "I swear these don't do a damn thing for me anymore. I took three, and I can't feel a thing."

"I'm good." The pills hadn't made much difference in my pain level either, and my makeshift ice pack was melting. I dabbed some more disinfectant on, then climbed into bed.

Heath switched off the lights and joined me; this time he kept a respectful distance. I spent a few minutes arranging pillows to elevate my foot before flopping back beside him.

"Aren't we a pair?" I said.

"A couple of geriatric has-beens, hanging on by a thread."

"Hey now, we would've been fine if it weren't for the fucking Volkovas."

Heath went quiet for a moment. "You're sure it's them?"

"Of course it's them." I turned to face him. "Who else would it be?"

"I don't know. Veronika's terrifying, but she usually takes her wrath out on her own skaters. And Yelena . . ."

I tried not to bristle at the softness in his voice when he said her name.

"She's not what you think," he said. "When I was in Moscow, she was the only person who was kind to me."

"Because she wanted you to be her partner."

"Even before that, when she was still with Nikita. She helped me learn the language. She stayed late to give me tips on my skating technique."

"So she wanted to sleep with you."

"Maybe." Heath turned toward me too. "Or maybe she needed a friend as much as I did. Although I wasn't a very good friend to her, in the end."

"What do you mean?"

"I left without saying goodbye, right when we were supposed to start training together. Knowing Veronika, I'm sure she put all the blame on Yelena, made her believe she'd driven me away or something."

"Earlier, you said . . ." I swallowed. Before Bella called, he'd been on the verge of telling me the truth he'd kept locked up tight for all those years. "If Veronika didn't hurt you, then who did, Heath?"

He was silent for so long, I thought he'd fallen asleep. Then he whispered to me, like we were teenagers again, wrapped up in each other under the covers, trying not to get caught.

"I've done a lot of things I'm not proud of, Katarina. To get back to you."

Somehow, we'd drifted close again. His hand was on my pillow, buried in my damp hair. I found the edge of his jaw and traced up to the scar under his eye.

"So have I," I said.

"But I also made my whole existence about you, for far too long." Heath's words came out in a rush, as if he'd been storing them up for ages. "I grew up without a family or a culture or anything of my own, so when I found you . . . it wasn't fair to either of us. I had to figure out my own passion, my own purpose in life."

He wasn't going to give me the answers I wanted. Not tonight. Maybe not ever.

"And you've found that?" I asked. "Your purpose?"

"I'm working on it."

In Los Angeles. With Bella, and their baby. Whether or not they were in love, soon Heath and Bella would be family in a way he and I had never been.

His lips brushed my hand. "We've wasted so much time, haven't we?"

We had. Years and years we could never get back. If we won the gold medal, would it all be worth it? Not so long before, I would have said yes without hesitation.

"We're here now," I told him. "Let's not waste any more."

KIRK LOCKWOOD: By the morning, word had spread about the latest attack on Shaw and Rocha. My producer still wouldn't let me point any fingers, but I had my suspicions.

VERONIKA VOLKOVA: I am tired of talking about this. Move on, or we are finished here.

ELLIS DEAN: There was speculation that Kat and Heath might not show up for the free dance.

FRANCESCA GASKELL: I blocked it all out. I was totally focused on the final. On the gold.

ELLIS DEAN: And then there was speculation about *that* speculation—people saying they'd staged the whole thing themselves to save face and create an excuse to withdraw, since they knew they couldn't win.

GARRETT LIN: No one who really knew them would've believed that crap for a second. Nothing could have kept them from competing that day.

VERONIKA VOLKOVA: We are not here to rehash all this baseless speculation, are we? No. We are here to talk about what happened next.

CHAPTER 79

On the day of the Olympic final, I slept late for the first time in years.

A knock at the door woke me mid-morning. I sat up, and Heath's arm, which had ended up across my waist in the middle of the night, slid away into the rumpled bedding. The sun sparkled over the Black Sea outside our window, and I felt rested, limber, ready.

Until I put my foot down on the carpet, and a starburst of pain flared out to my toes.

Another knock. "I'll get it," Heath mumbled.

He went to the door, rolling his neck, which set off a series of harsh cracks, like chain link unraveling. His back was always at its worst first thing in the morning, but not *that* bad. Maybe his body had acclimated too much to the meds.

All we needed to do was get through the four minutes of our free dance. One way or another, by the end of the day, our competitive careers would be over.

I checked my phone and found two texts from Ellis. The first said he was going out to brunch with Kirk, so we'd have the room to ourselves until the afternoon—followed by a suggestive winky smiley face. He'd be so disappointed to know that all we'd done was sleep.

The second was a heads-up that our relocation to the Radisson had leaked, and there were reporters outside waiting for us. Great.

Heath returned carrying a large white box. I shifted back, immediately suspicious.

"What is that?" I asked.

"I don't know. The card says it's from . . ." His eyes widened. "Yelena."

He set the box on the bed and showed me the note, handwritten in pretty Cyrillic script.

"Read it," I said.

"It says she had this couriered overnight from Moscow. For you."

I ran my fingers over the smooth edge of the box, half expecting it to spring some sort of trap, metal teeth clamping down on my hand.

"'We are competitors, but we do not have to be enemies,'" Heath read. "'I look forward to competing with you today. May the best team triumph.'"

"You really trust her?" I asked.

"More than the rest of them." He set the card down. "You want to open it, or should I?"

"I'll do it." I dug a nail under the tape holding the box shut. "But if there's blood in here, I'm bringing it to the Skating Palace tonight and going full *Carrie* on this bitch."

Heath watched over my shoulder as I lifted the lid and peeled back the tissue paper.

Inside was a skating costume—intended to replace my ruined one, I assumed. A lovely gesture, but there was no way in hell I could fit into Yelena Volkova's clothes.

Heath held the garment up for a closer look. Sunlight caught the gilt trim, and I gasped.

"What?" he said.

I took the dress from him and held it against my body, running my hands over the fine fabric. Amazingly enough, it looked like a perfect fit.

"You were right," I said. "Yelena is not at all what I thought."

Although I would *absolutely* be checking the lining for thorns or poison spikes or any other sign of treachery before I actually put the thing on; I'd learned my lesson.

"I hate that she has to skate with that psycho," Heath said.

"Dmitri?" I laid the dress on the unmade bed. "He seems kind of full of himself, but—"

"Trust me," Heath said. "My one regret about leaving Russia is that Yelena was stuck partnering with him. The guy is a nightmare, and even Veronika won't discipline him."

"Because his grandpa's a big-shot mob boss or whatever?"

"Not just his grandfather. His whole family. They're bad people."

"Your scars," I said. "Did Dmitri have anything to do with . . . with what happened?"

Heath hesitated. I watched the warring desires skirmish on his face. A part of him longed to surrender to my curiosity; another part wanted to keep defending the barriers he'd built up to protect himself. I couldn't force him. I couldn't rush him. He had to be the one to tear down the walls, brick by brick—and whenever he was ready, I'd be waiting on the other side.

He paced toward the window and stared out at the sea. Then, finally, he began to speak.

"Around the time Nikita retired, Dmitri's previous partner quit the sport. So Veronika invited him to try out with Yelena. That old church building was impossible to heat, and Dmitri came on one of the coldest days of the year."

I tried to picture Heath there, but all I could think of was him shivering in the stable—only without me to bring him blankets, to press my body close to his and rub life back into his ice-cold hands.

"Yelena kept making mistakes, and Dmitri wouldn't stop berating her. Veronika stood there and let him do it. So I took him aside and told him to knock it off." Heath finally looked at me, fresh rage still smoldering in his eyes. "And he shoved me through a stained-glass window."

"Jesus."

"I think it was Saint Andrew, actually."

"Very funny." I pushed against his arm. He grimaced. "Shit, sorry."

"Don't worry about it. That merciless pummeling you gave me last night helped."

"You're welcome." I considered what he'd told me. "What if it's Dmitri? Maybe *he's* been the one sabotaging us all along, and the Volkovas didn't have anything to do with it."

Thorns in skates and butcher shop blood on the bed seemed like extreme measures to rattle your opponents, even in a notoriously dramatic sport like skating. For the Russian mob, though? That was child's play.

Heath shook his head. "Dmitri's not smart enough to put together a plan like that. Not on his own. He reminds me of your brother, actually—all dumb brute force, zero impulse control."

He reached for the bottle of painkillers on the nightstand, tapping out two white pills.

"You want any?" he asked.

I waved him off. "They didn't do much last night. Guess I'll just have to tough it out."

"If there's one thing you're good at, Katarina Shaw, it's toughing it out."

I touched his arm again, sure to be gentle this time.

"I'm sorry that happened to you," I said. "I'm sorry I wasn't there."

"I'm sorry too." He laid his hand over mine. "Cause you'd've kicked that pretty boy's ass, and I would sure have loved to see that."

I thought about the way Dmitri came at us before the short dance, the chilly menace in his eyes. After I shoved him, he refused all forms of help, growling like a feral dog at anyone foolish enough to approach him—the medics, his coach, his partner, even sweet little Francesca Gaskell.

I hadn't been there when he gave Heath those scars. But the best revenge would be kicking Dmitri's ass today—and now, thanks to Yelena, I'd look damn good doing it.

"Better get moving," I said. "We have gold medals to win."

The final group of ice dancers are introduced before the free dance at the 2014 Winter Olympics.

ELLIS DEAN: Talk about an entrance.

"Representing the United States of America, Katarina Shaw and Heath Rocha!"

KIRK LOCKWOOD: I couldn't believe my eyes.

Katarina and Heath skate out hand in hand, looking strong and formidable, unswayed by the turmoil of the past twenty-four hours. Katarina lifts her arms and spins to show off her new costume. The dress is red velvet, trimmed with golden embroidery.

She's wearing Veronika Volkova's Catherine the Great costume from the Calgary Games.

VERONIKA VOLKOVA: I suppose it was *similar*, from a distance. But *my* Catherine the Great gown was much grander.

Backstage after the warm-up, Veronika and Yelena Volkova have a heated argument. This time, there are no tears from Yelena. She gives her aunt an imperious smirk and struts away.

GARRETT LIN: I didn't recognize the dress, but my sister did, right away.

VERONIKA VOLKOVA: It was much too tight on her. She looked like overstuffed kielbasa.

GARRETT LIN: Kat looked beautiful, but not because of the dress. It was the way she carried herself, the look on her face.

The camera zooms in on Katarina's face, echoing the close-up of Sheila Lin before her 1988 gold medal skate. Like Sheila, Katarina looks totally confident, as if she's already triumphed.

ELLIS DEAN: Katarina Shaw was in the building, and that bitch had come to *win*.

CHAPTER 80

Less than thirty minutes left.

We'd already warmed up and triple-checked every piece of equipment, from our skate blades to the bobby pins in my hair. All we could do now was wait for our turn on the ice.

Heath's back still hurt, and my foot still throbbed, but I knew we could push through the pain. We were stronger than ever—as individuals and as a team. We could win.

I left my skates under Heath's watchful eye as I headed backstage for a final makeup touch-up. Right as I reached the women's dressing room, the door swung open. I stood aside to let the person exit, focusing on the floor tiles rather than meeting their eyes. I had no interest in trying to psych out my competitors; this was about me and Heath, no one else.

Then I saw the black skates. Only men wore black skates in competition.

I looked up. Into the cold hazel eyes of Dmitri Kipriyanov.

He held my gaze for a second—face slack with surprise, full lips flushed pink—before walking away, leaving the door swinging in his wake. Yelena must be in the dressing room. She'd needed something, and he brought it to her. That was the only explanation.

But when I went inside, the only person there was Francesca Gaskell.

She stood at the mirror, applying another coat of rosy lipstick. The same color smeared across Dmitri's mouth. When she saw me, she smiled.

"Love the dress," Francesca said. "How'd you find another one so fast?"

"It's a long story." I stepped closer. "Look, I saw Dmitri."

She capped the lipstick tube and turned to face me.

"I don't know what's going on between you two," I said. "But he's not a good guy."

Francesca only blinked at me, the picture of wide-eyed innocence.

"Maybe he's different with you, but if he ever hurts you, or—"

"I appreciate your concern. You don't have to worry, though."

Her voice was all warmth. Something colder glinted in her eyes.

"Dmitri would never hurt me."

Dmitri's not smart enough . . . not on his own.

But Francesca was. Smart enough to plot behind my back while smiling in my face. Skilled enough at playing so sweet that no one would suspect a thing.

Don't trust anyone.

"I thought you of all people would understand," she said.

"Me?" I took a step back. "Why?"

"Because you're *Katarina Shaw.* You'll do anything to win."

"That's not—"

"You and Heath are *clearly* bad for each other, and yet you keep reeling him back again and again so you can use him to get what you want."

She zipped up her makeup bag. The metallic slide set my teeth on edge.

"Not that I'm judging," she said. "It's inspiring, honestly, how thoroughly you've got him wrapped around your little finger."

"You don't know anything about me and Heath."

"Maybe not." Francesca shrugged. "But I know I'm going to take that gold from you today. You can't win, Kat. This comeback of yours was doomed from the start."

Her words should have riled me up, incited me to respond with trash talk of my own.

But all I felt was a deep, aching sadness.

Francesca had grown up watching me, like I'd grown up watching Sheila. She said I was *inspiring,* but what had I inspired? There was no joy left in her, no light. Those smiles were a mask, concealing a molten core of grasping ambition.

I wanted to shake her by the shoulders and tell her it wasn't too late. She could wake up. She could realize there was more to life than winning.

Happiness couldn't be won. It couldn't be hung around our necks while a crowd of thousands cheered. It wasn't a prize, something we had to suffer and toil to earn. If we wanted happiness, we had to create it ourselves. Not in one shining moment on a medal stand, but every single day, over and over again.

I could have told Francesca all that, but it wouldn't have mattered. She'd have to learn for herself, like I did.

So instead, I wrapped my arms around her.

She stiffened, probably afraid I was about to bury a knife in her back. I didn't let go.

"Good luck today, Frannie," I whispered.

Francesca stared after me, caught between fury and confusion, as I walked out.

I was confused too, about why such a promising young skater would risk her own career for the sake of petty sabotage. Between Francesca's family money and Dmitri's criminal connections, all of it would have been easy enough to pull off.

But to what end? They couldn't really believe that was enough to stop me and Heath, not after all we'd been through. Then again, they weren't like us. They'd both grown up rich and coddled. Everything in their lives had worked out in their favor thus far, so why wouldn't this?

You can't win, she'd told me, but it hadn't sounded like a threat— and that, more than anything, was what troubled me. Francesca had said the words with such supreme, chilling confidence, like the outcome was already decided. Like she already held an unbeatable hand, and all she had to do was lay her cards on the table.

Heath leaned against a pillar in the backstage area, our skate bags at his feet. As I approached, he clapped a hand over his mouth, then took a swig from his water bottle.

More painkillers. He'd taken a dose in the morning. Another before we left for the arena.

"Your back is still bothering you?" I said.

"Yeah. I swear it's like the meds are making it worse instead of taking the edge off." He winced as he bent down to stow his water bottle. "Don't worry, though: I only took one. I'm still below the maximum daily—"

"Let me see."

"See what?"

"The bottle."

He handed it to me. I twisted off the cap and took out one of the white tablets. Francesca and Evan were about to take the ice. Then it would be Yelena and Dmitri's turn. Then ours.

"What's the matter?" Heath asked.

I studied the pill, running my thumb over the chalky edge. I thought of the sequins I'd found on the ice at the Grand Prix in Moscow—tiny white discs, so like the ones on my dress. But not quite the same.

Not quite right.

"We have a problem," I said.

CHAPTER 81

Heath and I went outside to talk, so we wouldn't be overheard.

Right between the Skating Palace and the steel carapace of Fisht Olympic Stadium was a patch of scrubby brown grass and evergreen shrubs, surrounded by a grove of yew trees. I'd walked past many times that week, assuming it was a garden—though it seemed a bit unkempt in comparison to the rest of the manicured Olympic grounds, and I never saw anyone enter.

As we hurried toward it in the dark, hoping for a few minutes of privacy, I realized the space wasn't a garden at all.

It was a graveyard. A few rows of headstones stood under the trees like sentries.

"Francesca and Dmitri," I said in a hushed voice. "They're working together."

"*What?*" Heath exclaimed. Then, softer, "But what does that have to do with—"

"I think . . ." I took a deep breath of the bracing night air. "I think they might have tampered with your medication."

Francesca Gaskell was rich, coddled—and the heiress of a pharmaceutical empire with labs and stockpiles on every continent.

"You think they swapped them out for placebos or something?" Heath said. "And that's why they're not working anymore?"

The night of the short dance, he'd left the bottle in our hotel room. It would have been easy enough for whoever was doing Francesca and Dmitri's dirty work to empty the bottle and refill it with something else.

We'd been so worried about the blood, the dress, the break-in. Maybe those things had only been a distraction, to keep us from noticing the *real* treachery.

"They wouldn't go to so much trouble to trick us into taking sugar pills," I said. "I think whatever's in that bottle is—"

"A banned substance." Heath buried his head in his hands. "Fuck."

You can't win, Francesca had said. If we won the gold, or made it onto any step of the podium, we'd have to submit to drug testing—and then they'd detect the substance, and we'd have our medals stripped. We could try to fight it, say we didn't know what we were taking, accuse Francesca and Dmitri directly. But they would deny it, and given our reputations, who would believe us over them?

Heath paced back and forth, processing all this. Francesca and Evan must be done by now. The Russian team would be starting their free dance any second. We had to go back inside. We had to decide what to do.

"Are you feeling anything strange?" I asked. "Any other symptoms, or—"

"No. Just the pain in my back. You?"

I shook my head. Aside from my injured foot, I felt fine. Normal. But I'd only taken two pills, and none since last night. Whatever the stuff in that bottle was, Heath had far more in his system than I did.

"We should withdraw, right?" he said. "Even if we win, we lose. So what's the point?"

Withdrawing was the smart move. But it meant all our hard work over the past year was for nothing. Our careers would end with a whimper instead of a bang, and we would never know whether or not we could have won. And what if I was wrong? The pills *could* have been placebos. Or I could've simply spun myself into a paranoid frenzy over nothing.

I swept my eyes over the graveyard. It reminded me so much of the family plot back home—a sliver of raw, rough nature in the midst of all this shiny newness. Sacred ground not even the global machine of the Olympic Games could bulldoze into submission. It had been there for a century already, and it would survive long after we were all bones in the dirt.

414

"We can't quit. Not now." I held out my hand. "What do you say?"

"I say . . ." He smiled and interlaced his fingers with mine. "I'm skating with Katarina Shaw, and there's nothing she can't do."

"We're Shaw and Rocha," I said. "And there's nothing *we* can't do. Together."

KIRK LOCKWOOD: They stepped onto the ice, and everyone in the Iceberg Skating Palace held their breath. Myself included.

Katarina Shaw and Heath Rocha take their opening positions for the free dance at the 2014 Winter Olympics. They don't smile up at the crowd. They're focused solely on each other.

ELLIS DEAN: Remember, no one had seen this updated program before.

INEZ ACTON: Taylor Swift! Fucking iconic. Too many people sleep on "The Last Time," but real Swifties know it's a total bop. My girls and I were ready to sing along.

NICOLE BRADFORD: My husband and I watched live. It was incredible seeing how far they'd come, from little kids clomping around the ice to Olympic superstars.

VERONIKA VOLKOVA: Yelena and Dmitri left the door wide open for both American teams. I have no idea what had gotten into that girl; it was as if she *wanted* to fail.

GARRETT LIN: Gaskell and Kovalenko were sitting in first place, Volkova and Kipriyanov in second. If Kat and Heath skated well, the gold was theirs for the taking.

FRANCESCA GASKELL: We'd done everything we could. All any of us could do was wait.

Closeup of Katarina and Heath staring into each other's eyes right before their music begins. A reverent hush has fallen over the stands.

GARRETT LIN: This was it. Four minutes, and it would all be over.

CHAPTER 82

Our music was about heartbreak, but that's the last thing I felt as Heath and I skated.

We'd created most of the program's choreography ourselves during those long winter days in Boston, and so it was perfectly suited to us, each element a knife's-edge balance between tenderness and power.

Searing eye contact as we slowly circled each other during the darkly romantic piano intro. Legs pumping in time with the vigorous bow strokes of the strings, while Heath cupped my chin with whisper-soft hands. Pressure building as the song pulled back to only vocals and a violin tremolo, and we launched into a lift that peaked along with the orchestration.

That free dance was the story of us: Heath and me, spinning away from each other one second, only to clutch each other close the next. Never still, never simple, always pushing and pulling, shattering each other and putting the pieces back together again.

We were adults, and we were children, and we were skating at the Olympics and also on the frozen lake back home, laughing and twirling and holding each other tight. It felt like flying and falling and being caught, all in the same instant.

It felt like seconds and hours and years, and then we were finished. The music still vibrated in my bones, and Heath pressed his forehead to mine, and I could think of only one thing that might make the exquisite moment even better.

So I did what I had stopped myself from doing the night before.

I kissed him.

ELLIS DEAN: The whole crowd was on its feet. Even the Russian fans.

GARRETT LIN: Bella and I were screaming, crying, hugging each other—until I told her to settle down before her heart rate got too high, and she hurled a pillow at my head.

INEZ ACTON: Watching at home, you could *feel* the energy in that arena. It was electric.

FRANCESCA GASKELL: I didn't watch. I couldn't watch.

NICOLE BRADFORD: I wish I could have been there. I can only imagine how thrilling it must have been in person. I was so proud of them.

JANE CURRER: Shaw and Rocha could be arrogant, inconsistent, insubordinate, outright reckless. But when they were on, they were *on*. And that night, they were flawless.

VERONIKA VOLKOVA: The scores had not even come through yet, and everyone was acting as if they had already won. The Olympics are not a popularity contest.

GARRETT LIN: They'd done it. They'd really done it. When they kissed, I thought . . . well, I won't pretend to understand Bella's relationship with Heath, but I thought she might be upset. She wasn't. She never stopped smiling.

KIRK LOCKWOOD: We didn't need to see the scores. We were all certain—one hundred percent, no doubt in our minds certain—Shaw and Rocha would be the Olympic champions.

CHAPTER 83

Even with everything going on around us—the screaming fans, the flashbulbs, the flowers and plush toys raining down—it felt like we were alone.

My whole world narrowed to the heat of Heath's lips, the sweat on the back of his neck slick under my palm, the weight of him leaning in like he couldn't get near enough to me.

I drew him closer, deepening the kiss. I didn't give a damn who was watching. All that mattered was him and me and what we'd just done on that ice together.

By the time I tasted the blood, he was already falling.

As the crowd goes crazy after their free dance in Sochi, Katarina and Heath share a passionate kiss. He bends toward her, hands on her waist.

Then his legs crumple, and he collapses to the ice.

KIRK LOCKWOOD: No one knew what the hell was happening.

INEZ ACTON: At first it looked like he had lipstick on his mouth. That red shade Kat always wore. I was wearing it too, actually, for the viewing party.

The camera zooms in on Heath. His skin is wan, and bright red paints his lips.

FRANCESCA GASKELL: I never expected—I mean, he was coughing up blood.

ELLIS DEAN: The mood shifted from triumph to Greek tragedy *real* quick.

Katarina sinks to her knees, cradling Heath as he's wracked with heaving coughs.

GARRETT LIN: I put my arms around my sister, and we just . . . sat there, frozen in horror.

KIRK LOCKWOOD: For the first time in my career, I had no idea what to say.

The shot cuts to the crowd in the Iceberg Skating Palace—first a wide view, then focusing on individual spectators. A bewildered-looking little boy cries, smearing his red, white, and blue face paint. A woman in a Team Russia sweater holds her hand over her mouth, like she might be sick. A young couple stands slack-jawed, an American flag hanging limp between them.

GARRETT LIN: We were thousands of miles away. There was nothing we could do.

Heath spits out a mouthful of blood, right onto the Olympic rings. Tears slip down Katarina's cheeks, and she clings tighter to him. He falls still, staring into her eyes.

ELLIS DEAN: There was nothing anyone could have done.

CHAPTER 84

When he dropped to his knees like a horrible echo of the night he proposed to me five years earlier on the ice in Cleveland, once again all I could think was, *No, please no.*

We'd won, I was sure of it. This should have been the happiest moment of our lives. We should have been smiling and waving and skating to the kiss and cry, not sprawled across the ice. I should have been holding Heath's hand, not clutching him to my chest as he coughed and spattered blood across the gleaming gold trim of my borrowed costume.

Not like this.

People rushed in around us—medics, officials, media, who knew. In all the chaos, Heath's eyes never left me, like he wanted to make sure my face was the last thing he saw.

I refused to let go, even as hands emerged from the swarm around us to pry my fingers loose. I refused to believe this was really happening.

There was so much I hadn't told him. I hadn't told him how much I loved him, even when I hated him. I hadn't told him that no matter how many changes I made to that old stone house where we grew up, where we fell apart, where we fell in love—I could never bring myself to touch the headboard where we'd carved our names.

We couldn't end like this.

Katarina Shaw sits on the bloodstained ice in Sochi with Heath Rocha in her arms.

ELLIS DEAN: We all feared the worst.

Medics rush onto the rink and load Heath's limp form onto a stretcher.

INEZ ACTON: We thought we'd just watched an Olympian drop dead on live TV.

The other ice dancers stand behind the boards, bewildered. Yelena and Dmitri look shell-shocked, while Francesca openly weeps on her partner Evan's shoulder.

FRANCESCA GASKELL: It was awful. Nothing at all like I'd imagined it.

PRODUCER (Offscreen): What do you mean? Imagined what?

FRANCESCA GASKELL: *(She blinks, then smiles.)* My first Olympics, of course. *(Her smile falters.)* Why, what did you think I was talking about?

KIRK LOCKWOOD: By the time Shaw and Rocha's winning marks appeared, they were in an ambulance speeding up Triumfalnaya Street to Sochi's closest emergency room.

U.S. team physician Dr. Kenneth Archer holds a press conference outside the hospital in Sochi.

"Mr. Rocha suffered a cardiac event with pulmonary distress, including significant bleeding in the lungs. Tests indicated the presence of an unidentified substance in his bloodstream."

A whirlwind of questions from the reporters in attendance. Dr. Archer calls on one, who asks, "Is it possible this 'unidentified substance' was some sort of performance-enhancing drug?"

"I'd prefer not to speculate," he replies. "Mr. Rocha is far from out of the woods yet."

ELLIS DEAN: "Performance enhancing" my *ass*.

GARRETT LIN: It's a miracle he made it to the end of the program, let alone gave a gold medal–worthy performance.

VERONIKA VOLKOVA: Rules are rules. Heath Rocha cheated.

ELLIS DEAN: No way did he take that shit on purpose. No fucking way.

GARRETT LIN: Someone drugged him, and they got away with it.

FRANCESCA GASKELL: And Kat refused to take a blood test herself— which makes you wonder, doesn't it?

KIRK LOCKWOOD: I've never seen the wheels of skating bureaucracy spin so fast.

JANE CURRER: We had to proceed with a disciplinary hearing. It's protocol.

ELLIS DEAN: They didn't even wait until Heath got out of the damn hospital.

GARRETT LIN: I wanted to be there to support them, but I couldn't leave my sister.

Several weeks later, Katarina arrives at the International Olympic Committee's headquarters in Lausanne, Switzerland, for the IOC Disciplinary Commission hearing. She's dressed in a sharp black suit and does not spare the reporters gathered outside so much as a glance.

GARRETT LIN: Kat didn't leave Heath's side either. Not until she was forced to.

CHAPTER 85

Heath and I requested a public hearing, delayed until he was well enough to attend.

The International Olympic Committee, in its infinite wisdom, denied our request. The fate of our careers would be decided behind closed doors in a glorified conference room, and I would have to speak for both of us.

"Remember what we talked about," my lawyer said as we took our seats. The table was oval, probably intended to convey equality and transparency, but it looked like a noose to me.

The rules he'd sternly laid out in our meeting before the hearing were similar to the rules for skaters in competition: Stay respectful and polite. Never speak out of turn. And no matter what happens, don't forget to smile.

The members of the disciplinary commission entered the conference room single file: first, the jowly, bespectacled president of the IOC, there to supervise the proceedings. He was followed by two other middle-aged men I didn't recognize. And finally, there was Jane Currer, her shock of dyed red curls framing a stern expression I knew well from her years sitting at the judges' table. She had always scored Heath and me harshly, and I couldn't imagine she'd be feeling any more generous on this occasion.

"Thank you for joining us today, Ms. Shaw," Jane said. "I hope Mr. Rocha's condition continues to improve?"

As soon as he'd been deemed stable enough for transport, we'd moved him from the Russian state hospital to a state-of-the-art private facility in Geneva. Even under their expert care, though, he remained weak and bed-bound, waking dozens of times per night to cough up more blood from his damaged lungs. Needless to say, I wasn't getting much sleep either. After the first few nights, he started pleading with me to check into a hotel so I could get some rest. But there was no way in hell I was leaving him again.

"I appreciate your concern," I told Jane—so respectful and polite my jaw ached with the effort. "Heath is on the mend. He sends his sincere regrets that he couldn't be here."

"Of course," she said. "Shall we get started?"

A representative of the World Anti-Doping Agency was summoned to speak first. He displayed a bunch of slides and chemical equations to explain that the substance found in Heath's bloodstream could not be definitively identified by any current laboratory tests.

"It appears to be a designer drug of unknown origin," he said, "which taken in excess could certainly cause the cardiovascular damage Mr. Rocha has suffered."

The fact that the drug was unidentifiable and therefore not specifically included on WADA's Prohibited List didn't get us off the hook. Far from it. Any drug not already approved for medical use, no matter its effects, was automatically considered banned in competition.

Then it was my lawyer's turn. He laid out the case that Heath and I had been the victims of sabotage in Sochi—though he refrained from making any accusations about *who* might have vandalized our belongings and tricked Heath into ingesting a harmful substance without his knowledge or consent.

"As the records we've provided clearly show"—my lawyer paused so the commission members could shuffle through the folders in front of them—"Ms. Shaw and Mr. Rocha were tested in Boston before leaving for the Games, and tested again upon their arrival in Russia. Both of those tests were clean."

There was no proof that I had taken anything, but my refusal of a post-competition drug test meant I was considered in violation of the doping rules too. I'd been so overwhelmed, between the camera flashes and the sirens and then the crush of doctors shouting in Russian, trying to shove me out of the way. Away from Heath, unresponsive on the stretcher, his face so ashen I feared he was already gone. I refused to leave his side, refused to let anyone touch me. It wasn't until later that I thought about how it would look.

Whatever Heath had taken, I'd taken too—though apparently my dose had been small enough that I suffered no noticeable ill effects. We had skated well in spite of those drugs, not because of them. But it didn't make a damn bit of difference.

"Unfortunately," Jane said, "regardless of how or why Mr. Rocha ingested the substance in question, the fact remains that it was found in his bloodstream during Olympic competition. So I'm afraid we have no choice but to—"

"How do you explain the other clean tests?" I blurted out. My lawyer cringed beside me.

"You must understand, Ms. Shaw," Jane said. "If we make an exception to the rules for you, then we'll be expected to make exceptions for everyone."

My lawyer laid a firm hand on my elbow. I ignored him. I was tired of all this politeness and propriety. All this pretending anything about this situation was fair. I was so tired.

"You seriously think," I said, "we made it all the way to the Olympic final and then decided to do some dangerous drugs just for the hell of it?"

Jane pursed her lips. "Ms. Shaw, if you could please refrain from using profanity in—"

"Heath almost *died.* You really believe he took that shit on purpose?"

My lawyer's grip tightened. "Katarina, I suggest you—"

"Oh, like it fucking matters what I say." I shook him off and turned to face the commission members. "You know exactly who did this, but why tell the truth when you have Heath and me to take the fall? You all made up your minds about us years ago."

We weren't enough, and then we were too much. We would never be worthy of the gold in their eyes, no matter what we did.

"I assume you're referring to the claims posted by Ellis Dean," Jane said. "His theories are certainly quite . . . imaginative. But we must rely on the facts, not wild, libelous conjecture."

So far, Ellis had been the only one willing to point fingers at Francesca and Dmitri, at least in public. They'd both stayed above the fray since the Games, releasing separate statements conveying their hopes that this matter would be resolved swiftly, and their total confidence in the IOC arriving at the right decision.

"If his claims are so 'wild,'" I shot back, "then why did Gaskell Pharmaceuticals slap him with a cease and desist and try to shut his site down?"

"Ms. Shaw," Jane started.

"Why is he getting middle-of-the-night phone calls from men with Russian accents? He's changed residences twice in the last month, and he's *still* receiving threats."

"We are not here to discuss Mr. Dean, or your competitors." Jane fixed me with a stern look. "We're here to discuss—"

"We were sabotaged, and we still won." I stood. My pencil skirt had ridden up, and I didn't bother to tug the hem back into place. "Those gold medals are rightfully ours. You know it, and everyone who saw us skate that night damn well knows it too."

"Sit down, Ms. Shaw," Jane said. "We're not finished here."

"Yes," I told her. "We are."

I took the next train to Geneva. By the time I reached Heath's hospital room, the IOC committee had sent out a press release with their decision.

The ruling had been unanimous. We would be sanctioned. Our medals would be stripped, our winning score stricken from the record books. We were no longer the Sochi gold medalists.

Heath was looking better that afternoon, sitting up in bed, the bright alpine sunshine lending his complexion a little color. From the expression on his face, though, I could tell he'd already heard the news.

"Are you all right?" he asked.

The question sounded so absurd in his hoarse, feeble voice, I almost laughed.

"Don't worry about me." I flung my suit jacket on the chair in the corner, where I'd spent the majority of my time the past several weeks. "How are you feeling today?"

"We can still appeal the ruling. Take it to the Court of Arbitration for Sport, or—"

"No." I sat on the bed, my hip brushing his. "Let them do what they want. I don't care."

"Sure," Heath said.

Then he realized I was serious. He stared as if he were seeing me for the very first time.

"But . . ." He swallowed. "We won."

"We did. I know it, you know it. The whole world knows it." I took his hand. "So who cares if we don't have some shiny hunks of metal to prove it?"

I meant every word. I didn't care about the medals anymore. I didn't care if we were immortalized in the record books, or forgotten tomorrow. A bunch of washed-up bureaucrats in some bland Swiss conference room didn't get to decide if we were champions or not. I decided who I was. I decided what I wanted.

"Are you sure, Katarina?" Heath asked. "Are you sure that will be enough for you?"

You're my home, Heath had said to me once. Despite all the years we'd spent apart, all the time we'd wasted, he was my home too. He always had been.

"We have the rest of our lives," I said. "That's more than enough."

INEZ ACTON: Good for her.

JANE CURRER: Ms. Shaw was given every opportunity to provide a reasonable explanation for what happened in Sochi. She did not avail herself of those opportunities.

INEZ ACTON: She gave her whole life to that sport, and this is how they repay her? Fuck 'em.

JANE CURRER: In the end, she left us no other option.

Kirk Lockwood reports on NBC: "American ice dancers Katarina Shaw and Heath Rocha will be stripped of their win at the recent Winter Olympics in Sochi, Russia—although, as Mr. Rocha has been hospitalized since the night of the ice dance final, they never actually received their gold medals. U.S. Figure Skating will meet in the coming months to consider future disciplinary measures, including a potential ban from the sport."

VERONIKA VOLKOVA: The medal ceremony was delayed for weeks.

A perfunctory ceremony is conducted for the remaining ice dance medalists. Francesca Gaskell and Evan Kovalenko are given the gold, while Yelena Volkova and Dmitri Kipriyanov are bumped up from bronze to silver.

FRANCESCA GASKELL: That wasn't how I wanted to win. Believe me.

As soon as the ceremony ends, Yelena throws her medal at her aunt's feet and storms off.

VERONIKA VOLKOVA: It was an emotional time for us all.

The image freezes on Yelena's retreating figure and fades to black and white. Superimposed text reads: "In the aftermath of the Sochi Games, Yelena Volkova abruptly quit the sport. We attempted to contact her before production began, but her current whereabouts are unknown."

ELLIS DEAN: So after all that, little Frannie Gaskell got to be Olympic champion.

FRANCESCA GASKELL: Would I have agreed to this interview if I had anything to hide?

ELLIS DEAN: And the next season, the Gaskells tripled their usual annual donation to U.S. Figure Skating. Totally aboveboard and not infuriatingly corrupt at all.

FRANCESCA GASKELL: The question you should be asking is: if Kat and Heath are so innocent, why did they refuse to talk to you? Why am I here, and they aren't, huh?

JANE CURRER: We may never know the truth for certain. We made the best decision we could, given the circumstances.

INEZ ACTON: Kat and Heath were robbed. I don't care what anyone says.

FRANCESCA GASKELL: I for one would love to know what they have to say for themselves. Since apparently I'll be spending my *entire life* defending my accomplishments.

ELLIS DEAN: I know what *really* went down in Sochi. The rest of the world deserves Shaw and Rocha's true story too.

FRANCESCA GASKELL: I'm an Olympic champion. I'm a philanthropist. I'm a *good person.*

PRODUCER (Offscreen): No one said you weren't, Ms. Gaskell. But back to my question: how *would* you define your relationship with Dmitri Kipriyanov?

FRANCESCA GASKELL: You know what? *(She starts to remove her mic.)* That's enough.

PRODUCER (Offscreen): Ms. Gaskell, please, we—

FRANCESCA GASKELL: I should have known you people weren't interested in the truth.

ELLIS DEAN: But I guess that's up to you now, huh? *(He winks at the camera.)*

Back to Francesca's interview, as she stands up and walks out of frame, leaving an empty chair in front of a row of rosebushes. The shot zooms in tight on a golden yellow cluster of blooms.

GARRETT LIN: I don't think Kat and Heath cared about the medals anymore. That's the truth.

KIRK LOCKWOOD: A few days after the hearing, Heath's doctors determined it would be safe for him to travel back to the United States.

Security camera footage shows Katarina and Heath arriving incognito at Logan International Airport in Boston. Heath appears thin and weak, and Katarina pushes him in a wheelchair.

KIRK LOCKWOOD: They got back just in time for the birth.

Candid snapshots from the hospital show Bella and Heath cradling their infant daughter. Garrett, Andre, and Kirk take turns holding her too. Finally, the baby is placed in Katarina's arms. Katarina looks stiff and uncomfortable, but she smiles at Heath.

GARRETT LIN: She was so freaking tiny! The most beautiful baby I'd ever seen, and it's not even close. Bella and Heath decided to name her after our mother. Not the name everyone knew her by, but her given name. Her real name.

A Kiss & Cry post announces the birth of Mei Lin-Rocha and wishes the family well.

GARRETT LIN: I figured we'd all go back to California. But when my sister told us what she had in mind, she shocked everyone.

KIRK LOCKWOOD: Bella didn't want her baby raised in the Hollywood limelight like she and Garrett had been. So she decided to move to Illinois and start a new skating school there.

GARRETT LIN: There had never been some great romance between Bella and Heath, but they turned out to be great co-parents. And Kat was a surprisingly excellent stepmom.

ELLIS DEAN: I'm not saying they were a throuple, but it seemed like they were a throuple.

GARRETT LIN: As for Kat and Heath . . . I won't claim they lived happily ever after. I'd say they'd proven, though, to themselves and everyone else, nothing could keep them apart for long.

PRODUCER (Offscreen): So what do you think is the true legacy of Katarina Shaw and Heath Rocha?

JANE CURRER: They had such promise, and it's a shame they never lived up to it.

KIRK LOCKWOOD: I've noticed definite changes in ice dance over the past ten years. More skaters taking creative control, asserting agency, pushing the limits of the sport. I can't say it was all due to Shaw and Rocha's influence, but they certainly had an impact.

INEZ ACTON: Katarina Shaw set an example for women—not only female athletes, women everywhere—that you can speak your mind, do things your own way, and win on your terms.

ELLIS DEAN: Kat and Heath were themselves, always. Whether you loved them or hated them, you sure as hell couldn't ignore them.

NICOLE BRADFORD: Even as children, they were so *intense*. That was their greatest strength, and their greatest weakness. But they loved each other, and they loved skating. I think that's what people will remember most: their love.

GARRETT LIN: I don't like that question. You're making it sound like they're dead or something. As far as I'm concerned, if you think Katarina Shaw and Heath Rocha are done, you don't know them at all. I wouldn't be surprised if they're just getting started.

EPILOGUE

"Oh my god, did you watch it?"

The sun isn't even up yet, and two girls sit beside the rink, lacing their skates.

"*Yes*. It was *wild*, right?"

They're too busy gossiping to notice my presence. I ease the door shut behind me and lean against it, listening to their animated voices ping back and forth.

"The part about the thorns in her boots? *Ouch.*"

"That Francesca lady seems super sus. The way she stormed off at the end?"

"Totally. Oh! And what about that video of Coach Shaw throwing a chair at—"

"You think that was wild?" I say.

The girls startle at the sound of my voice. They're so young. They remind me of myself and Bella—except we never spooked that easily.

"Trust me, you don't know the half of it." I point toward the fresh ice. "Go warm up."

"Yes, Coach Shaw," they mumble in unison.

When Bella asked me to join the staff at her new school, she wouldn't take no for an answer. And, shortly thereafter, when skaters' parents started threatening to withdraw their children rather than let them work with the notorious Katarina Shaw, Bella gave them two choices: shut up or fuck off. Lest my scandalous reputation prove *too* distracting, I don't accompany her to competitions, but I can't say I miss that high-stress, always-on-the-go life. These days, I'd much rather stick close to home.

Madison Castro arrives at the rink next, with Bella right behind her carrying a travel mug of coffee. Madison has been helping out with the younger teams, for a stipend and an assistant coaching title. She and her partner, Jacob, competed in the 2022 Olympics and came in tenth. They're hoping for better in 2026, but if not, she has a real future as a coach.

Bella and I watch as Madison starts putting the skaters through warm-up exercises, stroking back and forth across the ice. The old North Shore rink where Heath and I got our start is hardly recognizable; Bella gave it a gut rehab after she took over. Now there's natural light instead of low-hanging fluorescents, and definitely no hot dog smells or traffic cones.

"Were they talking about that damn documentary again?" Bella asks.

"Oh yes. Don't worry, they'll lose interest eventually."

"Yeah, until the twentieth anniversary." Bella sips her coffee. "Maybe I'll let them interview me for that one. I'll tell everyone the shocking truth that Katarina Shaw actually isn't that scary, once you get to know her."

I gasp. "You wouldn't dare."

We'd been surprised when Garrett agreed to participate in the documentary. Out of all of us, he loathed the spotlight the most. But he said it was important to him to show the humanity behind the scandal—and to shine a light on the extreme pressure elite athletes face.

Bella hands me her coffee so I can try a sip. For the past several years, she's been seeing a prominent Chicago restaurateur who's a wizard with an espresso machine. He travels a lot and keeps his own studio apartment in the city, which is an ideal arrangement for Bella. She gets companionship when she wants it, independence when she doesn't.

As the swirl of complex spices washes over my tongue, I moan with pleasure.

"You better marry that man," I say. "Or I will."

"I think Heath might have a few objections," Bella says.

"Objections to what?" Heath asks.

He's just come through the door, holding his daughter's mittened hand.

Mei tugs on his arm. "Can I go skate?"

"Sure, sweetie," he tells her.

When he was her age, Heath looked world-weary and serious. Now, at forty, he's always smiling—especially when Mei is around. He's never regained his full strength, though; we skate together sometimes in the private rink in the woods behind my—now our—house, but Heath gets winded after only a few minutes. Then he sits back and watches me.

"Aunt Katie, watch!" Mei shouts at me as she races onto the rink and bends into a perfect Biellmann spin, pigtails blurring.

"Be careful!" Bella calls out. I whoop and applaud, ever the bad influence.

Heath and Bella's daughter is a fearless skater, far better than I was at nine years old. Who knows, maybe she'll be the member of our strange little family who finally brings home the Olympic title.

Or maybe she'll do something completely different. It's up to her.

After we came home from Sochi, I resumed wearing the engagement ring Heath gave me, but we've never gotten married. A piece of paper means nothing compared to what we share. Over the past decade, we've been off and on and everything in between. One way or another, Heath Rocha and I will be in each other's lives until we die. Even if we end up killing each other.

Right now, though, I have no complaints. Sunrise streams through the skylights, turning everything golden. Bella passes me her coffee again, and Heath slips his hand into mine.

So say what you want about me. Call me a bitch, a cheater, a loser, a whore. I may not have an Olympic gold medal, but I have something better: a life where I spend every day with my favorite people in the world, doing exactly what I love.

If that's not winning, I don't know what is.

ACKNOWLEDGEMENTS

Before writing *The Favourites,* I abandoned not one but TWO other novels after years of work, tens of thousands of words written, and several existential crises. So to start off, I'd like to thank anyone and everyone who listened to me bitch and moan during this personal Dark Night of the Soul—especially my agent, Sharon Pelletier, who responded to all my unhinged emails and tearful phone calls with grace, compassion, and unfailingly wise advice. Sharon, you have the patience of a saint, and you deserve to be personally serenaded by Harry Styles himself.

I recognize how tremendously fortunate and privileged I am that I could afford to give this book (and myself!) the necessary time and space to grow. Thank you to my grandparents, June and Howard, for your generosity and support, not only during this strange and stressful time but throughout my entire life. Thanks also to my former employer, for subsidizing my creative passions for a decade plus and sending me off with good wishes—and stock options!—when I decided to make the leap to full-time writing (in March 2020 . . . but that's another story).

When I finally (FINALLY) finished *The Favourites,* I had a feeling it was something special. But the book's publishing journey so far has exceeded even my most delusional expectations. Caitlin McKenna, you were the first editor I spoke to during my whirlwind submission/birthday week, and by the end of our chat I was pretty damn sure you were the one. Every day we've worked together has proven that initial gut instinct 100 percent correct. You and Kaiya make the ultimate dream team, and if they gave gold medals for editing, you'd both deserve to stand on top of the podium. Much gratitude also to Noa Shapiro for all your expertise and badass organizational skills; this has been the smoothest, calmest publishing experience of my career, and I know that is in no small part because of your hard work behind the scenes!

To the rest of the team at Random House—Andy Ward, Rachel Rokicki, Ben Greenberg, Alison Rich, Erica Gonzalez, Rebecca Berlant, Benjamin Dreyer, Robert Siek, Windy Dorresteyn, Madison Dettlinger, Keilani Lum, Maria Braeckel, Rachel Ake, Denise Cronin, Sandra Sjursen, Caroline Cunningham, and Pamela Feinstein—thank you for the incredibly warm welcome, and for all you have done and will do to make *The Favourites* a success. I am beyond thrilled to be a Random House author, and I hope we'll be working together on many more books to come. Also thrilled (or should I say chuffed?) to be publishing in the U.K. with the legendary Chatto & Windus, so massive thanks to Kaiya Shang, Clara Farmer, and the entire team there.

Thank you to Lauren Abramo for filling my book's passport with plenty of stamps; every time I see your name in my inbox, I do a little happy dance. Thanks as well to Gracie Freeman Lifschutz, Andrew Dugan, Nataly Gruender, Kendall Berdinsky, and everyone else at Dystel, Goderich & Bourret who works so tirelessly to make it one of the best agencies in the biz.

Thank you to my film agent, Dana Spector, and her fantastic assistants, including Eliza Jevon and Oliver Sanderson, for setting up meetings I'm still pinching myself over. Hopefully by the time this book hits shelves, I'll no longer be sworn to secrecy about them!

Halley Sutton, thank you for believing in this book even when I didn't, and listening to me ramble about all the different versions of it that eventually led me to this one. Thank you to my work wife/critique partner/platonic soulmate Wendy Heard, who is always right. Megan Collins, thanks for being a phenomenal agent sister and all-around cheerleader, and for always being ready to gossip in the group chat. Much love to the Young Rich Widows (aka Kimberly Belle, Cate Holahan, and Vanessa Lillie) for being the very best collaborators; I've learned so much from all three of you, and writing our books together kept me sane (not to mention financially solvent) while I figured out *The Favourites*.

To my friend/teacher/favorite good witch Andrea Hannah: I'm a different person than I was when I met you. I truly don't know where I'd be without your guidance, and I don't want to know. Thank you to Taylor Jenkins Reid, not only for writing novels that inspire me to keep leveling up my own skills but for your amazing research webinar, which is what made me believe I could pull off a project this ambitious in the first place. Every time I rewatched the recording or reviewed the many, many notes I took, your words gave me the boost of confidence I needed to keep going. And getting to meet you, however briefly, at the 2022 Writer's Digest conference in Pasadena was truly one of the highlights of my life.

Wendy Walker, thank you for sharing your figure skating past with me, and for the way you've supported my books from the very beginning. Thank you to Danielle Earl, Jordan Cowan, and all the other photographers, videographers, and skating fans who've posted content that let me imagine myself rinkside even when I was locked in my house with a pandemic raging. And whoever scanned and archived all those old issues of *Skating* magazine . . . bless you, you have no idea how much nerdy joy I got out of reading them. Shout-out to my favorite skaters, including but not limited to Madison Hubbell, Kaitlyn Weaver, and Amber Glenn, for all the incredible things you do both on and off the ice. And an extra-special thanks to Jason Brown, because this book might have ended *very* differently if I hadn't had the pleasure of seeing you skate at Stars on Ice. I was absolutely mesmerized by your artistry and palpable joy, and I hope my own creative joy comes across in the same way to everyone who reads *The Favourites*.

Last but most certainly not least, heartfelt thanks to my nearest and dearest: my mother, Linda—you can actually read this one, Mom!—and my partner, Nate, who has watched more figure skating than perhaps any straight man alive. You're really something, honey.

Finally, thank you to Cymbalta, because a depressed person could *not* have made this.

ABOUT THE AUTHOR

Layne Fargo has a background in theatre, women's studies and library science, so it's only fitting that she now writes deliciously dramatic, unapologetically feminist stories for a living. She's the author of psychological thrillers *They Never Learn* and *Temper*, as well as co-author on the bestselling Young Rich Widows series, and her work has been translated into over a dozen languages. Layne lives in Chicago with her partner, their pets and an ever-expanding collection of books she's definitely going to read before she dies.